Ulla Kriebernegg, Roberta Maierhofer (
The Ages of Life

The series **Aging Studies** is edited by Heike Hartung, Ulla Kriebernegg and Roberta Maierhofer.

ULLA KRIEBERNEGG, ROBERTA MAIERHOFER (EDS.)

The Ages of Life

Living and Aging in Conflict?

[transcript]

Gedruckt mit Unterstützung der Universität Graz

Bibliographic information published by the Deutsche Nationalbibliothek
The Deutsche Nationalbibliothek lists this publication in the Deutsche Natio-nalbibliografie; detailed bibliographic data is available on the Internet at http://dnb.d-nb.de

© 2013 transcript Verlag, Bielefeld

Cover layout: Melissa Milis/Tamara Tepfer, Netherlands,
   and Kordula Röckenhaus, Bielefeld
Proofread by Barbara Ratzenböck
Typeset by Katharina Wierichs, Bielefeld
Printed by Majuskel Medienproduktion GmbH, Wetzlar
ISBN 978-3-8376-2212-6

Inhalt

REPRESENTATION OF AGES OF LIFE IN LITERATURE

The Ages of Life
Living and Aging in Conflict?

Ulla Kriebernegg/Roberta Maierhofer

Representations determine how we understand age and aging and influence the way we perceive others and define ourselves over the life course. Iconographies and representations mark changes in social and cultural perceptions and have very real consequences in terms of social, political and cultural practice. From Ptolemy's cosmology of the seven ages of life and Galenic medicine's four elements to the ladder of years, which identified ages of life with social roles during the eighteenth century, redefinitions of living and aging can be chartered. In contemporary Western societies, ages of life have been seen as opportunities and challenges to construct individual biographies. In this process, the category of 'youth' has continually been extended towards the end of the life course, turning living and aging into apparently conflicting processes. These conflicts provide the basis of re-conceptualizations of the concept of aging, deconstructing the binary opposition of 'young' and 'old.' Bio-gerontological models of aging as decline can be redefined from a cultural studies perspective as the ambiguity of living and aging. This cultural ambiguity enables an analysis of the social functions of images of aging in order to provide a basis for interdisciplinary exchange on gerontological knowledge. Images of positive or 'successful aging' target and empower the affluent and healthy 'young old,' but exclude and stigmatize those of the 'oldest old' who face the realities of illness in old age. Apparently negative images of old age as physical decrepitude and disease are deconstructed when life even in the oldest age is appreciated as a form of 'successful frailty.'

Although consensus exists that any studies on aging and the life course have to bridge the gap between the abstract and the concrete, the personal and the political, theory and practice by providing an interdisciplinary platform for research, only recently the field of 'cultural gerontology' – also known as 'aging studies,' 'age studies,' 'humanistic or narrative gerontology' – has gained acceptance as enabling such an interdisciplinary discourse. Even if many of the essays found here are firmly rooted within specific disciplines, by contributing to the third volume of *Aging Studies* an interdisciplinary discussion on aging and the life course is encouraged. In the humanities and social sciences, there has been a proliferation of identity-based studies. Age as an identity marker has so far been mostly ignored, although in contrast to other categories, the boundary of 'age' is always fluid providing a basis for deconstruction. By determining in what way 'youth' and 'age' come to have certain meanings at a particular place and time, and stressing the necessary interrelatedness of these meanings, an understanding of what is considered typically 'young' in a given society depends in part on being different from what is 'old,' and what is 'old' on 'not being young.' This understanding can lead to the conclusion that what is considered age-neutral, i.e. 'universal' is implicitly often male and young, and exclusive of the female and old. Kathleen Woodward argues in her book *Aging and Its Discontents* (1991)[1] that Western society has not been culturally inventive in producing age gradations, but merely distinguishes a single binary, young and old, which is hierarchically organized, youth being the valued term, the point of reference for defining who is old. Cultural representations of age remain locked in primarily negative stereotypes, whereas youth, subjectively speaking, remains a remarkably fluid and seemingly almost infinitely expandable category, it is a moveable marker (Woodward 6). Contrary to popular conceptions of old age, which tend to define it as a distinct period in life, old people themselves emphasize the continuity of the ageless self amid changes across the life span. It is, however, necessary to analyze representations of age and aging across the life course from a cultural perspective in order to regain an understanding of this fluid definition of identity.

Regardless of the different approaches and disciplines presented by the contributors in this volume, all share the conviction that there is a lack of understanding concerning cultural, social and political representations of age and aging. The approaches presented in this volume of the *Aging Studies* series take an interdependent life course perspective, thus explaining

---

1 | Kathleen Woodward. *Aging and Its Discontents. Freud and Other Fictions*. Bloomington: Indiana UP, 1991.

the seeming paradox of autonomy and interdependence of individuals and age groups as they move through life. When talking about family structure and cultural change, the questions of life course, personal development and aging are of central concern. The aging individual and the conflicts, passions, and joys, exemplify more than any other stage in life the interplay between the private and the public, the individual and the communal, and stress the importance of relationships and connections. For a culture, permeated as it is with images of youth, our own aging is experienced through the mirror of others. The question how age is mediated in our culture is related to semantics of form. The 'narrative turn' has affected the theoretical foundations of both the humanities, social and life sciences. History, storytelling and images of aging are linked by narrative genres that are invested with cultural meanings. Focusing on the individual life story, the question is how the aging process, memory and the experience of time are incorporated into cultural narratives of aging.

LANDSCAPES AND CONTEXTS

The idea for this volume in the *Aging Studies* series was developed out of a program under the heading "Encounters in Bad Aussee" initiated by Irmtraud Fischer, former Vice Rector for Research at the University of Graz, who having grown up in the Salzkammergut, decided in 2009 to take the university to the region. At the turn of the 20th century, this Austrian lake region had become a summer meeting place for intellectuals, writers and artists from Vienna and Berlin. Through representations in art and literature this landscape became an almost iconic place of longing. Fischer's idea was to continue the tradition of cultural, intellectual and artistic encounters by taking up discussions on contemporary issues and offering a platform for exchange in the context of a landscape – both real and imaginary – inscribed by history. In 2010, these "Encounters in Bad Aussee" were devoted to the topic of "Ages of Life," where the topic of aging was discussed as a perceived contradiction to living. In a keynote address, Anne D. Basting, director of the Center on Age & Community (http://www.ageandcommunity.org/) spoke on the topic of memory and imagination, and how to link generations through creative engagement in art. Basting, both educator and artist, has developed research methods to embed arts into long-term care with a special focus on people with cognitive disabilities. Basting's emphasis on improving the quality of life for communities and individuals as well as bridging the gap between academia and care-taking embodied well the intentions of these "Encounters in Bad Aussee." In her talk, Basting stressed the potential of creative engagement in care-giving and brought together theoretical and practical aspects of living and aging.

Combining the abstract and the concrete, "Encounters in Bad Aussee" not only offer stimulating talks and academic presentations for an inter-ested public but also integrate 'life outside of the classroom.' All activities are accompanied by music, and the contemporary musician and composer Bertl Mütter played short pieces of music in-between the talks, during the hikes through the woods, and as a closing statement after the discussions. It is therefore not surprising that one picture taken of the musician play-ing his trombone, sitting on a stone in the middle of one of the lakes in the region was recently added to the picture-gallery of *TimeSlips Creative Storytelling* (http://www.timeslips.org/). *TimeSlips* is an interactive website founded by Anne Basting in 1998 featuring over a hundred images en-couraging creative encounters by presenting different representations of life. Under the heading "Let your imagination soar. Start telling stories," *TimeSlips* aims at inclusion in both telling and creating stories triggered by various images. The pressure to remember is replaced, as the website states, by the freedom to imagine.

Fig. 1: Bertl Mütter playing the trombone at "Encounters in Bad Aussee"

STRUCTURE, METHODS AND APPROACHES

The book is structured in three parts. The first section deals with methods and approaches and more general introductions to aging from the perspectives of different disciplines. Contributions in the second and third part of this volume devote themselves to specific investigations concerning representations of the ages of life in media, art and literature.

In his contribution, Marvin Formosa raises the question, "Positive Aging in an Age of Neo-liberalism: Old Wine in New Bottles?" While in the 1970s and 1980s, older people were generally expected to embrace a passive lifestyle wholly dependent upon state welfare policy, common neo-liberal ideology encourages individuals to become 'entrepreneurs of themselves' and to behave according to the ideal of economic markets. Positive aging thus overlooks how in capitalism the drive of human beings to self-develop tends to be captive to the ideological hegemony of the commoditization of culture.

Karin Lövgren explores limitations and possibilities of a cultural studies approach to aging studies in her article entitled "Celebrating or Denying Age? On Cultural Studies as an Analytical Approach in Gerontology." Analyzing popular magazines intended for an older female audience, Lövgren discusses the interflow of cultural notions between readers and different cultural intermediaries, and comes to the conclusion that both producers and consumers are sensitive to shared cultural notions. These notions are reflected, produced, and reproduced in mediated texts and ads, and are then used as resources in constructing the self. Lövgren encourages an analysis of these cultural concepts of aging in order to determine what 'doing age' means in cultural and social terms.

Sharon-Dale Stone challenges in her contribution "Age-Related Disability – Believing is Seeing is Experiencing" the common assumption that aging and disability go hand in hand. The ubiquity of this common-sense notion that old age and disability are coterminous underpins the taken-for-granted construct of 'age-related disability,' a notion suggesting that the aging process itself is disabling and prevents us from questioning its validity. This article proposes that we need to question the idea that the aging process causes the acquisition of disabling impairments. Given the lack of convincing evidence to support the belief that aging causes disability, but considering the propensity of people to more easily notice disability in elders, we need to ask how much of our bodily experience is materialized as a result of our imaginations.

Cultural constructions also play an important role when considering legal structures concerning age. Jürgen Pirker and Nora Melzer-Azodanloo discuss in their essay, "Aged by Law? Ages of Life in Austrian Law," how rules and regulations create reality and contribute to our perceptions of age and life phases. This article analyzes various Austrian legal provisions on age and deals with their development and justification. In a very specific discussion of the Austrian situation, the authors provide an overview of age limitations and discuss in which ways law makes us young or old, and which images of life phases are constituted by age regulations.

REPRESENTATIONS OF AGES OF LIFE IN MEDIA, ART AND LITERATURE

Recognizing the importance of cultural interpretations of media, art and literature, various representations of aging have been analyzed in the second and third section of this book in order to establish a basis for understanding the implicit meaning of aging. The process of aging has often been evaluated in relation to dominant culture, suggesting there is one and only one life course which necessarily involves a period of progress and a resulting time of decline. Cultural manifestations such as in media, the arts and literature have often reflected this perception of aging and contributed to this archetypal representation of the aged, but have also offered interpretations on how to transcend and subvert conventional and stereotypical notions of aging.

MEDIA AND ART

In the article "'The Journey into the Land of Forgetfulness:' Metaphors of Aging and Dementia in the Media," Heinrich Grebe, Welf-Gerrit Otto and Harm-Peer Zimmermann provide an insightful discussion on the use of metaphors of aging and dementia in media. Their data analysis shows the meaning making capability of such metaphors. In order to reduce the complexity of neuromedical research and making issues involved accessible to a wider social debate, the metaphor of a container or a hard drive is used. However, orientational knowledge created by such metaphors limits our perceptions linking dementia to concepts such as absence, loss, regression, or darkness. Rather than substituting public demonization of dementia by an idealized image of the condition, this article calls for greater social inclusion of people with dementia by showing the variety of possible experiences. In this way, living and growing old with dementia might be reconciled rather than being seen as a contradiction in terms.

The contribution "Representation of Old Age in Media: Fear of Aging or Cult of Youth?" by Julian Wangler discusses how age discourse in German speaking countries changed over the past three decades and now presents much more variety. In this article, Wangler focuses on relevance, specifics and potential of images of old age in media representations. This analysis does not restrict itself to an analysis of representation of the old, but calls for an expansion of the scope of research to images and representations of all age groups and all stages of life.

Age-specific distinctions have always been present in advertisements in the regional Austrian province of Styria, as Eva Klein's essay, "Age Images in Advertising. An Art-Historical Analysis of Advertisement Images in the Austrian Province of Styria" shows. These distinctions have always been very clearly defined in terms of gender difference. Since 1900, women have been presented as constructed ideal types, and present-day advertising has continued with this gendered portrayal of young women. Currently, attempts have been made in advertisement campaigns to counteract the established practice of focusing on youth and its medial staging. Although these attempts are exceptions to the rule, these efforts can be seen as a conscious challenge of the norm practiced in advertising illustrations dominating public space for more than a century.

Thomas Küpper's essay "Of Mimicry and Age: Fashion Ambivalences of the Young-Old" seeks to show how changes in perception of age(ing) influence the fashion discourse with implications for the fashion industry. Homi Bhabha's term 'mimicry' is of imminent value for these considerations as it can describe unintentional subversive practices. These effects (intended or not) constitute the ambivalences that are characteristic for the fashion of the young-old.

LITERATURE

Cynthia Skenazi's essay, "The Irony of the Ages of Life: Etienne Pasquier's *Les Jeus Poetiques* (1610)," is about an ironic tale of the ages of life.
The 81-year-old French poet Etienne Pasquier playfully questions abstract
accounts of the life cycle as a repetitive and timeless sequence of ages.
Throughout his collection, age is not only thought of as simply a measure
of time between birth and death, but as the way people perceive themselves
and the way others see them. Pasquier used stereotyped and abstract accounts of the stages of the life cycle to promote a varied notion of aging as
a social and literary process.

Perceptions of age are dependent on culture, Marta Miquel-Baldellou
argues in her contribution "Past the Mirror of Victorian Aging and Beyond: Recurring Transatlantic Archetypes of the Aged." Based on Teresa
Mangum's understanding that the Victorian period invented the concept
of old age, Miquel-Baldellou discusses historical, political and cultural differences between English and American narratives of age by focusing on
male and female aging archetypes. In Victorian England, aging characters
were often associated with positive images, whereas in American narratives old characters were often perceived as personifications of the past
subjection to the Old World, symbolizing an old order that had to be left
behind.

In her paper "Beyond *Dis*-Ease: Positive Female Aging against the Cult
of Invalidism in Ellen Glasgow's Last Two Novels," Emma Domínguez-Rué
examines the relationship between illness and invalidism. Taking an autobiographical approach, this essay contends that the two novels *In This Our
Life* and *Beyond Defeat: An Epilogue to an Era* served Glasgow to imagine
a fictional homeland in which characters recover and find fulfillment in
maturity and age.

Recent fiction of the twenty-first century has provided new narratives
on the experience of aging, Helen Chupin asserts in her contribution to
the volume with the title, "Growing Old and Searching for Identity in Anne
Tyler's *Noah's Compass* (2009) and Umberto Eco's *The Mysterious Flame of
Queen Loana* (2004): A Contemporary Semantics of Aging." Chupin argues
that the numerous images of aging that these otherwise very different novels share (physical shocks, amnesia, returns to childhood homes, attempts
to combine the past and the present) reflect the difficulties encountered in
giving meaning to the transitional stage of life of sixty-year-old men.

In her essay "Man, Interrupted: Intersections of Masculinity, Disability, and Old Age in John Coetzee's *Slow Man*," Katharina Zilles discusses a powerful narrative of aging corporeality. Zilles reads bodies – including those written or told – as a major site of construction and concretization of age(ing) and the basis of the production of the age-other. As her analysis of *Slow Man* shows, the experience of age(ing) significantly alters notions and images of gendered identity. 'Coming of age' remains unaccomplished, since the protagonist fails to find and adapt to a new age role in order to resolve the process of becoming other.

Salman Rushdie's interest in women and aging are explored by Dana Bădulescu in her essay "Too Old To Rock? Rushdie's Vina Apsara 'Surging into Her Mid-Forties Full of Beauty and Courage.'" Rushdie, detecting a growing tendency towards 'masculinism' in Indian society due to the availability of ultrasound tests to determine the gender of unborn children, has focused in his work on strong and aging women. Bădulescu discusses Vina Apsara as an exceptional woman who is magnified by mythical associations and lifted to iconicity while she is alive, and to a cult after her death. This protagonist is shown as a woman in transition to middle-age whose association with rock 'n' roll provides the backdrop for a discourse on age and aging.

This collection of essays aims to explore the relationship between living and aging as a productive antagonism which focuses on the interplay between continuity and change as a marker of life course identity. Aging and growing old are processes which cannot be reduced to a chronology of years but which are shaped by the individual's interaction with changing circumstances of life. To the degree that it enables agency, living and aging – as the contributions to this volume show – allow for subversive deconstruction of normative age concepts.

FIGURE

Photo credits: Brad Lichtenstein

Methods and Approaches

Positive Aging in an Age of Neo-liberalism
Old Wine in New Bottles?

Marvin Formosa

The discourse of positive aging has become the central plank upon which international and national aging policies are constructed. Moreover, an increasing number of popular writers are advocating positive aging as a means to age actively, successively, and productively. These include authors of self-help books, media personalities, as well as writers from psychology and the social sciences (Lane; Devall). As Gilleard and Higgs (141) point out, rationales supporting positive aging convey a common message that later life is a time of opportunity and 'old age' a state to be resisted, whilst treating 'disengagement' from society or the marginalization of 'pensioned retirement' as a moral or personal failing. Such a stance is a sharp turn away from modern visions of aging policy, popular during the 1970s and 1980s, where older people were generally expected to embrace a passive lifestyle wholly dependent upon state welfare policy. One key problem, however, is that rationales advocating positive aging are generally embedded in a neo-liberal ideology that encourages individuals to become 'entrepreneurs of themselves,' behaving according to the ideal of economic markets, and choosing the optimal courses of action that maximize their interests. Positive aging thus overlooks how in capitalism the drive of human beings to self-develop tends to be captive to the ideological hegemony of the commoditization of culture. This argument is presented in four sections. Whilst the first part focuses on the genealogy and key tenets of positive aging, the second section presents some international policies advocating the goal of positive aging. The third section provides a constructive critique of positive aging, stressing its neo-liberal bias, and hence, its limitations as a social change program. The final part forwards recommendations that function to improve the democratic credentials of positive aging.

THE GENEALOGY OF POSITIVE AGING

Positive aging represents a new model of aging policy that positions elders as potentially productive participants, and therefore, they are to be included in broader social agendas rather than be solely perceived as passive care recipients. This shift in perspective occurred as the result of a profound restructuring of social life that operates at both a global level and at the level of what has been described as the institutionalized life course. In Bauman's words,

[society] is being transformed by the passage from the 'solid' to the 'liquid' phases of modernity, in which all social forms melt faster than new ones can be cast [...] their allegedly short life-expectation undermines efforts to develop a strategy that would require the consistent fulfillment of a 'life-project.' (Bauman 303)

Such transformations have a profound impact on retirement and later life. In the past, the aging self was based on occupational biographies and incumbents' relationships to the welfare state. However, in contemporary times "the old have moved into a new 'zone of indeterminacy,' so that growing old is itself becoming a more social, reflexive, and managed process, notably in the relationship between the individual, the state, and a range of public as well as private services" (Phillipson and Powell 22). It was precisely to protect older people from the possible risks emanating from the coming of global capitalist economies as well as the shift of state welfare to the privatization of services, that governments and non-governmental organizations began advocating for aging policies to be based on the tenets of positive aging. Positive aging refers to the following:

[...] a new vision of ageing [...] that accepts the realities of a fundamental genetically driven bio-molecular process leading to death, but with the prospect of achieving healthy, active, productive, successful and positive ageing to the very end through lifestyle modification and interventions that work. (Andrews 1)

The discourse surrounding positive aging challenges assumptions about later life as a period of inevitable decline and focuses on the modifiable effects of lifestyle, attitude, skills, and technologies (Davey and Glasgow). It harbors a rejection of the assumption that adjustment to 'old age' is best achieved through a mutual withdrawal of individual and society, and instead, underlines the need to remain actively engaged in society in order to adapt successfully to older age. Although a number of terms are being used to describe this 'new' approach to aging, the notions of active aging, successful aging, and productive aging are dominant and widespread. The World Health Organization advocates a multi-dimensional definition of "active ageing" as "the process of optimizing opportunities for health, participation, and security in order to enhance quality of life as people age" (12). Active aging thus refers to continuing participation in social, economic, cultural, spiritual, and civic affairs, rather than just the ability to be physically active or to participate in the labor force. In Rowe and Kahn's influential work, 'successful aging' is defined as including three main components: low probability of disease and disease-related disability, high cognitive and physical functional capacity, and active engagement with life. However, successful aging is more than the absence of disease, it is their combination with active engagement with life that represents the concept most fully. Finally, "productive ageing" refers to any activity "that contributes to producing goods and services or develops the capacity to produce them" (Caro et al. 6). Such activities "are social valued in the sense that, if one individual or group did not perform them, there would be a demand for them to be performed by another individual or group" (Bass and Caro 37). Productive aging, therefore, includes paid employment, unpaid volunteer work, family care, but excludes enriching activities such as physical exercise, spiritual encounters, and learning for personal growth. The next section demonstrates how such ideas guide and inform national policies on aging.

POLICY FRAMEWORKS

Rationales celebrating positive aging have been highly attractive in policy circles as they draw inspiration from radical streams in gerontology as well as the age movement itself (Biggs 97). To governments, positive aging suggests a means of countering negative stereotyping of aging and promising the possibility of being critical of such stereotypes of decline, whilst still conforming to wider values in society. The policy discourse of positive aging generally includes the need for older individuals to be responsible for the outcomes of their life choices (particularly in relation to health and income), the necessity for communities to provide the social support required for individuals to make better choices over their life-course, and the urgency for governments to provide the infrastructure for both individuals and communities to give 'life' to these better choices (Asquith 256). Indeed, a concluding statement submitted to the United Nations Second World Assembly on Ageing reads:

A new vision of ageing was proposed that accepts the realities of a fundamental genetically driven bio-molecular process leading to death, but with the prospect of achieving healthy, active, productive, successful and positive ageing to the very end through lifestyle modification and interventions that work. (Andrews 1)

Rationales in favor of positive aging have also made significant in-roads in the European Union where it was stated:

The EU approach to ageing aims at mobilising the full potential of people of all ages [...]. This results in an orientation towards *active ageing policies and practices*. Core active ageing practices include lifelong learning, working longer, retiring later and more gradually, being active after retirement and engaging in capacity enhancing and health sustaining activities. (European Community 5-6; bold in original)

The New Labour government in the United Kingdom (1997-2010) has been particularly enthusiastic in its redefinition of adult aging (Biggs 100). One consolidating document states that "unless we encourage older people to remain actively engaged in socially valued activity, whether paid or unpaid, everybody in Britain will miss out on the benefits of their experience and social commitment" (Cabinet Office 1). Four key areas were identified for change namely to raise the expectations of older people and stop making judgments based on their age rather than their 'true value.' They wanted to encourage people aged 50 or older to stay in the work force, reverse incentives to retire early, and increase volunteering among older people. More recently, the policy paper *Opportunity Age* sought a 'new view' of aging as an "extension of opportunities for individuals and society" (HM Government 3). It explicitly stated the following:

[In] the years after 50 we all want three main things: the opportunity to continue our career, or the choice of starting a new one that better suits our family circumstances, to play a full and active role in society, with an adequate income and decent housing; and later to keep independence and control over our lives as we grow older, even if we are constrained by the health problems that sometimes affect the final years. (HM Government 3)

On the other side of the Atlantic, Canada set up a public committee to review public programs and services for seniors, to identify the gaps that exist in meeting the needs of the country's aging population, and as a result, make recommendations for service delivery in the future. Highlighting how difficult it is to talk about aging in a positive way in a society, capitalist countries are assailed with advertising which promises eternal youth. It was argued that

[m]indsets have to be changed if we are to go beyond our obsession with defying aging and youth-oriented society [...]. Social attitudes and marketing practices that are based on ageism create demographic silos where age groupings are pitted against each other in the workplace, in health care and in the media. This situation must change. (Special Senate Committee on Ageing 14)

On the basis of the abovementioned recommendations, positive aging made strong inroads in Canadian provinces. The *Nova Scotia Strategy for Positive Aging* (Seniors' Secretariat) emphasizes how aging is both a personal and a societal issue. It highlights the urgent need for policy statements that focus on promoting individual responsibility such as improving lifestyle choices that influence positive aging, while also addressing the broader role that families and communities play in ensuring seniors receive the support they need to age positively. Accordingly, the strategy stipulates nine key goals for positive aging, namely celebrating seniors, financial security, health and well-being, maximizing independence, housing options, transportation, respecting diversity, employment, life transitions, and supportive communities.

In Australasia, New Zealand launched a *Positive Aging Strategy* in 2001 with the objectives to improve opportunities for older people to participate in the community in whatever way they choose (Ministry of Social Development, *Positive ageing indicators report*). It was stated that such a goal will be achieved through identifying barriers to participation and working with all sectors to develop actions to address these and other difficulties, while balancing the needs of older people with the needs of younger and future generations. The New Zealand government highlighted that the *Positive Aging Strategy* is directed by ten key goals:

1. empowering older people,
2. providing opportunities for older people to participate in and contribute to family and community,
3. reflecting positive attitudes to older people,
4. recognizing the diversity of older people,
5. affirming the values and strengthen the capabilities of older Maori,
6. recognising the diversity and strengthen the capabilities of older Pacific people,
7. appreciating the diversity of cultural identity of older people,
8. recognising the different issues facing men and women,
9. ensuring older people, in both rural and urban areas, live with confidence in a secure and service-oriented environment, and
10. enabling older people to take responsibility for their personal growth and development.

(Ministry of Social Development, *New Zealand Aging Positive Strategy* 1)

A Critical Interlude

Rationales advocating positive aging constitute a breath of fresh air since, in place of disengagement and structured dependency perspectives, they highlight how retirement now offers the opportunity to develop a distinct and personally fulfilling lifestyle. However, policies overlook that later life does not arise in a social vacuum. Similar to younger peers, older people are living their lives in late modern societies which operate according to the socio-economic and political principles of neo-liberalism. Although Marxism has gone out of fashion, many theorists are noting how record levels of human agency have led to the fading of social inequalities, however, the truth could not be more opposite. As Mayo affirms, current societies are still characterized by a "scenario of mass impoverishment in various parts of the world [...] besides the persistence of structures of oppression in terms of class, gender, race, ethnicity, sexuality, and ability" (42). Research finds that the experience of older people is far from that of flying freely into space free of the fetters of structural inequalities (Formosa 17). Suffice to say here that as much as 19 percent of the people in the European Union (16 million) are living at the risk of poverty (Zaidi 1). One feature of retirement in late modernity is the growth of new inequalities alongside the continuation of traditional social divisions. Far from class, gender, and other types of inequality becoming less important, it is more a question of social division becoming redefined and experienced in different ways to earlier periods. In this respect, one finds two key lacunae in the planning and practice of positive aging.

ECONOMIC BIAS

Despite the emphasis on participation and holistic routes to well-being in later life, policy instruments and funding opportunities are biased in favor of increasing the number of older persons in employment. Unfortunately, the notion of productive aging has taken precedence over the concepts of active aging and successful aging. As Walker highlights, this may be due to a limited understanding of the concept of active aging beyond its application to the labor market. For example, according to the Organisation for Economic Cooperation and Development, active aging is "the capacity of people as they grow older to lead productive lives in the society and economy" (29). At the same time, the prevailing concept of successful aging is highly idealistic and strongly North American culture-bound, so that it fails to locate much empathy and affinity in a cross-cultural scenario. Although policy directives that provide older workers a better chance of continuing work beyond statutory retirement age are highly warranted today. The productive aging approach has been criticized for an overemphasis on economic activity that fails to incorporate notions such as work/ life balance and the societal benefits of recreational, creative, and spiritual pursuits (Formosa 2). The overall emphasis on workforce participation detracts from a holistic approach to wellbeing and limits the visibility of those who by choice or circumstance are no longer active workers or volunteers. Writing from an Australian perspective, Asquith claims that governments demanding from individuals to continue working to assist future generations

is a breach of the social contract in place for 100 years. While some older Australians may want to continue working, these are often workers who have jobs

that they enjoy and can continue doing beyond the age of 65. For manual workers, who have literally put their bodies on the line for Australian economic security, the promotion of additional working years contradicts the first component of
positive ageing – healthy ageing. (Asquith 263)

Indeed, positive aging is unashamedly economic, and uses 'efficiency' as
its main argument. Other evidence constitutes the EU's extensive drive to
improve the e-learning skills of older people. Although this is not in itself
wrong, one has to query the EU's strong interest in meeting the needs
of the dominant service industries and the relative neglect of the whole
range of abilities needed by the extensive assortment of productive sectors. As Borg and Mayo underline, "private and public interests, concerns
and agendas are slowly becoming one" (213). As such, positive aging is
characterized by a liberal avoidance of purpose, where older adults find
personal value through becoming a pool of surplus value although it is
an economic justification, rather than an ideological justification because
the claims of productivity is absent (Cole 440). Indeed, positive aging falls
short of challenging the contemporary economic dynamic. This is a social
inclusion based only on the terms of work and work-like activities and is
a position that appears limited when compared to alternative possibilities
for an aging identity, as has been identified through gerotranscendance
and the mature imagination (Biggs 110). Furthermore, it is questionable to
what extent productive aging is compatible with the lives, needs, and interests of older women. As Holstein noted, "since an older woman's market
value and contribution to the system of economic productivity is already
negligible, she can be further devalued if participation in that work culture becomes the new and valued norm for old age" (23). Of course, this
is not the same as saying that positive aging should shift its focus to the
activity and successful aging rationales as both positions include various
limitations. Activity theorists are criticized for their narrow focus on individual adaptation and satisfaction to the neglect of larger structural issues
and differences, with cultural critics pointing to the kinship between positive activity models of aging and consumerist ideologies (Katz, *Busy Bodies*
140). As Moody claims, active aging celebrates the 'frenzy of activity' whilst
masking the need for meaning. On the other hand, the focus of successful
aging in creating healthier older people must shift to healthier lifestyles
in childhood and adulthood, since "waiting for the arbitrary chronological
marker of 65 is the equivalent to closing the stable door after the horse has

bolted" (Asquith 262). Moreover, successful aging divides the population as 'wellderly' and 'illderly,' whilst giving the wrong impression that aging is a manageable problem (Estes et al. 70).

AGENTIC BIAS

Positive aging also fails to acknowledge the structural limitations that older people face in everyday life (Davey and Glasgow). Its emphasis on independence and activity functions to underplay the experience of people who for various reasons cannot age positively. Critics argue that the discourse of positive aging fails to acknowledge the limitations and difficulties that many older people face, and as a result allows society to avoid thinking about and creating a respected place for elderly people in society (Katz, *Busy Bodies* 145). Whilst there is no doubt as to the strong arguments present in social constructionist theories of the life course, it remains to say that "social constructions of old age have real consequences for those so defined" (Calasanti and Slevin 17). Indeed, the positive discourse on aging presents an image of active and healthy older age that for some may not be achievable. As Davey and Glasgow claim, the positive aging discourse portrays older people as able to counteract the effects of aging through personal effort. One can never underestimate the extent to which older adults inhabit a life-world typified by unique structural inequalities that limit their potential to age positively. Although all aging people experience some level of ageism and age discrimination, there are some sectors whose lives are characterized by other lifelong 'otherisms' as a result of which they experience even more intense levels of social exclusion. Research highlights a strong positive relationship between class and quality of life, with older people in working-class positions generally holding relatively lower levels of financial, social, physical and cultural capital – all of which hinder their success in aging actively, successfully, and productively (Formosa 141). The same can be said with respect to women and members of ethnic minorities whose life course is characterized by sparse opportunities compared to male and white peers respectively, so that they generally underperform in terms of socio-economic resources, bridging forms of social capital, and health status, whilst experiencing double and triple jeopardies of age, sex, and race discrimination (Formosa). Positive aging, in this sense, is geared towards "middle-class whites with sizable pensions and large automobiles...marked by 'compulsive tidy loans' and populated by 'tanned' golf-ers'[...] attained only by men whose race and class make them most likely to afford it" (Calasanti 202).

Furthermore, positive aging appears insensitive to the vulnerable and frail status of older people who are experiencing physical and cognitive difficulties. As Opie (cited in Davey and Glasgow 25) states, positive ag-ing renders the aging body invisible, hence, relying on "the very negatives which it ostensibly and ostentatiously denounces" (Davey and Glasgow 25). Similarly, Katz points out that positive aging does not make us deal well with issues of decline and death, both of which are highly integral to the aging transition (*Disciplining* 22). Positive aging is, therefore, guilty of age-denial. It focuses its energy and efforts on celebrating and propagating the so-called 'third-age lifestyle,' and in doing so, promotes its ethos at the expense of older and more defenseless people, namely those in the fourth age. As Karpf underlines,

Sustaining this age-denial is magic thinking that with enough Sudoku and per-sonal training you'll manage to bypass the fourth age altogether. By creating a new stereotype out of the mobile, healthy and affluent, you demonise the immo-bile, sick and poor. You also foment the belief that, through discipline and self-control, the body can always be transcended. It can't. (1)

RENEWING POSITIVE AGING

There is an urgent need for policy documents to provide an improved infra-structure for both individuals and communities to age positively. It is im-portant that rationales advocating positive aging adopt a realistic approach, namely one that does not blame the individual for unsuccessful or negative aging experiences. The following broad recommendations emerge from the discussion herein in hope of strengthening and furthering the demo-cratic credentials of positive aging policy.

Transformational agenda. Policies that act as catalysts for higher levels of positive aging should be directed to aid older people gain power over their lives. Positive aging must not be viewed as an end in itself, but as a vehicle for retraining or adjusting to technological change, improving strategies of self-fulfillment and a sense of purpose, and above all, a catalyst for indi-vidual and social empowerment. In sum, positive aging must arise as potential counter-hegemony to the current political scenario marked by neo-liberalism and the effect that this ideology has on daily living in later life.

Social inclusion. Positive aging must adopt a 'widening participation' agenda. Policy makers must think out of the box so that initiatives promoting active/successful/productive aging attract older adults with working class backgrounds, older men, ethnic minorities, and frail and vulnerable elders. There must be serious attempts in outreach work to reach older adults who could or would not usually participate in positive aging activities. It is fundamental that positive aging dismantles those barriers which exclude older people, other than middle-class white urban females, from aging actively/successfully, and productively.

Lifelong policies. Following Asquith, positive aging must be based on creating good health choices and opportunities for social inclusion during childhood and adulthood. Rather than simply focusing on retirement age, policies must focus on lifelong healthy living, ranging from childhood nutrition to reduction of drug use (including smoking) to physical exercise. At the same time, it must be realized that active and productive aging will only be achieved if people reach later life following extensive periods in active employment and learning environments that equip them with the necessary skills and mental attitude to age positively.

Fourth age. Positive aging must drop its obsession with enabling older people to remain active at all costs and at maintaining a mid-life focus. Instead, rationales are to propose policies and action plans that emphasize that, despite physical and cognitive difficulties, people are still able to age successfully. As an emergent body of literature strongly demonstrates, the quality of active and learning participation amongst older people in the 'fourth age' is impressive and exceeds all expectations (Findsen and Formosa 112).

These policy directions point towards the need for positive aging to embrace the concepts of 'social integration' and 'social inclusion' in both its planning and coordination stages. In particular, policy makers must raise their concerns as how the most vulnerable sectors of the aging population are to be empowered to reach higher levels of active, successful, and productive aging, to counter societal and legal imperatives promoting disengagement later in life. There is an urgent need for policies to configure how positive aging can be achieved through strategic alliances between state welfare, private entities, non-governmental organizations, community relationships, and most especially, older people themselves. For positive aging policies to be successful, they must be constructed by older persons for older persons.

Conclusion

Following Asquith, it can be stated that "despite the fact that the discourse of positive aging sounds positive, it is not" (266). Positive aging is destined to fail, not because its goals and objectives are not commendable. There is no doubt that positive aging (as expressed in the ideals of active aging, successful aging and productive aging) constitutes a good way forward. It is destined to fail because it is built on a wrong premise, namely presuming that if people are incapable of meeting the benchmarks of a positive aging experience, they have negatively (or unhealthily, unsuccessfully, or unproductively) aged. This is tantamount to a 'blame the victim' approach where vulnerable and disengaged elders are made to "bear the weight of failure as it is represented in the terms opposed to healthy, successful, and productive" (Asquith 266). Positive aging is also unethical in neo-liberal times because it transforms the 'public' issue of aging into a 'private' one where aging citizens themselves are expected to solve challenges that arise out of the political economical contexts of globalization and late capitalism (Mills 2). As Asquith notes, "positive ageing requires more than an individual response to the biological process of decay" (266). A more equitable way forward is a bottom-up approach that is sensitive to the social constructionist nature of aging and later life, and also attempts to direct more socio-economic and political resources towards the most vulnerable and frail members of the aging population. The recommendations posted in the penultimate section of this paper should surely serve as initial step towards such a goal.

References

Andrews, Gary. *Statement*. Second United Nations World Assembly on Ageing, Madrid, Spain, 8-12 April, 2002. Web. 12 December 2012.

Asquith, Nicole. "Positive ageing, neoliberalism and Australian sociology." *Journal of Sociology* 45.3 (2009): 255-69. Print.

Bass, A. Scott, and Francis G. Caro. "Productive aging: A conceptual framework." *Productive Aging: Concepts and challenges*. Ed. Nancy Morrow-

Howell, James Hinterlong, and Michael Sherraden. Baltimore: The John Hopkins University Press, 2001. 37-78. Print.

Bauman, Zygmunt. *Liquid life.* Cambridge: Policy Press, 2005. Print.

Biggs, Simon. "New ageism: Age imperialism, personal experience and ageing policy." *Ageing and diversity: Multiple pathways and cultural migrations.* Ed. Svein Olav Daatland and Simon Biggs. Bristol: Policy Press, 2004. 95-122. Print.

Borg, Carmel, and Peter Mayo. "The EU Memorandum on lifelong learning: Old wine in new bottles." *Globalisation, Societies, and Education* 3.2 (2005): 203-25. Print.

Cabinet Office. *Winning the generation game.* London: Cabinet Office, 2000. Print.

Calasanti, Toni. "Theorising age relations." *The need for theory: Critical approaches to social gerontology.* Ed. Simon Biggs, Ariel Lowenstein, and Jon Hendricks, Amityville, NY: Baywood, 2003. 199-218. Print.

Calasanti, Toni, and Kathleen Slevin. *Gender, social inequalities, and aging.* Walnut Creek, CA: AltaMira Press, 2001. Print.

Caro, G. Francis, Scott A. Bass, and Yung-Ping Chen. "Introduction: Achieving a productive aging society." *Achieving a productive aging society.* Ed. Francis G. Caro, Scott A. Bass, and Yung-Ping Chen. Westport, CT: Auburn House, 1993. 1-25. Print.

Cole, Mark. "The Issue of Age in The Learning Age: A Critical Review of Lifelong Learning in the United Kingdom under New Labour." *Education and Ageing* 5.3 (2000): 437-53. Print.

Davey, Judith, and Glasgow. "Positive aging: A critical analysis." *Policy Quarterly* 2.4 (2006): 21-27. Print.

Devall, Donna. *The power of positive aging.* Bloomington, IN: Xlibris Corp, 2010. Print.

Estes, L. Carroll, Simon Biggs, and Chris Phillipson. *Social theory, social policy, and ageing: A critical introduction.* Berkshire: Open University Press, 2003. Print.

European Community. *Europe's response to world ageing: Promoting economic and social progress in an ageing world: A contribution to the 2nd World Assembly on ageing.* Brussels: European Community, 2002. Print.

Findsen, Brian, and Marvin Formosa. *Lifelong learning in later life: A handbook on older adult learning.* Rotterdam, Netherlands: Sense Publishers, 2011. Print.

Formosa, Marvin. *Class dynamics in later life: Older persons, class identity and class action.* Hamburg: Lit, 2009. Print.

Gilleard, Chris, and Paul Higgs. "The third age: Class, cohort or generation?" *Ageing and Society* 22.3 (2002): 369-82. Print.

Holstein, Martha. "Productive aging: A feminist critique." *Journal of Aging and Public Policy* 4.3.4. (1993): 17-34. Print.

HM Government. *Opportunity Age: Meeting the challenges of ageing in the 21st century,* London: HM Government, 2005. Print.

Katz, Stephen. *Disciplining old age: The formation of gerontological knowledge.* Charlottesville, VA: The University Press of Virginia, 1996. Print.

Katz, Stephen. "Busy bodies: Activity, aging, and the management of everyday life." *Journal of Aging Studies* 14.2 (2000): 135-52. Print.

Karpf, Anne. "In this golden age of ageing, old people are met with fear and loathing." *The Guardian* 28 June 2011. Web. 1 Sept. 2011.

Lane, John. *The art of ageing: Inspiration for a positive and abundant life.* London: Green Books, 2010. Print.

Mayo, Peter. "A rationale for a transformative approach to education." *Journal of Transformative Education* 1.1 (2003): 38-57. Print.

Mills, Wright Charles. *The sociological imagination.* Oxford: Oxford University Press, 1959. Print.

Ministry of Social Development. *New Zealand positive ageing strategy.* Wellington: Ministry of Social Development, 2001. Print.

Ministry of Social Development. *Positive ageing indicators report.* Wellington: Ministry of Social Development, 2007. Print.

Moody, R. Harry. *Abundance of Life: Human development policies for an aging society.* New York: Columbia University Press, 1988. Print.

Organisation for Economic Cooperation and Development. *Ageing in OECD countries. A critical policy challenge.* Paris: Organization for Economic Cooperation and Development, 1996. Print.

Phillipson, Chris, and Jason L. Powell. "Risk, social welfare and old age." *Old age and agency.* Ed. Emmanuelle Tulle. New York: Nova Science Publishers, 2004. 17-26. Print.

Rowe, W. John, and Robert L. Kahn. "Successful ageing." *The Gerontologist* 37.4 (1997): 433-40. Print.

Seniors' Secretariat (Nova Scotia). *Strategy for positive aging in Nova Scotia.* Novascotia.ca. Communications Nova Scotia, 2005. Web. 1 Sept. 2011.

Special Senate Committee on Ageing. *Canada's aging population: Seizing the opportunity. Special Senate Committee on Ageing Report.* The Senate of Canada. The Special Senate Committee on Aging, 2009. Web. 1 Sept. 2011.

Walker, Alan. "Commentary: The emergence and application of active ageing in Europe." *Journal of Aging and Social Policy* 21.1 (2009): 75-93. Print.

World Health Organization. *Active ageing: A policy framework*. Geneva: World Health Organization, 2002. Print.

Zaidi, Asghar. *Poverty risks for older people in EU countries – An update*. Austria, Vienna: European Centre for Social Policy and Research, 2010. Print.

Celebrating or Denying Age?

On Cultural Studies as an Analytical Approach in Gerontology

Karin Lövgren

This article explores the limitations and possibilities of applying a cultural studies approach to aging studies and gerontology. The chosen empirical material consists of popular magazines targeted at an older female audience. These glossy commercial magazines in many ways resemble magazines intended for younger women or lifestyle magazines; what is new and different about them is that the targeted audience is older. This press genre is a fairly new phenomenon in Sweden and saw a boom in 2006, as several such magazines were launched. Since then, some titles have been discontinued.

In media, small narratives or cultural messages – for example, on aging – are created, circulated, repeated, and mirrored. Yet, while media may set the agenda for the debate (Edström 31-46; Gripsrud 64), it does not control it, which instead is done in interaction with audiences who spread news, discuss current topics, or simply leave a news item to fade away into oblivion. It is impossible to separate media messages from other messages or forms of communication between people. We are all enmeshed in our cultures, so that although the impact and influence of mediated messages are readily discussed in theoretical and philosophical terms, it is difficult, if not impossible, to establish the same empirically. Users sift the mediated messages they encounter during the day, adopting different reading positions, rejecting some messages, reading other messages oppositionally, negotiating some and adapting or latching onto others (Hall 130; Featherstone and Hepworth, "Images of Aging" 735). Even though the direction of influence or impact cannot be determined, cultural studies can contribute to the analysis by shedding light on how messages are communicated and negotiated.

In this article, I commence by describing the research design, method, and materials used, and continue with an overview of messages about age and aging communicated in this commercial genre of the popular press. I then discuss the usefulness of a cultural studies approach in such an analysis, but also its limitations.

RESEARCH DESIGN, METHOD, MATERIAL

The research design used for this study is a modified version of the "cultural circuit" used in cultural studies (Du Gay 3; Radway).[1] There were three vantage points for developing an understanding of communication of cultural notions on aging. Magazines targeting women over forty were used as the point of departure. Interviews with representatives of the marketing and advertising industries were undertaken in order to understand how the market talks about addressing consumers who are older than the norm. The magazines are dependent on income from advertisers, so these cultural intermediaries are important. The sampling strategy for interviewing cultural intermediaries was to follow a chain of production: representatives for cosmetics companies; marketing experts and researchers; advertising agencies – one specifically aimed at a senior market and one at a youth market as well as those working with different customers; media brokers; publishing companies – and there specifically representatives in charge of finding potential advertisers for the magazines, doing analyses of the market and segmenting targeted audiences, and finally journalists and editors, both freelance and contracted. 18 representatives with many years of experience in trade were interviewed.

---

1 | For a more detailed description of the research design see Lövgren, *Se lika ung*. Radway's by now classic cultural study of romance deals with the publishing and retailing system of romances, interviews with readers on their thoughts and feelings about romances, and a text analyses of the romances, thus covering a cultural circuit.

Second, the magazines – both texts and images, both editorial content and ads – were analyzed, primarily in order to examine what cultural messages on aging their readers encounter.

The third vantage point was to interview women in the targeted age category. 14 women were interviewed, five of them in a group interview. An additional four women wrote letters on their thoughts on aging, magazine reading and advertising. The women lived either in Stockholm and surroundings or in smaller cities in Central Sweden, and were mainly from a middle class background, working for instance as nurses, nurses' aides, as assistants at companies or as teachers. Five were either granted early retirement due to sickness or were partly on sick leave. They were between 43 and 63, the age category targeted by these magazines.

The interviews were loosely structured, using an interview guide and a conversational style that left the informants to choose the direction. A checklist was used to ensure that the same basic topics were covered: biographical background; everyday life; thoughts on being in this stage of life and on aging; media consumption habits and opinions on advertising. During the interviews, interviewer and interviewee together looked at magazines and ads. Informants were asked to point out the ads that caught their attention, and to show their favorite sections of the magazines in order for the interviewer to capture how different cultural values came into play in order to draw conclusions about the meaning, influence, and impact of representations, and ultimately to analyze cultural notions of age and aging.

The interviews were transcribed verbatim, and detailed field notes were taken when analyzing the magazines. The documents emerging from this process were read several times and recurring themes, discrepancies and contradictions were marked. The themes were used as guidelines in the interpretative work, at which point various analytical questions concerning the material were raised. The main questions regarding the mediated material were how older or middle-aged women were represented, under which circumstances they were depicted, in what ways, in what kind of relations to others, and how: whether they were depicted as equal or as subordinated to others, as powerful or subjugated (O'Barr 3-4).

In the analyses, what was said was equally important as how it was expressed. Informants very often referred to age and aging in ambivalent terms, both underscoring its relevance and denying its importance. The same was true concerning how age was presented in magazine texts and images; on the one hand, aging was disavowed by extolling the forever young; on the other, aging was celebrated for the experience and self-confidence it was claimed to bring.

In terms of theory, the concept of "doing age" (West and Zimmerman 126; Calasanti and Slevin 12; Lövgren, *Se lika ung* 48) was used to emphasize that the manner in which meaning is ascribed to age and aging is a cultural negotiating process undertaken not only in communication between people, but also on an institutional level. Parallel to a gender order, there is an age order: people and institutions distinguish between different age categories and ascribe different norms and expectations to each. Individuals grow older, and as they do so, they change places in the age order, but the age-divided stages are more static and less prone to change (Bytheway 6-9; Närvänen 22-24). Age can be construed both as something to be accomplished – done in relation to expectations and norms – and also as something that is institutionalized.

A CULTURAL STUDIES APPROACH

The cultural studies approach used in this article follows a model of first establishing how the magazine producers talked of age and aging; second, identifying the messages on this theme in the magazines; and, finally, listening to what women, the readers, had to say about late middle age and their own readings and interpretations of the magazines and ads. It is important to stress that this disposition does not imply causality with messages flowing from a sender to a passive receiver. Instead, there is a complex interflow of cultural messages in different directions.

PRODUCERS

There is evidence that marketers are increasingly interested in the so-called 'grey market of older consumers.' As early as in the 1980s, marketers were talking about the importance of going by demographics and addressing the baby boomers, the large cohort born between the 1940s and early 1960s who had grown up in a consumer society and was considered affluent (Carrigan and Szmigin 219; Gunter 6; Sawchuk 177-78). With this in mind, one can only conclude that it has taken the market a long time to begin advertising and marketing to older target groups. The industry representatives who were interviewed displayed an ambivalent approach to older consumers, seeing them as uninteresting and arguing that they might negatively impact the image of a company. Being associated with older consumers was even referred to as "a kiss of death" (Szmigin and Carrigan 136; Carrigan and Szmigin 219; Lövgren, *Se lika ung*; Lövgren, "See themselves" 334). One media consultant, for example, used the phrase "geriatric mags" when talking of the glossy magazines for women of fifty and over. This devaluation of the older consumer is also evident in statistics on media habits of older people – consumers older than seventy-nine have been excluded. Companies advertising products on Swedish television do not have to buy airtime used to reach them, they are only paying for slots for television ads that target younger viewers (Lövgren, "See themselves" 57). The elderly are considered a stagnant market, stuck in their ways, incurious, and less given to trying new products. One informant used the phrase "coagulated" when describing them.

In contrast to this denigrating attitude towards older consumers, there are marketers who emphasize that there is now a golden opportunity to reach a hitherto ignored target group with both money and the leisure to spend it. That Swedish baby boomers own 80 percent of the wealth and represent 70 percent of the country's spending power was a mantra repeated both in the texts of the magazines and in the informants' accounts of whom to address and target (Lövgren, *Se lika ung* 11, 85, 183). The magazines' marketing departments pointed out what they saw as misconceptions about older consumers, claiming that the elderly are just as good consumers as anyone. Thus, it is for their affluence, spending power, and competent consumption that the elderly are being targeted and constructed as 'forever young' or 'youthful.' Address all consumers as if they were young, and you will reach everyone, has been the underlying assumption, since both the chronologically young and those young at heart will be attracted by such ads. The result, somewhat paradoxically, is a number of circumscriptions of definitions of the older consumer. In trying to target this demographic and economic category, the marketers avoid addressing them as 'old' or including them in the age category of 'old people.'

MESSAGES IN THE MAGAZINES

What are the messages about age and aging in these magazines? In the texts and ads, there are allusions to a discrepancy between chronological age and subjective, felt age – a notion that has been examined in gerontology (see, for example, Featherstone and Hepworth, "Mask of Aging;" Hurd Clarke; Fairhurst; Öberg, "Images;" Öberg and Tornstam, "Body Images;" Öberg and Tornstam, "Youthfulness;" Öberg and Tornstam, "Attitudes"). The magazines also display some ambivalence towards the notion of aging. This is hardly unique to magazines that have a given age as their selling point, as it is common to all 'women's magazines:' articles claiming to boost the reader's ego and self-confidence are interspersed with articles on the self as an object for constant refashioning, dieting, and bodily improvements. In midlife magazines, articles on how to dye your hair are followed by texts claiming to expose the myth that having grey hair ages you; there are articles criticizing the way beauty work leaves you working three shifts – employed work, household work, and beauty work – and articles on the importance of never neglecting your beauty routine, and how to clean and pamper your skin around the clock; there are articles criticizing what has been coined as 'chronic youth syndrome,' where only youth is valued, and articles on how to keep young and how to come across as youthful, in fact, on being young regardless of age.

The texts contend that women should look as young as possible without coming across as desperate and trying too hard. A woman should preserve her looks, but not spend an exaggerated amount of time on her body. Cultural body work should look natural and doing it should be pleasant and enjoyable. There is a certain moral condemnation expressed of those who do not adhere to its norms. The arguments in its favor are health and well-being, and it is stated that it demands discipline and privation. In both their visual and editorial content, the magazines perform a delicate balancing act when it comes to the cultural meaning of aging.

The magazines make older women visible, something that is achieved in two different ways. One is to use glamorized images of older women. Here, age is not an issue. The women are presented as looking youthful and beautiful. The other way is to work with images of actual older readers in order to increase reader identification. These images represent ordinary people. The images, just like the texts, have an upbeat tone. And it should be noted that they in particular celebrate the baby boomers who are described as 'too young to be old,' and are said to be growing older in a different way than previous generations. From this it can be deduced that it is the demographically large cohort of the baby boomers that is targeted by marketers and publishers.

The message in the magazines is that older people are still young – and are, as consumers, as good as anyone. Aging is in fact denied. This plays out in individualistic messages on aging common to magazines directed at older people. Successful aging – that is, staying young in mind and body – is presented in the texts as a question of choice. Moreover, the magazines' balancing act includes never positioning the process of aging as one of decline. Instead, the texts are full of advice and encouragement. This leaves the reader positioned differently vis-à-vis the images and the texts: role models to aspire to or fantasize about, and models to identify with. Age is denied by claiming that age does not matter, and yet age is enforced by the simple fact that it is one of the targeting issues and a constant focus point.

The magazines discuss certain issues, yet they never truly challenge the status quo. They can be understood as part of a feminist, consumerist logic, appropriating feminism and anti-agism whilst selling commodities both in the form of advertised products and in the form of narratives (Gill 83-84, 94-95).

READERS ON THEIR READING

When the informants talked about reading magazines, they stressed the *act* of reading.[2] Several women talked with sensuous delight of slitting open the crinkly wrapper on a new, fresh, unread magazine and of the pleasure of curling up on the sofa, taking time for themselves, indulging in time free of demands.

When they were asked about media material, the editorial content, and the ads, a clear pattern of different reading positions emerged. One can be described as a rather critical stance prompted in part by the interview situation itself. Informants distanced themselves from the reading material. They pointed to the contradictions and criticized messages on aging or on gender relations; they stressed that the images seemed photoshopped and often portrayed glamorized celebrities: in sum, they showed a keen

---

2 | This is also found in Radway's study of romance reading (86-118).

awareness of the genre and its requirements. One informant compared the magazines to a bag of mixed candy, emphasizing all that was lightweight, glossy, glamorous, and by implication contrasting this reading with "healthier," more nutritious reading matter. Another touched on her disappointment at the very unattainability of the consumer products advertised or the lifestyle flaunted, although she, too, acknowledged the element of fantasy, the pleasure of dreaming while reading:

I always get disappointed when I buy a magazine. They are more like catalogues. At the same time, it can feel luxurious just sitting there and dreaming, fantasizing about being somewhere else. I wouldn't want socially realistic reporting either. That seems boring; you get enough of it anyway, I think.

In a group interview, some women commented, "These magazines are supposed to make women feel good." The informants joked about the ambivalences and contradictions of the magazines, saying, for instance, that whilst they read articles on dieting, they would be reaching for cookies. The different contradictory messages were described as offers that could be read, or just browsed through, or ignored. The women had noted the contradictions, but instead of seeing them as a problem, they saw them as more of an asset. They claimed that in this sense, the magazines had something for everyone: if you are not attracted by the message in the text, you simply ignore it, quite literally turning the page. The advice given on beauty work or boosting self-confidence might justify the time spent by reading it as being beneficial and enlightening, educational even.

Another informant pointed out, "They've got to have something you can aspire to, something unattainable." She shows an awareness of how women's bodies are positioned culturally as in constant need of being redone or made over, and that this relentless 'project of the self' is an impossible task. One way of reading is to identify with the text; another is to find it inspirational, a reading in which the representations are used as role models to aspire to or as fantasy objects to dream about. This illustrates different forms of reading: with the text, in opposition, or in negotiation (Hall 136).

Another recurring reading position was more difficult for the informants to verbalize, and they fell back on words such as "nice," "feels good," "treat," "pleasure," and "enjoyment," using incomplete sentences and letting their intonation convey pleasure and indulgence.

The readers came across both as shrewd analysts, able to distance themselves from the texts, which they criticize in detail, and as pleasure-seekers prepared to spend money and time on themselves.

CIRCULATING CONCEPTIONS

The main cover line of *Tara*, one of the glossy magazines targeting women in middle age and older proclaims, "Look 10 years younger." It proffers advice on how to achieve this by sartorial means, by beauty work, and by body work. The feature elaborates:

You can't become younger. Of course. But you can look as young as you feel. In this number's fashion and beauty special you'll get advice on how to update yourself. It happens to most people. One day you look in the mirror and see someone looking older than you feel. In the quest for beauty some make the mistake of trying to look much younger than they are. [...] What you can do is rediscover yourself. Which in a magical way results in those extra ten years that appeared in the mirror just falling away. (*Tara* 37)

This is a good example of the double standard of women's magazines. "You cannot deny your age," the article begins. Yet, the discrepancy between how old you look and how old you feel needs to be minimized. This requires a balancing act – looking as young as you feel, but doing so in a way that appears effortless. In the analyzed articles, "young" and "youthful" are synonyms for "curious," "modern," "evolving," "attractive," and "desirable". Youthfulness is not the same as actual youth, but instead it is a cultural quality that conveys societal value. The message of inner youth is also echoed in ads, especially in those for anti-wrinkle and anti-aging products. "Look as young as you feel" is the recurring slogan, albeit in different versions. The concept of "ten years younger" also recurs in ads, as do the allusions to an exact time frame for how rapid the promised youthifying transformation will be, ranging from one hour to overnight.

The feeling of different ages – felt age and apparent age – was also referred to by the interviewed readers who claimed that they sometimes did not recognize themselves in the mirror. They described surprise and astonishment at seeing themselves. "Who is that woman? She looks so grouchy and morose," one woman explained her reaction to her image in the mirror, referring not only to her sense that her inner self was not reflected in age terms, but also to the perception that her looks failed to properly convey her mood and her feelings. This illustrates the concept that age identification and chronology differ, and advertisers and commercial magazines make use of this gap by providing advice on how to present a younger self. The ad asks, "Is your inner self no longer reflected by your outward appearance?" and promises a remedy, if you use their particular products.

Several different cultural conceptions of age and aging recur in the empirical material: that people feel younger than their chronological age; that this difference is approximately ten years; that sometimes people do not recognize themselves in the mirror; that aging entails a transition into invisibility that must be avoided at all costs. The trope of the 'little old lady' is used as a marker of aging, warning women of the type of aging that should be avoided. The message of the ads is echoed and reinforced in the editorial content and the images. All these elements were mentioned by the informants, not only those working in advertising or magazine publishing, and also reinforced by the messages in the magazines. There was an occasional note of ambivalence regarding how aging was talked about. There was a longing to let things slide, to give up constantly monitoring your appearance, and to prioritize comfort over looks, and a stress on how aging brought experience, increased self-confidence, and an ability to state your mind and no longer defer to others. Yet, there was also a constant awareness of a culture that puts a premium on youth, so that in order to be taken into account, you must appear youthful. The advertising and media rhetoric has become a resource for people in their quest to understand themselves and to become culturally understandable beings.

Supplying Demand

When discussing ads, there was also a contradictory discourse. On the one hand, readers stressed that the ads mostly failed to catch their attention, and instead their interest might be caught by images of shoes or purses, while ads for anti-aging creams might go unnoticed. Advice by beauty columnists would be read, but ads were rarely talked of as triggering interest in a product. Instead, several of the women talked knowingly of airbrushing, retouching, and photo shopping pictures, pointing out different ads where they thought this was evident in the visual imagery.

The informants said they did not buy products because of the promises made in the ads, claiming instead that their consumption was guided by price, previous experience with a product or advice of a professional. Even so, they felt confident that ads worked. They stressed that if advertising did not work, there would not be any, arguing that the mere fact of its existence confirmed its efficacy. Some thought that ads functioned unconsciously, subliminally; others argued that ads worked particularly well on younger people, but that their experience allowed them to better evaluate commercial promises. Here, a higher chronological age was talked of as an asset that allowed them to be more independent and less vulnerable to mediated messages and pressure.

The interviewed advertisers also spoke in contradictory terms about the impact of advertising. They happily represented themselves as qualified manipulators, well aware of which buttons to push in order to create a certain feeling or to encourage consumption, yet they claimed that what worked was unpredictable, describing most advertising expenses as "money down the drain." They argued that it was impossible to foresee what would catch public attention. They sometimes even said in a self-deprecating mood that companies had to advertise in order to show their belief in their products, and that advertising worked because there was a tacit agreement that it worked.

Did the readers think that media influences them? That mediated messages have an impact? The answer is yes and no. They believe that media matters, but still there was a certain ambivalence in the way they talked about it. The informants felt that at their age, media no longer had the same impact it had on young women. In fact, young women were consistently considered to be victims of media pressure and mediated ideals that would be impossible to live up to. It is interesting to note how youthfulness was seen as a desirable quality in the editorial content of the magazines, in contrast to the descriptions of actual young people as exposed and vulnerable, and youth as a horrific time of life.

When it came to discussions of media responsibility, there was a twofold contradictory discourse. This duality was evident in the interviews both with professionals – advertisers and magazine editors – and with middle-aged women. Media was spoken of as being powerful, influencing people's perceptions and self-images, and impacting young, vulnerable women in particular. However, media was also talked of as merely responding to audience needs, supplying demand by providing a pleasurable read. Media ideals were described as being impossible to live up to, but nevertheless it was also said that these messages and representations existed because the audience demanded and expected them.

IS MEDIA THE CULPRIT?

The elderly are by far the most underrepresented age category in media (von Feilitzen 34, 48, 55, Edström 97-98). They are thus almost invisible relative to their actual number. Once gender is factored in, the pattern becomes even more disturbing: elderly women are practically inexistent.

To be rendered invisible in a mediated landscape is a form of subordination, even annihilation, as media researcher Gaye Tuchman (173) puts it. Tuchman described media's annihilation of women in terms of omission, trivialization, and condemnation (173). Media has an impact by setting the agenda for current debates and discourses, which in turn does much to determine levels of interest. In sight, in mind: visibility mirrors cultural values, influences how a category is perceived, and represents symbolic value. Some media researchers claim that media stereotypes enforce a symbolic order of subordination and the distribution of power and influence (Lumme-Sandt 46). The fact that youthful looks and young role models are overrepresented thus has an impact, as it demonstrates what is culturally valued, which in turn affects people's aspirations. Mediated images reflect the symbolic power structure of a culture in which white, middle-aged men of productive age have the most power. Symbolic oppression in the form of invisibility can lead to low self-esteem, less solidarity and identification with other members of the same category, and an acceptance of subordination (Laws 113). Referring to Iris Marion Young's work on media representation, Glenda Laws discusses ageism as a form of cultural imperialism (113): subordinated groups are made invisible or represented as ridiculous. It is in the same fashion that media represent older members of the public.

By targeting older women, the press has contributed to their visibility in the mediated landscape. This can be interpreted as empowering. The norm for those depicted visually in media is young, and there is reason to believe that this influences how people identify with someone who is chronologically younger. This dominance of younger visual representations entails that there are fewer opportunities for representation of diversity, such as images of different body shapes and different forms of aging. Instead, people are forced to compare themselves to, identify with, or distance themselves from those who are younger. This partly explains why people feel a discrepancy between their felt and apparent ages.

The informants working for glossy, commercial magazines that target women in older age categories stressed that they had problems finding images of older people (Lövgren, *Se lika ung* 133-43). In an interview, the chief editor of one of the magazines targeting middle age women stated that when asking image agencies or advertising agencies for pictures of someone in their sixties, she might get photos of a frail, elderly woman heavily leaning on a walking frame, as their concept of older is vague (Unsgaard 66). The fact that older women are not only visible in the magazines, but are also presented as attractive and conscious about their appearance, was one of the merits that the readers pointed out. They felt seen and acknowledged. As several informants referred to their feelings of becoming more invisible as they aged and stating that they were no longer seen as sexually attractive or worth taking into account, being seen was acknowledged as the antidote to being made invisible.

It is empowering when older women are made visible in a mediated landscape, especially when they are usually invisible – in fact, annihilated, to use Tuchman's term (173). However, it is problematic that there is an underlying commercial logic wholly concerned with 'good' consumers. When defending the idea that ads and media should be directed at older age categories, the aspect that consumers over fifty represented 70 percent of Sweden's spending power and 80 percent of total wealth was often mentioned.

In commercial media, emphasis is on norms of agelessness, for it is imperative to appear as young as possible. This reinforces a denial of aging rather than encouraging a celebratory stance, and this in turn impacts age identification: if consumers/readers are forced to identify with role models who look young for their age, this may well displace the norms of how one should look at a certain age. Glenda Laws claims that popular culture is of importance because of its impact and mass appeal (116). It informs people and shapes their self-images and conceptions of their own bodies as well as of that of others. She claims that we respond to representations as we respond to real people, but as the way in which representations are read and interpreted is not well understood, this is a difficult claim to sustain. Featherstone and Hepworth (*Images* 735) stress the flexibility with which images operate and the way they are always open to different interpretations. They argue that images of old age should be viewed as prescriptive social texts

(*Images* 739). Visual representations of people of youthful appearance can be taken to signal norms and imperatives. In turn, this may further enforce a separation between the aging body and the eternally young inner self.

Evidently, there is a variety of different cultural conceptions in circulation: the informants drew on them when talking about aging; there were references to them also in the media texts; ads made use of this with advice on how consumption can offer a strategy to handle aging. However, this cannot fully explain how cultural concepts are conceived and communicated. Thus, it cannot be inferred that it is copywriters and advertisers – the media – who influence readers and consumers. It would be incorrect to assume that readers automatically compare concepts and notions in media to themselves, and that media is solely responsible for any adaptions on part of the consumers. This jump to conclusions ignores the argument that media depends on generally accepted concepts in texts, referring to common notions of aging. Media and advertisers feed on notions that are spread in different ways across society, and they know how best to appeal to notions that already have their readers' interest. They respond to a need they claim their readers have, in this case the aim of conveying their inner, young selves. But in so doing, media also spreads notions perpetuating views and constructions of aging that in turn influence readers who are trying to come to terms with their own aging.

POSSIBILITIES AND LIMITATIONS
OF A CULTURAL STUDIES APPROACH

The model of the cultural circuit, with sender, text, and receiver, is an over-simplification of the role of the different cultural intermediaries involved, as is the concept of message transmission, such as the so-called "injection model" (Gripsrud 49-75; Hall 128). Most researchers agree that there is no such thing as one-way transmission, but instead a complex interflow of cultural meaning.

A cultural studies approach has certain benefits in that it emphasizes context, one example being the dimensions of production. In a context of selling magazines, or selling advertising space to keep a commercial magazine in business, there are certain limits as to what and how something may be said. There is a tendency of the genre for the messages to be upbeat and stick to a certain agenda. Advertisers, magazine editors, and journalists are sensitive to the *Zeitgeist*, but, as many of the informants pointed out, they are also conservative when it comes to the representation of gender and age. This conclusion also explains readers' ambivalent responses: the act of reading itself can be intense and pleasurable, and yet the readers are aware and critical of the underlying ideologies. Readers can identify with or aspire to, fantasize, reject, and ignore: the negotiation process is nothing if not complex. It has been stated that images in media are important, because we measure ourselves against them, and these images shape attitudes towards old people (Lumme-Sandt 45). My analysis, however, has shown that the process is more complex than a one-way communication of media messages to a passive audience who merely reacts to the senders' construction. Granted, it is difficult to assess how reading material influences a person's self-image or perception of aging, yet a close reading of the magazine texts can reveal contradictions and paradoxes – multifold discourses.

Although all dimensions of the cultural circuit are equally important, it is worth dwelling on the role of the sender. I think it does matter who conveys a message and who has the right to define and verbalize. As far as aging as an asymmetric power relationship goes, one of the problems is that it has mainly been others who have spoken for, in this case, older people. Who has so far been given the opportunity to report from 'deep old age'? In this context, it is of relevance that people are reluctant to think of themselves as old, as individuals have a sense of continuity in selfhood or personhood. They are the same, though older (Fairhurst 268-69; Jones 86). Another explanation focuses on status loss and threat associated with being seen as old (Calasanti and Slevin 12, 14), leaving people keen to avoid being included in an elderly category with the stigma associated with it (Featherstone and Hepworth, "Images of Aging" 740). Age as a number does not capture the feeling or the many-layered meanings that are ascribed to it when doing age, using it as description and explanation, both denying it and insisting on its relevance.

Images of old age are changing. In conjunction with changing demographics and the state of the market, it is far more common now to encounter representations of older people as golf-playing hedonists, enjoying their leisure, and consuming experiences and adventures as well as commodities. They are described as healthy and wealthy. This is an argument used by market representatives as a reason to address older consumers. These representations capture a change in the image of older people as fragile and in need of care to one where they are free to indulge in consumption and leisure. It also illustrates how the old are now positioned as privileged and thought to have benefited – even profited – from the generational transference of wealth. The mediated image of older people is accomplished by a combination of changing factors: in demography, in health, in the state of the market, in politics, and in global as well as local events. The mediated image is neither solely the result of media's efforts, nor does it exert influence in an isolated way. Instead, there is a complex interplay between economy, politics, media, and communication between readers or consumers on an everyday basis. These changes regarding representation of old age can be compared with how media represented housewives, when after the Second World War women were strongly encouraged to return to the home leaving waged work to bread-winning men. Later, when there was a shortage of labor, the homemaker era ended. These changes went hand in hand with changes in representation. However, it cannot be claimed that media influences readers by mere force of imagery. Rather, changes in representation went hand in hand with changes in economics, demography, the state of the market, and policy issues. An economic change was reflected and shaped in different mediated images.

Media matters. Cultural studies can help shed light on everyday use of images of aging acknowledging how the media industry operates, taking into account different contexts and the demands of genre. The cultural meaning ascribed to aging can be questioned in terms of how people negotiate and draw meaning from media. Cultural studies can help analyze the production and reception process of commercial messages. Still, it is also important to keep in mind other aspects of age segregation and discrimination and how they interact and intersect with media representation.

CONCLUSION

In conclusion, media constitutes and contributes to cultural building blocks indispensable to the meaning that is ascribed to aging; however, such messages cannot readily be distinguished from other forms of communication, whether politically or interpersonally. There are different reading positions or stances. Readers negotiate and interpret texts in different ways: aspiring, dreaming, fantasizing; for pleasure, to escape, as a treat; or – in opposition to the text – ignoring messages from the producer, sometimes comparing themselves with role models, and at other times skipping over messages. It is of interest to focus on the readers' own meaning-making. There are economic interests in the production of popular culture: the need to turn a profit must be taken into account. Popular culture is sensitive to the *Zeitgeist* and conservative in its approach to gender and age. In analyses, it is important to focus on the genre in question and on how it influences the narration, both visually and verbally. At the same time it is important to consider the demands of the genre and examine the mediated messages critically. There is an interflow of cultural notions between readers, consumers, editors, and advertisers – between different cultural intermediaries. Both producers and consumers are sensitive to shared cultural notions. These notions are reflected, produced, and reproduced in mediated texts and ads, and are then used as resources in constructing the self. In returning to the model of the cultural circuit, it is difficult to establish causal links – to state where the notions emanate. It is nevertheless important to analyze messages and cultural conceptions on aging. By doing so, the manner in which age is done can be identified and questioned.

ACKNOWLEDGEMENTS

This article has been written as part of the work at "Aging and Living Conditions," an interdisciplinary research project financed by the Swedish Research Council's "Linnéstöd."

REFERENCES

Bytheway, William R. *Unmasking Age: The Significance of Age for Social Research.* Bristol: Policy Press, 2011. Print.

Calasanti, Toni M., and Kathleen F. Slevin, eds. *Age Matters: Realigning Feminist Thinking.* New York: Routledge, 2006. Print.

Carrigan, Marilyn, and Isabelle Szmigin. "Advertising in an Aging Society." *Aging and Society* 20 (2000): 217-33. Print.

Du Gay, Paul, ed. *Doing Cultural Studies: The Story of the Sony Walkman.* Open University: London: SAGE, 1997. Print.

Edström, Maria. *TV-rummets eliter: föreställningar om kön och makt i fakta och fiktion.* Gothenburg: Gothenburg University, 2006. Print.

Fairhurst, Eileen. "'Growing old gracefully' as opposed to 'mutton dressed as lamb.' The social construction of recognising older women." *The Body in Everyday Life.* Ed. Sarah Nettleton and Jonathan Watson. London: Routledge, 1998. 259-75. Print.

von Feilitzen, Cecilia. "Barn, ungdomar, vuxna och äldre i TV", in *Folket i TV. Demografi och social struktur i televisionens innehåll.* Stockholm: Centrum för masskommunikationsforskning, Stockholm University, 1989. 27-57. Print.

Featherstone, Mike, and Mike Hepworth. "The Mask of Aging and the Postmodern Life Course." *The Body: Social Process and Cultural Theory.* Ed. Mike Featherstone, Mike Hepworth, and Bryan S. Turner. London: SAGE, 1991. 371-89. Print.

—. "Images of Aging." *Encyclopedia of Gerontology.* Ed. James E. Birren. Amsterdam: Elsevier, 2007. 735-42. Print.

Gill, Rosalind. *Gender and the Media.* Cambridge: Polity, 2007. Print.

Gripsrud, Jostein, *Mediekultur, mediesamhälle.* Göteborg: Daidalos, 2000. Print.

Gunter, Barrie. *Understanding the Older Consumer: The Grey Market.* London: Routledge, 1998. Print.

Hall, Stuart. "Encoding/Decoding." *Culture, Media, Language: Working Papers in Cultural Studies, 1972-79.* Ed. Stuart Hall. Centre for Contemporary Cultural Studies, University of Birmingham; London: Hutchinson, 1980. 128-40. Print.

Hurd Clarke, Laura. *Facing Age: Women Growing Older in Anti-Aging Culture.* Lanham, MD: Rowman and Littlefield, 2011. Print.

Jones, Rebecca. "'Older People' Talking As If They Are Not Older People: Positioning Theory as an Explanation." *Journal of Aging Studies* 20 (2006): 79-91. Print.

Laws, Glenda. "Understanding Ageism: Lessons From Feminism and Postmodernism." *The Gerontologist* 35.1 (1995): 112-18. Print.

Lumme-Sandt, Kirsi. "Images of Aging in a 50+ Magazine." *Journal of Aging Studies* 25 (2011): 45-51. Print.

Lövgren, Karin. *"Se lika ung ut som du känner dig": kulturella föreställningar om ålder och åldrande i populärpress för kvinnor över 40.* Linköping: Linköping University, 2009. Print.

—. "'They See Themselves As Young:' The Market Addressing the Older Consumer." *Representing Aging. Images and Identities.* Ed. Virpi Ylänne. London: Palgrave Macmillan, 2012. 53-67. Print.

M Magasin 2 (2007). Print.

Närvänen, Anna-Liisa. "Ålder, livslopp, åldersordning" *Åldrande, åldersordning, ålderism.* Ed. Jönson, Håkan. Norrköping: Nationella institutet för forskning om äldre och åldrande, Institutionen för samhälls- och välfärdsstudier, Linköpings universitet. 2009. 18-29. Print.

O'Barr, William M. *Culture and the Ad: Exploring Otherness in the World of Advertising.* Boulder: Westview Press, 1994. Print.

Öberg, Peter. "Images Versus Experience of the Aging Body." *Aging Bodies: Images and Everyday Experience.* Ed. Christopher A. Faircloth. Walnut Creek, CA: AltaMira Press, 2003. 103-39. Print.

—, and Lars Tornstam. "Body Images Among Men and Women of Different Ages." *Aging and Society* 19.5 (1999): 629-44. Print.

—. "Youthfulness and Fitness – Identity Ideals For All Ages?" *Journal of Aging and Identity* 6.1 (2001): 15-29. Print.

—. "Attitudes Towards Embodied Old Age Among Swedes." *Aging and Human Development* 56.2 (2003): 133-53. Print.

Radway, Janice. *Reading the Romance: Women, Patriarchy, and Popular Literature.* Chapel Hill: University of North Carolina Press, 1984. Print.

Sawchuk, Kimberley. "From Gloom to Boom: Age, Identity and Target Marketing." *Images of Aging: Cultural Representations of Later Life.* Ed. Mike Featherstone and Andrew Wernick. London: Routledge, 1995. 173-87. Print.

Szmigin, Isabelle, and Marylin Carrigan. "Does Advertising in the UK Need Older Models?" *Journal of Product & Brand Management* 9.2 (2000): 128-43. Print.

Tara 13 (2004). Print.

Tuchman, Gaye. "The Symbolic Annihilation of Women by the Mass Media." *The Manufacture of News. Social Problems, Deviance and the Mass Media.* Ed. Stanley Cohen and Jock Young. Rev. ed. London: Constable, 1981 (1978). 169-85. Print.

Unsgaard, Edvard. *När Amelia behöver hemtjänst.* Stockholm: Timbro, 2011. Print.

West, Candance, and Don Zimmerman. "Doing Gender." *Gender & Society* 1.2 (1987): 125-51. Print.

Age-Related Disability

Believing is Seeing is Experiencing

Sharon-Dale Stone

Aging and disability are commonly assumed to go hand in hand (Stone). So much so, in fact, that it can be difficult for someone to understand themselves as aging, if they do not over time experience reduced physical or intellectual abilities, let alone understand themselves as old in the absence of the experience of disability. Consider, for example, the vehemence with which people of advanced age often deny that they are old (for example, see Degnen; Lund and Engelsrud). Typically, they are able to sustain the belief that they are not old because they do not experience themselves as disabled. They take care to distinguish themselves from the amorphous group of "others" who have clearly entered the final life stage of decline into disability and decrepitude. They will commonly give voice to the platitude "you're only as old as you feel," thereby reinforcing the already well-entrenched ideological construction of old age being equivalent to disability.

The ubiquity of this common-sense notion that old age and disability are coterminous underpins the taken-for-granted construct of "age-related disability," a notion suggesting that the aging process itself is disabling and prevents us from questioning its validity. This article proposes that we need to question the idea that the aging process causes the acquisition of disabling impairments, and we also need to examine the extent to which we are encouraged to understand the aging process through the lens of this belief. There are far-reaching and harmful consequences attached to the assumption that aging and disability are coterminous.

CULTURAL DIFFERENCES IN THE VALUATION OF OLD AGE

The notion that old age and disability go together seems to be a phenomenon peculiar to modern Western societies. From a non-Western perspective, such as the perspective on old age that tends to be found operative in indigenous communities around the world, disability is not seen as a defining feature of old age. In Western cultures, we are largely understood to be aging successfully to the extent that we avoid disability; hence the celebration of phenomena such as oldsters who run marathons, but in non-Western cultures, bodily condition is irrelevant to successful aging. Instead, factors such as emotional and spiritual well-being or connections to others come to the fore as defining features of successful aging (Lewis; Oakley; Torres). It is also significant that in traditional, non-Westernized cultures, elders tend to be revered for their knowledge about the past. These are societies that value all things old.

In contrast, anyone living within the context of contemporary mainstream Western culture is surrounded by messages that highlight aging as a process of decline into disability and decrepitude. Not that this is a new message. In Western culture, it goes back a very long way and was given especially clear expression by Shakespeare who identified the seven ages of man as ending with second childhood, "sans teeth, sans eyes, sans taste, sans everything," but in contemporary times it is a message that is thrown at us with a vengeance.

AGED POP STARS, FAMOUS INDIVIDUALS, AND THE REST OF HUMANITY

In part, we get the message that aging brings increasing disability thanks to the culture's unrelenting valorization of youth and the appearance of being youthful. Mick Jagger of *The Rolling Stones*, for example, turned 68 in 2011, but onstage he can still out-rock people young enough to be his grandchildren (Fig. 1). Indeed, he gave quite the energetic performance at the 2011 Grammy Awards celebration[1]. For that matter, singer Barbra Streisand was also a featured entertainer at the 2011 Grammy Awards. Streisand turned 69 in 2011, but she looked much the same as she did forty years prior.

---

1 | The American awards ceremony for the best musical performers of the year.

These are not people we can easily recognize as old. Jagger's face may have the wrinkles and leathery skin we associate with old age, but there is not a speck of grey hair to be seen, and definitely no evidence that he is slowing down. Streisand, meanwhile, shows no evidence of wrinkles or leathery skin on her face. Neither Jagger nor Streisand are recognizable icons of old age. Rather, they are each in their own way icons of eternal youth, carefully packaged perhaps to help the great mass of baby boomers to feel youthful themselves. Significantly, both Jagger and Streisand are themselves a little too old to be counted as baby boomers, yet it is very interesting that both performers were featured at the Grammys in 2011, the year that the first baby boomers turned 65. One wonders whether the association was intentional, a way of assuring baby boomers that life does not end at 65?

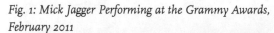

Fig. 1: Mick Jagger Performing at the Grammy Awards, February 2011

It is not at all difficult to find images of people who actually look old. We can look, for example, to august individuals such as Mother Teresa who died in 1997 at age 87, Desmond Tutu who announced his intention to retire in 2011 at age 79, or Queen Elizabeth of England who at age 85 keeps up a busy schedule of public appearances (Fig. 2). Each of these people is famous for reasons unrelated to age, physical appearance, or ability to entertain, and so now that they are old, no one needs to hide evidence of their aged bodies to ensure continued public approval. Even so, when any of these people are discussed in the media, commentary does not focus on their age. It is as though each is granted honorary status as youthful. Thus, even as these famous individuals display their aged status for all to see, their difference from the great mass of humanity is simultaneously (and no doubt unintentionally) reinforced.

Fig. 2: Queen Elizabeth II of England, April 2011

Similarly, there are old people in the news precisely because they are old, yet have accomplished an unusual feat. Fauja Singh, 100 years old, for example, became the world's oldest marathon runner after finishing a race in Canada in 2011 (Fig. 3). Apparently, Mr. Singh took up running at age 89 and trains by running ten miles every day. Individuals such as Mr. Singh are held up as marvelous wonders because they are so different from what one expects. He is clearly not a typical old man, and his newsworthiness underlines his difference from others.

The existence of neither aged pop stars who in one way or another appear youthful, nor famous individuals who are unashamedly old but apparently able-bodied, is enough to challenge the idea that disability is to be expected in old age. These are not the images that readily come to mind when we think about old age.

Fig. 3: Marathon Runner Fauja Singh,
Age 100, October 2011

Indeed, studies show that despite all the hoopla attached to the idea of "successful aging", most people do not expect to achieve this Western ideal. Rather, they expect to experience both physical and cognitive decline (Sarkisian et al. 1841).

HEGEMONIC IDEOLOGY

In contemporary Western societies, it becomes difficult to really see images of old people engaged in activities usually associated with youthfulness. The hegemonic imagery of old age as decline into decrepitude is too pervasive to allow most people to recognize evidence to the contrary. When such evidence exists, dominant ideology encourages the dismissal of these people either as too unusual to be taken as exemplars of old age, or as not really old.

Fig. 4: Nursing Home Residents

Fig. 5: Elderly Crossing Road Sign

With regard to holding on to the idea that disability is a natural part of old age, we notice those who are both old and disabled because we are primed to do so, which continually re-confirms our pre-existing belief. At the same time, we are able to avoid cognitive dissonance by not noticing those whose existence challenges entrenched beliefs. Thus, when those steeped in dominant ideology think of old age, it is easy to think of images of old people sitting in wheelchairs in nursing homes (Fig. 4), or elderly people who have difficulty walking (Fig. 5), because these are the images that are reinforced in society.

A further point to be considered is that as a society, we encourage old people to segregate themselves in locations such as retirement villages or seniors centers. This segregation ensures that:

1. When we see old people in such places we are able to easily recognize them as seniors because this is where we expect to find them.
2. The fact that there are so many of them in such places makes it easy to notice the ways in which they differ from younger people.
3. Their presence in places other than where we expect to find them is not so easily noticed.

Indeed, it can be difficult to notice old people while going about daily routines. Should we happen to notice them we are primed to either recognize them as old and out of place because they are visibly disabled, or we do not recognize them as old or out of place because they are not visibly disabled and seem to be going about their business in an efficient manner. In the latter case, the fact that they blend in with everyone else makes it unlikely that they will be recognized as old.

THE RELATIONSHIP BETWEEN AGE AND DISABILITY

Just as most people have a hard time recognizing someone as old in the absence of disability, it can be difficult to recognize that large numbers of children and young adults are disabled, because it is not common to be routinely exposed to evidence of this. Thus, when confronted with a young person who is clearly disabled, we are primed to understand that person as a tragic exception to the rule that young people are able-bodied. The impulse to regard disability as tragic for children and youth works to reinforce the idea that disability and old age go hand in hand. If we were to collectively acknowledge that impairment and disability are a routine part of human experience across the life course, then we would need to change our ideas about who is likely to be disabled. But there are powerful forces at work that prevent most people from recognizing that age and disability are not necessarily related.

The suggestion that age and disability are not necessarily related appears, at first glance, to contradict the evidence. Consider, for example, official Canadian statistics drawn from a post-censual survey based on self-report (Table 1):

Table 1: Canadian statistics on disability rate according to age

AGE	RATE	AGE	RATE	AGE	RATE
0 to 4	1.7%	25 to 34	6.1%	55 to 64	22.8%
5 to 14	4.6	35 to 44	9.6	65 to 74	33.0
15 to 24	4.7	45 to 54	15.1	75 and over	56.3

2006 Total - All ages 14.3 % (2001 12.4 %)
Adapted from: Statistics Canada, 9

These statistics clearly suggest that the prevalence of disability rises with age, and it is particularly likely to be present for those over the age of 55 (more than 1 in 5 people). Yet, there are several matters that need to be taken into account to fully appreciate the meaning of this table.

As indicated, the disability rate for Canada as a whole in 2006 was 14.3%, up from 12.4% in 2001. Moreover, the disability rate increased across all age groups between 2001 and 2006 (14). *Statistics Canada* has computed the age-standardized rate for 2006 to compare statistics with 2001, to find that the aging of the population accounts for only 0.8% of the disability rate increase (13); this explanation does not account for 1.1% of the increase. Also even though one's chances of acquiring disability rise with age, it remains the case that it is not until age 75 and older that the majority of people report that they are disabled and even then, 43.7% do not report being disabled – a substantial minority. If disability was a factor of aging, then the majority of people over the age of 65 should be reporting disability, rather than saying that they are disability-free.

Still, it appears that the disability rate rises with age, even if only slightly. There are at least two considerations that go a long way towards explaining the increase. First, the older one is, the more chance one has had to be in situations that are likely to cause disability e.g. repetitive strain injury is caused by making the same motions in rapid succession over a protracted period of time; disabling impairments such as spinal cord injury or brain injury are entirely unrelated to age but are caused by external forces; the chances of becoming disabled as a result of a car accident are increased the more often one rides in a car; etc. Thus, it is not surprising to find that in an objective sense the older one is, the more likely one is to have become disabled. The mistake is to assume that it is age that creates such disability.

A second consideration is that disability statistics are greatly influenced by perceptions. Indeed, *Statistics Canada* recognizes this by noting: "How respondents perceive their limitations, and willingness to report them, greatly influences the type of answers they provide. Perceptions of disability are fluid and ever changing" (14).

When this recognition is paired with the fact that mainstream society is ageist, it makes sense that people are more likely to report disability at older ages. The older they are, the more likely they are to notice their disabilities. All people have limitations of one sort or another, but most people have limitations that do not significantly interfere with their daily lives. Accordingly, when asked whether they are limited in their ability to carry out activities (which is the way the question is posed for collecting Canadian disability statistics), few young people are likely to say that they are limited. The young person who can easily climb stairs but is unable to run a marathon is not likely to have this lack uppermost in mind when responding to a standard questionnaire about disability. The younger one is, the easier it is to ignore one's limitations, not for physiological reasons but because the younger one is, the harder it is to find one's experience of limitations represented in popular culture. Young people are not primed to pay attention to their limitations.

Conversely, the older one is, the easier it is to notice one's own disabilities, and the easier it is for others to notice them. Disability in old age is noticeable because hegemonic imagery primes us to notice this. For example, lapses in memory for a young person are often explained away as an indication of being too stressed. The *Globe and Mail*, a national Canadian newspaper, recently ran a feature story about the connection between stress and memory lapses (Pearce). Nevertheless, it remains the case that anyone over the age of 60 who experiences a lapse in memory is in danger of receiving sideways glances from others who are attentive to signs of incipient dementia, while the person in question is primed to laugh about having "a senior moment." It is disturbing that popular culture so easily allows us to explain away forgetfulness among those who are young, while we easily make ageist jokes when it happens to those who are old.

PERCEPTIONS, EXPERIENCE, AND ABILITY

Increasingly, researchers are finding that there is good reason to question the idea that disability is to be expected in old age. It is clearly not the case that everyone will become disabled if they only live long enough.[2] It is not at all unusual to learn of individuals such as Fauja Singh (Fig. 3) or Olga Kotelko, the 92-year-old Canadian who regularly and with gusto plays the strenuous sport of shot put ("Olga The Magnificent"). Increasingly, evidence is being found to suggest that at least some disability is acquired in old age because of the beliefs and attitudes held by elders.

Over the past decade, growing research attention has been paid to the ways in which ageist stereotypes influence not only perceptions but also what people can or cannot do. There is now a considerable body of research to show that old people can actually be primed to be forgetful, walk slowly, or otherwise engage in stereotypically old behavior (e.g. Hausdorff, Levy, and Wei; Horton et al.; Levy; Westerhof et al.). People "expect" to be disabled in old age. They expect to have their memories fail, they expect to slow down their movements, they expect to have ubiquitous aches and pains, and they even expect to experience a serious health crisis such as stroke or heart attack. The evidence of these expectations is overwhelming.

Beginning in childhood, we are all subjected to continual reiteration of ageist stereotypes. To the extent that we are immersed in popular culture, we grow up with relentless exposure to ageist ideas, and it is the rare individual who can escape internalizing these ideas. By the time people reach old age themselves, it can be very difficult to resist embodying the negative stereotypes they are accustomed to associating with old age. Elderly individuals have a choice: either downplay one's chronological age and reject the idea that one is old, or accept that the stereotypes are an accurate representation of reality. The first choice requires denying important parts of life experience not to mention constant vigilance to ensure that signs of age are

2 | Thanks to Kathleen Woodward for drawing attention to this issue (personal communication, March 27, 2011).

suppressed (Andrews). The second choice, however, can have devastating consequences.

Evidence from the Baltimore Longitudinal Study of Aging (BLSA) is beginning to accumulate to show the deleterious consequences of ageism. Since 1958, the BLSA has been collecting longitudinal data on the aging experiences of thousands of men and women (Ferruci). Levy et al. reviewed a subset of this data to examine whether there is a link between early life belief in ageist stereotypes and later life health. Upon recruitment in 1968, participants ranged in age from 18 to 49 and were in good health. Initial data gathered about their attitudes toward the elderly showed that they ranged from very positive to very negative. Over the course of the 40-year study, researchers examined participants' health histories with particular reference to cardiovascular disease. They found a significant association between ageist attitudes early in life and poor health later on. Participants who expressed negative views of old age were much more likely to experience some kind of cardiovascular disorder in the ensuing 40 years.

Of particular significance, Levy et al. also identified a group who experienced heart problems after reaching the age of 60 and also found that they tended to have been negative about aging from early on. The episodes of heart disease could not be explained by common risk factors such as smoking, depression, cholesterol or family history. As Levy et al. conclude, "age stereotypes internalized earlier in life can have a far-reaching effect on health" (297).

Other studies show that, compared with older adults who frequently felt useful to others, those who never or rarely felt useful were more likely to experience an increase in disability or die sooner (Gruenewald et al.); and Boyle, Buchman and Bennett found that among community-dwelling older persons, purpose in life is associated with a reduced risk of incident disability.

In a Danish study of 75-year-old and 80-year-old men and women, Avlund et al. found that "being embedded in a strong network of social relations provides protection against disability by reducing risk of developing disability" (97). These findings are similar to James et al.'s findings about the relationship between social activity in old age and disability, and Buchman et al.'s findings that there is an association between feelings of loneliness and the rate of motor decline in old age.

Altogether, the evidence is mounting to show the ways in which the mind and body are linked, so that attitudes and beliefs can actually create physical disability. Clearly, disability is not necessarily related to an aging body, but can be a consequence of myriad factors. To understand the prevalence of disability in old age, we must look beyond the assumed correspondence of these conditions, to examine social and psychosocial factors. Given the lack of convincing evidence to support the belief that aging causes disability, but considering the propensity of people to more easily notice disability in elders, we might even ask: how much of our bodily experience is materialized as a result of our imaginations?

ACKNOWLEDGEMENTS

This article is based on the paper "Age-Related Disability: Believing is Seeing is Experiencing" presented at the conference *Aging, Old Age, Memory, and Aesthetics*, University of Toronto, March 25–27, 2011.

LIST OF FIGURES

Fig. 1: Mick Jagger Performing at the Grammy Awards, February 2011. Source: http://www.wjsginternetradio.com/2011_02_27_archive.html
Fig. 2: Queen Elizabeth II of England, April 2011. Source: http://www.deccanchronicle.com/channels/world/europe/william-and-kate-become-duke-and-duchess-cambridge-153
Fig. 3: Marathon Runner Fauja Singh, Age 100, October 2011. Source: http://en.wikipedia.org/wiki/Fauja_Singh
Fig. 4: Nursing Home Residents. Source: http://www.farigo.com/choosing-a-nursing-home
Fig. 5: Elderly Crossing Road Sign. Source: http://www.telegraph.co.uk/news/newstopics/howaboutthat/2585801/Pensioner-groups-demand-elderly-road-sign-change.html

LIST OF TABLES

Table 1: Canadian statistics on disability rate according to age. Adapted from: Statistics Canada, 9.

REFERENCES

Andrews, Molly. "The Seductiveness of Agelessness." *Ageing and Society* 19.3 (1999): 301-18. Print.

Avlund, Kirsten, Rikke Lund, Bjørn E. Holstein, and Pernille Due. "Social Relations as Determinant of Onset of Disability in Aging." *Archives of Gerontology and Geriatrics* 34 (200): 85-99. Print.

Boyle, Patricia A., Aron S. Buchman, and David A. Bennett. "Purpose in Life is Associated with a Reduced Risk of Incident Disability Among Community-Dwelling Older Persons." *American Journal of Geriatric Psychiatry* 18.12 (2010): 1093-102. Print.

Buchman, Aron S., Patricia A. Boyle, Robert S. Wilson, Bryan D. James, Sue E. Leurgans, Steven E. Arnold, and David A. Bennett. "Loneliness and the Rate of Motor Decline in Old Age: The Rush Memory and Aging Project, A Community-Based Cohort Study." *BMC Geriatrics 10.77 (2010): 1-8. Print.*

Degnen, Cathrine. "Minding the Gap: The Construction of Old Age and Oldness Amongst Peers." *Journal of Aging Studies* 21 (2007): 69-80. Print.

Ferrucci, Luigi. "The Baltimore Longitudinal Study of Aging (BLSA): A 50-Year-Long Journey and Plans for the Future." *Journal of Gerontology*: Medical Sciences 63A.12 (2008): 1416-19. Print.

Gruenewald, Tara L., Arun S. Karlamangla, Gail A. Greendale, Burton H. Singer and Teresa E. Seeman. "Feelings of Usefulness to Others, Disability, and Mortality in Older Adults: the MacArthur Study of Successful Aging." *Journal of Gerontology*: Psychological Sciences 62B.1 (2007): 28-37. Print.

Hausdorff, Jeffrey M., Becca R. Levy and Jeanne Y. Wei. "The Power of Ageism on Physical Function in Older Persons." *Journal of the American Geriatric Society* 47 (1999): 1346-49. Print.

Horton, Sean, Joseph Baker, William Pearce, and Janice M. Deakin. "Immunity to Popular Stereotypes of Aging? Seniors and Stereotype Threat." *Educational Gerontology* 36.5 (2010): 353-71. Print.

James, Bryan D., Patricia A. Boyle, Aron S. Buchman, and David A. Bennett. "Relation of Late-Life Social Activity with Incident Disability Among Community-Dwelling Older Adults." *The Journals of Gerontology* Series A: Biological Sciences and Medical Sciences 66.4 (2011): 467-73. Print.

Levy, Becca. "Stereotype Embodiment: A Psychosocial Approach to Aging." *Current Directions in Psychological Science* 18.6 (2009): 332-36. Print.

—, Alan B. Zonderman, Martin D. Slade and Luigi Ferrucci. "Age Stereotypes Held Earlier in Life Predict Cardiovascular Events in Later Life." *Psychological Science* 20.3 (2009): 296-98. Print.

Lewis, Jordan P. "Successful Aging through the Eyes of Alaska Natives: Exploring Generational Differences Among Alaska Natives." *Journal of Cross Cultural Gerontology* 25 (2010): 385-96. Print.

Lund, Anne, and Gunn Engelsrud. "'I am Not That Old': Inter-Personal Experiences of Thriving and Threats at a Senior Centre." *Ageing and Society* 28 (2008): 675-92. Print.

Oakley, Robin. "Empowering Knowledge and Practices of Namaqualand Elders." *Contesting Aging and Loss*. Ed. Janice E. Graham and Peter H. Stephenson. Toronto: University of Toronto Press, 2010, 47-62. Print.

"Olga The Magnificent." The Sunday Edition. Canadian Broadcasting Corporation Radio One, 4 December 2011. Radio.

Pearce, Tralee. "Forgot Your Keys? You're Not Alone." *The Globe and Mail* 11 February 2011, L4. Print.

Sarkisian, Catherine A., Ron D. Hays, and Carol M. Mangione. "Do Older Adults Expect to Age Successfully? The Association Between Expectations Regarding Aging and Beliefs Regarding Healthcare Seeking Among Older Adults." *Journal of the American Geriatrics Society* 50.11 (2002): 1837-43. Print.

Statistics Canada. *Participation and Activity Limitation Survey 2006: Analytical Report*. Ottawa: Minister of Industry, 2007. Print.

Stone, Sharon Dale. "Disability, Dependence and Old Age: Problematic Constructions." *Canadian Journal on Aging* 22.1 (2003): 59-67. Print.

Torres, Sandra. "Different Ways of Understanding the Construct of Successful Aging: Iranian Immigrants Speak About What Aging Well Means to Them." *Journal of Cross-Cultural Gerontology* 21.1-2 (2006): 1-23. Print.

Westerhof, Gerben J., Karolien Harink, Martine Van Selm, Madelijn Strick and Rick Van Baaren. "Filling a Missing Link: The Influence of Portrayals of Older Characters in Television Commercials on the Memory Performance of Older Adults." *Ageing and Society* 30 (2010): 897-912. Print.

Aged by Law

Ages of Life in Austrian Law

Jürgen Pirker/Nora Melzer-Azodanloo

There are far more than one thousand regulations[1] concerning age in all areas of Austrian law, such as civil, criminal, labor, or administrative law, to mention only a few. It is inevitable that age limits are concerns of law making and legal regulations, but is it law that defines us as 'young' or 'old'? What influence does law have on our perceptions of age and life phases? Basically, we have to differentiate between chronological age and what society associates with the years lived, i.e. cultural age. Cultural age is a social definition (Maierhofer 82), and law contributes to how this is determined. Law uses chronological age (the number of years that we have lived) to assign specific rights and duties based on reasonable classifications. By doing so, law constitutes a social status (Ruppert 138, 141; Kaufmann 121, 123; Ehmer 169), and creates part of a cultural reference system to which everyone belongs (Haltern 207). Age limits thus generate images and social meanings of life phases. In addition, law contributes to aspects of social discourse on age und uses established research, such as developmental psychology, to set up markers as a condition to grant rights or assign duties. Therefore, law is not only a source, but an integral part of social discourse concerning age.

Age regulations affect all aspects of life, from school enrollment to retirement. Kholi talks about the 'institutionalization of the life course' (Kholi 1). This legally defined vita provides orientation to the members of a legal system and structures individual biographies through legal age limits (Haltern 207; Ruppert XXXI). In terms of the legal system, these limits

---

[1] | Laws and decrees are cited in German, and can be accessed through the Austrian Federal Law Information System: http://ris.bka.gv.at.

define who is 'young' and who is 'old,' and who may, may not yet, or is no longer allowed to exercise specific rights, and they determine which legal status applies to chronological age.

The following analysis can be seen as an interdisciplinary contribution to the overall topic of the book, *The Ages of Life: Living and Aging in Conflict?* Age as a cultural phenomenon addressing all phases of life can only be understood in connection to definitions of childhood, adolescence (youth), and adulthood (Hareven 165). On the basis of what it means to be 'aged by culture' (Gullette), this article explains what it means to be aged by law. Which age regulations and limits can be found in different sections of Austrian law, how did they develop and how are they justified?

INSTITUTIONALIZATION OF BIOGRAPHY

The link between a specific biographical age and rights or duties was established in the middle of the 18th century (Ruppert 142, XXIV), when life phases were specifically defined and differentiated by law. Law in modern societies treats cohorts equally, making generations of people pass simultaneously through phases of life on the basis of standardized assumptions (Ruppert 144; Hareven 176). By defining by law which behavior is allowed, norms of class were replaced by legal regulations (Ruppert XXIX). Legal age phases influence the use of age as an identity marker creating social norms and defining specific behavior adequate for a certain age (Kaufmann 123). In the 19th and 20th century, a decrease in infant mortality rate and an increase in life expectancy led to demographical changes that made structuring life phases important (Hareven 173; Ehmer 162, 169; Kaufmann 122). Based on the central period of employment, life phases were defined as childhood, adolescence, adulthood, and old age. This institutionalized life course was divided into three phases: education, employment, and retirement (Ehmer 169; Weymann 213). Extended compulsory education and the establishment of retirement systems determine the dividing lines of these phases. Individuals now pass through these life phases simultaneously and experience higher pressure to change their roles at the points of transition (Hareven 166, 176, 179; Kaufmann 122).

Childhood is constituted by compulsory education and prohibition of child labor. Definitions of the phase of childhood can be found as early as the 18th century. After the effective abolition of child labor, the welfare state organized childhood in a clear structure with a high concentration on regulations. Children usually spend their first years at home, followed by some years of kindergarten and school, before moving into a crossover phase of adolescence (Honig 25, 27-28, 43, 45; Hareven 167). At the beginning of the 20th century, development psychology declared adolescence a specific stage of life resulting in socialization of public schools and grouping adolescents by age groups. Laws directly addressing young people strengthened their identity as a group (Abels 113-14; Hareven 168). Granting rights and enforcing duties are connected to a pedagogic and psychological concept of maturity. However, different areas of law establish different connections between age and maturity. Therefore, adolescence is not defined consistently; its definition depends on whether physical or social maturity is taken as a basis (Abels 124).

Childhood and adolescence law serve mainly as means of protection. Extended periods of education can even cause longer periods of 'post adolescence.' Young adults are very often intellectually, culturally, and politically, but not economically independent (Abels 133-34). Therefore, transition phases are often difficult to determine. Adulthood is commonly characterized by employment and as the phase between adolescence and old age. At the end of the 19th and the beginning of the 20th century due to industrialization, old age was defined as a life phase following the phase of employment. General awareness of old age was encouraged by studies in gerontology, negative images of old age and regulations for retirement (Hareven 164, 168; Ehmer 167). In England at the beginning of the 19th century, sixty-five years of age was determined as retirement age. Other European countries followed this example granting special benefits to public servants and soldiers. Nowadays, the sixty-year-limit has become part of the age discourse (Göckenjan 194, 197; Ehmer 162, 165; Ruppert XXI).

Retirement regulations have created a new social age that is marked by two main elements: reward for former efforts free from labor and loss of central roles and perspectives in life (Saake 271; Göckenjan 198). As the period of retirement steadily extends, it is sometimes split into further categories: third and fourth age or young old and old old with a transition point between eighty and eighty-five years of age (Ehmer 163, 165-66). Typical for this final phase is loss or decrease of self-determination, sometimes due to physical infirmities.

LIFE PHASES IN AUSTRIAN LAW

Childhood

Childhood is constituted by various age limits. Social insurance claims are granted to children until the age of eighteen. In Austria, school or professional education can extend the phase of childhood to the age of twenty-seven (§ 252 ASVG), which in legal terms is the last year of being a child. In some specific cases, childhood can be extended for those who suffer from a mental or physical handicap, if retirement insurance is available through the parent or guardian. Retirement insurance may insure the parent or guardian until the child is forty years of age (§ 18a para 1 ASVG).

Childhood begins at birth, where a person earns certain rights which steadily increase with age culminating in the most important right according to civil law, the legal capacity to contract. Three phases determine the increase in rights: Until 2001, a person was defined as a child until the age of seven. The next phase was made up by nonage-minors ranging from seven to fourteen, and followed by minors that have reached the age of consent (fourteen years). This phase lasts from fourteen to eighteen (§ 21 para 2 ABGB). Usually, after the eighteenth birthday mentally healthy people reach the age of majority and then possess full legal capacity to contract. Before reaching the age of majority, people are under specific protection of the law determined by their physical, intellectual and emotional development (ErläutRV 296 21. GP). In contrast to adults, adolescents cannot be taken advantage of in business because of the assumed lack of common sense and experience and cannot be charged for neglect of duties (Koziol and Welser 50). Very often special needs are taken into consideration due to their weak economic position, as for example price benefits for public transportation. Many rules and regulations for childhood and adolescence prove the intention to protect. One of the first regulations focuses on the second year of life. Female prisoners, for example, are allowed to keep their children with them until that age (§ 74 para 2 Strafvollzugsgesetz) in order to make allowances for the specific needs of a child of that age. Passengers of this age group are exempt from flight taxes (§ 3 Flugabgabegesetz) if no separate seat is booked. After the age of five, reasoning capacity and self-determination are assumed. Children at this age have the right to be heard in a case of adoption (§ 181a ABGB). Compulsory education starts with September 1 following the sixth birthday (§ 2 Schulpflichtgesetz), and lasts for nine years (§ 2 Schulpflichtgesetz). From that age on, a broad spectrum of definitions and protective regulations for children are in place. Under the age of six, children are not allowed to use public transportation unaccompanied. With six years of age, children can escort younger children (§ 14 Z 4 Kfl-Bef Bed). From the sixth until the fifteenth birthday, public railway transports children for half the usual fare (§ 16 para 2 EBG). If parents with children under the age of twelve need to take care of their sick child, payment is continued by their employer (§ 16 UrlG). Children under fifteen are not allowed to be commercially employed. However, with thirteen years of age children can be hired for lighter work, if the working hours do not conflict with school (§§ 5, 5a KJBG). At fourteen, children have the right to consult records and obtain information, if fathered by sperm from a third party (§ 20 para 2 FMedG). Children of diplomats under twenty-one can under special conditions be exempt from employment regulations for foreign citizens (§ 1 Z 13 AuslBVO). How the phase of childhood is defined depends on the area of law analyzed. You can legally be considered a child at seven, fifteen, eighteen, twenty-one, twenty-seven, twenty-eight or forty years of age. Age markers, however, are defined on the second, fifth, sixth, twelfth and fourteenth birthday. Transition between childhood and adolescence is therefore fluid.

Adolescence

Criminal law defines an adolescent between the ages of fourteen and eighteen as a person deserving milder treatment (§ 1 Z 2 JGG). The term 'young adult' refers to people under twenty-one (§ 46a JGG). Social insurance law defines people between fifteen and eighteen as adolescents (§ 132a para 2 ASVG), while 'adolescent employees' refers to persons under eighteen as well as to interns under twenty-one (§ 123 para 3 ArbVG). Special discount air fares can be limited to adolescents until the age of twenty-five, while federal youth representation law and federal youth support law include everyone until the age of thirty. These laws intend to represent the interests of young people on a federal level and to support the development of mental, physical, social, political, religious, and ethical competences of children and adolescents (§§ 1, 2 Bundes-Jugendvertretungsgesetz, §§ 1, 2 Bundesjugendförderungsgesetz).

Definitions of adolescence range from fourteen to eighteen, twenty-one, twenty-five or even thirty reflecting protective intentions in specific areas of law. In Austria, fourteen is an age where a broad spectrum of regulations applies. From age fourteen on, people become legally responsible for their behavior. This basically applies to civil law (§ 153 ABGB) as well as criminal law (§ 4 para 2 JGG). In civil law, children can be made responsible even earlier, depending on their individual ability to realize and expiate (§ 1310 ABGB). However, in criminal law the age border is absolute: people under the age of fourteen are not punishable (§ 4 para 2 JGG). In criminal law, adolescents are also not punishable if under specific circumstances they are no able to realize what they did wrong (§ 4 para 2 Z 1 JGG). At fourteen, young people are responsible for certain decisions, for example, they can decide independently whether they want to continue with their religious education (§ 1 Religionsunterrichtsgesetz). Some protective regulations even apply to ages eighteen and older. The possession of explosives is only allowed after the age of twenty-one (§ 4 para 1 SprG). Advertisements for tobacco products specifically targeting adolescents, and presenting adolescents or people whose age cannot be clearly determined as being older than thirty is prohibited in cigarette ads (§ 11 Tabakgesetz).

Different fields of law draw different conclusions concerning the connection between age and maturity. Extending adolescence to the age of twenty-seven in terms of family insurance takes the economic situation of young people into account. In Austria, lowering the age for receiving family benefits from twenty-seven to twenty-four (§ 2 para 1 lit b Familienlastenausgleichsgesetz) shows that the economic aspect of regulations influences the legal definition of the phase of adolescence (Ruppert 141). Transition to the phase of adulthood is thereby fluid and dependent on the laws applied.

The dividing line between majority and voting age as well as compulsory military service (only for men) determine the transition phase. In 1811, the age of majority was reached at twenty-four, in 1919 at twenty-one (StGBl. 96/1919), in 1973 at nineteen (BGBl 1973/108), and in 2001 at eighteen (BGBl 2000/135). The downshifting of the limit for the age of majority has reduced the phase of adolescence. Results in child and adolescence psychology had impact on national legislation. Research showed that young people enter the phase of adolescence earlier and are ready to make independent decisions and bare responsibility at an earlier age. Austria was the last member of the European Council to lower the majority age limit, and thereby respond to requirements of increasing mobility and flexibility in education (ErläutRV 296 21. GP). In Austria, compulsory military service applies to all men of seventeen (§ 10 para 1 Wehrgesetz 2001). At the age of eighteen they can be drafted as long as they are Austrian citizens and have the necessary physical and mental abilities (§ 9 para 1 WG 2001).

In Austria, voting age, which entitles to political participation, is lower than the age of majority. Since 2007, sixteen is the age to vote for federal parliament (Art 26 para 1 B-VG, § 21 NRWO) making Austria the first member of the European Union to adopt a voting age of sixteen. The same voting age applies to elections for the European Parliament (Art 23a para 1 und 3 B-VG) and all regional elections (Art 95 para 2, Art 117 para 2 B-VG). As fourteen- year-olds are allowed to make important decisions about private and professional aspects of their lives, this right was extended to political decisions in order to support participation in democratic processes. Studies in psychology confirmed that people of that age already have the necessary understanding to vote. In addition, it is seen as a good way of balancing future interests of young and old. Another intention was that younger members of parliament would be elected by a younger voting public (StenProt NR 23. GP 24. Sitzung 06.06.2007). Age of candidacy at which a person can legally qualify to become a member of parliament is now eighteen (Art 26 para 4 B-VG).

Originally, voting age and the age of majority were closely connected (Ucakar 69-75). After the election reform in 1907, voting age was twenty-four, age of candidacy was thirty (Ucakar 353). After WWI, the statute on electing the constituting national assembly separated voting age from civil majority age, which was set at twenty. The main intention was to grant political participation to those who had served in WWI, but there was a contradiction in terms. On the one hand, majority age restricted access to full financial and economic freedom to the age of twenty-four and older. On the other hand, democratic and political participation in state affairs was allowed at twenty years of age (Ucakar 400). Further adjustments followed: In 1929, the voting age was twenty-one, the age of eligibility was twenty-nine (Ucakar 444), in 1949 the voting age was twenty, the age of candidacy was twenty-six (Ucakar 463), and in 1968 the voting age was nineteen, the age of candidacy was twenty-five (Ucakar 486-87). This led again to a discussion of the voting age centering on questions of 'democratization' and political maturity (Ucakar 486). In 1992, the request was fulfilled, and the voting age was lowered to the age of eighteen (BGBl I 2003/90).

Today, the age of majority and military enlistment mark the age of eighteen as a major transition to adulthood. The lowered voting age of sixteen, however, ends the phase of adolescence by determining participation in major political decision-making. Similarly, adolescence has been legally lowered in terms of marriage, which is closely linked to maturity and adulthood. According to the Austrian Civil Code of 1811, underage minors could not obtain a matrimonial contract without parental consent. In the Ehegesetz of 1938, the age of marriage was twenty-one for men, and sixteen for women. Dispensation was possible, but men needed to be eighteen (Floßmann 86-87). In 1973, marriage age was nineteen, however dispensation was possible for men of eighteen and women of fifteen (§ 1 EheG, BGBl 1973/108). From 2001 on, marriage age was determined at eighteen, regardless of sex. Dispensation is now possible for everyone of sixteen years of age if they seem mature enough and their partners are older than eighteen (§ 1 para 1 EheG). One reason for this reform was the lowering of the age of majority, the other was unequal treatment of men, which no longer could be justified (ErläutRV 296 21. GP).

Adulthood

Transition from adolescence to adulthood is closely connected to professional employment and full access to the labor market. Professions and careers are very influential for determining place and status in society within a life course. This strong influence explains why professional identity takes precedence over private aspects (Weymann 188, 197-98). Consequently, many provisions on age limits are to be found in occupational statutes determining professional education and training as well as career and employment, as for example integration into the labor market. Many occupational provisions ignore the civil age of majority and mainly apply to individuals over eighteen who have already attained all civil law capacities and are considered adults.

Some professional rules lay down special age limits which request a certain age in order to pursue a specific profession. Other professional rules provide supportive measures, as some adults are considered in need of special protection. Yet, a main reason for this support is not an assumed lack of understanding or physical status, but an assumption that this age group is affected by a weak economic position and lacks professional experience.

Concerning unemployment benefits, the qualifying period is usually fifty-two weeks of work. However, for under twenty-five-year-olds, twenty-six weeks in the last twelve months suffice (§ 14 para 1 AlVG). In terms of older adults, special protective measures apply. Night workers are provided with medical exams every two years, those over fifty are granted one medical exam per year (§ 12b para 1 AZG). So-called 'social plans' guarantee readjustment allowances and special severance payment to women over fifty and men over fifty-five, if jobs are terminated (see for example Supreme Court 8 Ob A 139/04-05). The duration of unemployment benefits also increases to twenty weeks from age forty or fifty with an increase to thirty-nine respectively fifty-two weeks with further age (§ 18 para 2 AlVG).

Pension and Retirement

Transition from adulthood to 'old age' is mainly characterized by retirement and pension; i.e. withdrawal from the labor market. The original idea of retirement regulations was to provide benefits for people too old or ill to earn their living. In Austria, the standard retirement age is sixty-five for men, and sixty for women. This rule applies to employees, farmers, and the self-employed (§ 253 ASVG, § 121 BSVG, § 130 GSVG.).[2] Physicians (§ 99 Ärztegesetz), judges (§ 99 Richter- und Staatsanwaltschaftsdienstgesetz), members of parliament (§ 27 para 1 Bezügegesetz), and military officers (§ 10 para 1 Wehrgesetz 2001) receive retirement benefits from sixty-five of age onwards, regardless of sex. Special retirement limits are set for state employed professors at age sixty-eight (§ 163 para 5 Beamten-Dienstrechtsgesetz 1979). However, in Austria people usually retire much earlier, women at the age of 56.5 and men at the age of 61.5 on the basis of pension contributions (37.5 years of insurance or thirty-five years of contribution; § 253b ASVG).[3] Another reason for early retirement is permanent night-shifts. In such cases, male workers may retire at fifty-seven and female workers at fifty-two (Art 10 para 1 Nachtschwerarbeitsgesetz).

Similar to other phases of life, the word 'elderly' comprises many meanings. Legal rules, especially those granting benefits, often associate 'old age' with various ages of retirement. Provisions on discount tickets for public transportation refer to the age of sixty-five for men and sixty for women

---

2 | From 2024 on with completion in 2033, retirement age for women is gradually being increased to sixty-five.

3 | Every three months, age is gradually being increased, for details see Resch 131.

(Anlage 1 Z 9 Kfl-Bef Bed). This law is expected to be changed very soon on grounds of being discriminatory. Federal statutes on representation of the elderly in politics and the public define 'elderly persons' as women of fifty-five and men of sixty (§ 2 Bundes-Seniorengesetz).

Yet, one can be legally 'old' even without being retired. Track and field instructors' examination boards grant people between forty and fifty, or fifty and sixty 'old age bonus points' (Anl 6 BGBl. II 2011/351).

Provisional Results

Not all phases of life receive equal attention in Austrian law. Whereas many rules exist for the young, with the exception of retirement there are few regulations for the old. Austrian law, however, does work on the assumption of three distinct age groups defined by the transition to the age of majority and retirement: the young (children and adolescents), working adults, and retirees (Ruppert XXXII-XXXIII; Ruppert 145; Kaufmann 122). From a mere constitutional point of view, Ruppert states a dichotomy in a life course, the phase of adolescence with limited rights followed by a phase where everything is possible and allowed. In Austria, no rights once granted can be revoked on the basis of age (Ruppert XXIX). A regular car driver's license, for example, cannot be revoked at a certain age and there are no medical exams required later in life. So far, no legal provisions exist which can deny certain rights to the elderly, such as medical treatment.

Age limits are fluid and closely linked to the intentions of the law concerning specific regulations, and are based on general schemes rather than individual or intentional abilities (Koziol and Welser 53). This is the reason why there is conformity concerning age limits in the European Union. These age regulations follow the human maturing process by legally reaffirming stereotypes in order to create consistent rules. Yet, there is a common understanding now that these stereotypical assumptions need to comply with principles of equal treatment (Pöschl Altersdiskriminierung und Verfassung, speech on November 24, 2011). Rules based on stereotypical notions increase discomfort on the part of citizens concerning these regulations. Age limits are often criticized because they do not sufficiently consider the gap between individual maturity/ability and chronological age. The young, for example, feel able to do so much more than the law allows, or the elderly are not always in need of financial support for public transportation. One of the few exceptions where individual capacity for rational understanding and not age limits is the basis for rules concerns a child's consent to medical treatment. Generally, individual decision-making is set at the age of fourteen, but even a teenager can decide on medical treatment on his/her own before the age of fourteen, if the physician considers the child mature enough for such a decision (§ 146c ABGB).

In cultural discourse, youth is – as Maierhofer shows – often a metaphor for energy, flexibility and desire, whereas old age often stands for inability, passiveness and helplessness (Maierhofer 85). Even if this applies to cultural and social perceptions, legal contexts are not affected, as phases of childhood and adolescence are seen as life stages requiring special protective regulations.

MINIMUM AND MAXIMUM LIMITS IN LAW

Some provisions lay down minimum age limits. Apart from rules on the age of majority, provisions on minimum age limits mainly regulate occupational provisions and determine access requirements to certain professions. Special physical or psychological abilities and a level of maturity, for example, are required, and the level of maturity and experience vary in different professions. Employees collecting road tolls have to be eighteen (§ 17 BStMG), certain mining employments require an age of twenty-one (§ 331 para 2 Allgemeine Bergpolizeiverordnung). Probation assistants (§ 12 Bewährungshilfegesetz), psychotherapists (§ 10 para 2 Z 2 Psychotherapiegesetz) or proprietors of gas companies (§ 44 para 1 Z 3 lit a Gaswirtschaftsgesetz 2011) have to be at least twenty-four. Cable car engineering requires an age of twenty-five (§ 109 para 1 Bergpolizeiverordnung für die Seilfahrt), and an arbiter must be twenty-eight (§ 9 para 1 Z 1 ZivMediatG). Furthermore, a person can only be elected federal president at the age of thirty-five (Art 60 para 3 B-VG).

Another category of rules that sets maximum age limits are those determining special benefits, such as family support and research scholarships, but also publicly financed in-vitro-fertilization (§ 4 para 4 Z 1 In-vitro-FertilisationsG). Membership to the constitutional court ends at seventy years of age (Art 147 B-VG). Some rules lay down minimum as well as maximum age limits for certain professions; members of the jury must be between twenty-four and sixty-four years old (§ 24 ASGG). However, as already stated, there are only a few general provisions revoking established rights. Reasons for the rules vary. Whereas minimum age limits are based on assumed lack of life experience and rational understanding, maximum limits argue on the basis of personal deficiencies, which reduce one's ability to work (Ruppert XXXIII). Youth is seen full of capacity and strength, the elderly providing professional life experience and wisdom. Some authors, therefore, refer to old age in legislation and jurisdiction as a 'model of competency' emphasizing the aspect of experience, but at the same time referring to a 'deficit model' associating age with illness and reduced abilities (Ruppert 145).

Today, 'typical' or 'traditional' age limits have to be specifically justified. Special jobs demand certain physical requirements, for example fire fighters. In other areas, it is important to consider age distribution, for example to secure general medical provision despite a great number of retirees.[4] Higher salaries for older employees are permitted if higher payment is based on professional experience (Marhold 89-90).

AGE, WORK AND VALUE

Supportive measures for (re-)integration of unemployed into the labor market take into account the central role of employment in an individual's biography. Unemployed under the age of twenty-five or over fifty have to participate in special training and educational programs (§ 38a AMSG). The well-known *Marienthal-Studie* 1931-1932 showed the negative consequences of unemployment and led to an understanding of the value of work in terms of self-worth and appreciation, and the destructive forces of unemployment concerning self-confidence and awareness of time. In addition to financial needs, one's position in society is challenged by unemployment (Weymann 191-92). These feelings might also occur at retirement, as capable people have to accept the loss of their professional identity and re-arrange their lives anew. Thus, retirement regulations also determine

---

4 | ECJ Rs C-229/08, *Colin Wolf*, Slg 2010, I-00000; ECJ Rs C-411/05, *Palacios*, Slg 2007, I-08531; EuGH Rs C-341/08, *Petersen*, Slg 2010, I-00000; ECJ Rs C-45/09, *Rosenbladt*, Slg 2010, I-00000; ECJ Rs C-250/09 ua, *Georgiev*, I-00000; ECJ Rs C-17/05, Cadman, Slg 2006, I-9583. See in detail also Rebhahn 173.

social roles and the 'usefulness' of individuals in terms of economic effectiveness and distributive justice.

POSITIVE FEATURES OF 'OLDER' PERSONS AND THE ELDERLY: LIFE EXPERIENCE AND WISDOM

In Austrian law, 'old' or 'higher' age is sometimes linked to specific responsibilities based on experience. Normally, such provisions do not lay down an absolute age, but the rules assign, for example, specific rights to the 'oldest' person of a group or a board. Many administrative and organizational provisions use this method. If a president is prevented from performing duties in the case of abolition of parliament, the oldest member of parliament takes over the presidency (§ 6 para 2 GOG-NR). In many chambers, such as of the pharmacists, the 'oldest' member of the board governs a session till the new president is elected (§ 34 para 1 Apothekerkammergesetz). In the board of lay judges in labor and social insurance matters, the votes are cast according to age, starting with the oldest member of the group (§ 13 para 1 ASGG).

GENDER AND AGE

Some categories of Austrian rules on age not only lay down age limits but combine them with further criteria such as gender. This applies mainly to the current rules on retirement (see above), which still differ between men and women. In 1990, the constitutional court abolished these rules, because women with the double burden of family and work did not profit from earlier retirement (VfSlg 12568/1990). Yet, the provisions are still in existence as constitutional law, despite objections by the European Court of Justice. Starting in 2024, these differences will gradually be adjusted (Melzer-Azodanloo 340).

The reasons for different legal treatment of men and women vary, but they are all of a social nature. At the beginning of the 20th century, according to the ministerial drafts concerning white collar workers insurance rules, a man's insurance contribution had to finance not only his own, but in case of his death also the widow's pension. Women's contributions were only dedicated to the women's own pensions. Yet, the statute of 1906 did not adopt the proposal that women would retire five years earlier than men. The discussion continued, and in 1914 women's age of retirement was lowered creating one main problem. Earlier retirement age meant less contribution, less contribution meant lower pensions (Haerendel 139). Another reason for women's earlier pension age, though not explicitly spelled out, was that couples could retire at the same time due to the average age difference in marriage, as examples from Great Britain in 1940 and in Portugal in 1973 show (Haerendel 139). In the 1970s, a third reason was mentioned, women's double burden of family and work (Haerendel 140). Gender age adjustments in terms of retirement were demanded, never aiming at lowering men's, but raising women's (Haerendel 141). Other age provisions concern biological aspects. Public financing of in-vitro-fertilization depends on age limits. Women must be younger than forty, and men younger than fifty (§ 4 In-vitro-Fertilisationsgesetz). Acceptance criteria for physical education teachers differ for men and women (Anlage 6 der VO BGBl. II Nr. 351/2011). Other distinctions – not as obvious – are, for example, that men must be at least thirty, women only twenty-eight when adopting children (§ 180 para 1 ABGB).

CONCLUSIONS

In the 1870s, the psychologist George Beard defined the time between thirty to forty-five years as the ideal age (Hareven 164). Nowadays, ideal age can be defined as a time without any age restrictions and limitations, open access to all sorts of professions and full economic freedom. In this context, antidiscrimination laws are very important. Since 2005, equal treatment rules have explicitly been applied to age (§ 17 Gleichbehandlungsgesetz). In principle, there is no protection of an absolute age or even old age, only of age as such. In Austria, limiting access to certain professions based on age is still allowed, but needs to be justified (Marhold 89-90).

Our overview of Austrian regulations on age confirms that law constructs and influences individual life courses. By granting rights and imposing duties, law assigns social status on the basis of age. Law is also essential for defining age in cultural discourses. For lawmakers, age limits are legal and necessary, as they allow and enable easy and general decisions. Furthermore, most age limits are historically grown and generally accepted. These regulations contribute to social peace, and are therefore not easily changed (Ruppert XXXII).

Social developments leading to a growing gap between individual maturity (adolescence), physical and mental abilities (retirement), and legal age limits will be the basis for further analysis leading to a reassessment of age limits as constituted by law.

REFERENCES

Abels, Heinz. "Lebensphase Jugend." *Lebensphasen. Eine Einführung.* Ed. Heinz Abels, Michael-Sebastian Honig, Irmhild Saake, Ansgar Weymann. Wiesbaden: Verlag für Sozialwissenschaften, 2008. 77-157. Print.

Arheidt, Sabine. "Der Jugendliche im Jugendhilferecht zwischen 1961 und 1991." *Lebensalter und Recht.* Ed. Stefan Ruppert. Frankfurt am Main: Vittorio Klostermann, 2010. 99-126. Print.

Ehmer, Josef. "Das Alter in Geschichte und Geschichtswissenschaft." *Was ist Alter(n)?* Ed. Ursula M. Staudinger and Heinz Häfner. Heidelberg: Springer, 2008. 149-72. Print.

Floßmann, Ursula. *Österreichische Privatrechtsgeschichte.* Wien, New York: Springer, 2008. Print.

Göckenjan, Gerd. "Vom Greis zum Rentner – Alter als soziale Leistung." *Lebensalter und Recht.* Ed. Stefan Ruppert. Frankfurt am Main: Vittorio Klostermann, 2010. 187-206. Print.

Gullette, Margaret Morganroth. *Aged by Culture.* Chicago: University of Chicago Press, 2004. Print.

Haerendel, Ulrike. "Die Frauenaltersgrenze in der gesetzlichen Rentenversicherung: Geschichte, Funktion, Vergleiche mit dem Ausland." *Lebensalter und Recht.* Ed. Stefan Ruppert. Frankfurt am Main: Vittorio Klostermann, 2010. 127-51. Print.

Haltern, Ulrich. "Notwendigkeit und Umrisse einer Kulturtheorie des Rechts." *ARSP* Beiheft 113 (2008): 193-221. Print.

Hareven, Tamara K. *Familiengeschichte, Lebenslauf und sozialer Wandel.* Frankfurt am Main, New York: Campus, 1999. Print.

Honig, Michael-Sebastian. "Lebensphase Kindheit." *Lebensphasen. Eine Einführung.* Ed. Heinz Abels, Michael-Sebastian Honig, Irmhild Saake, Ansgar Weymann. Wiesbaden: Verlag für Sozialwissenschaften, 2008. 9-76. Print.

Kaufmann, Franz-Xaver. "Was meint Alter? Was bewirkt demographisches Altern? Soziologische Perspektiven." *Was ist Alter(n)?* Ed. Ursula M. Staudinger and Heinz Häfner. Heidelberg: Springer, 2008. 119-38. Print.

Kholi, Martin. "Die Institutionalisierung des Lebenslaufs. Historische Befunde und theoretische Argumente." *Kölner Zeitschrift für Soziologie und Sozialpsychologie* 37 (1985): 1-29. Print.

Koziol, Helmut, and Rudolf Welser. *Bürgerliches Recht I.* Wien: Manz Verlag, 2006. Print.

Maierhofer, Roberta. "Mensch, Alte! Frauen, Altern und Identität. Eine kulturwissenschaftliche Einführung." *Beiträge von Vortragenden der Montagsakademie 2007/08.* Ed. Karl-Franzens-Universität, Graz: 2009. 81-97. Print.

Marhold, Franz. "Differenzierung nach dem Alter." *Arbeitsrechtliche Diskriminierungsverbote.* Ed. Theodor Tomandl and Walter Schrammel. Wien: Braumüller Verlag, 2005. 83-92. Print.

Melzer-Azodanloo, Nora. "Unzulässige Differenzierung nach dem Geschlecht bei Kündigung wegen Erreichens des gesetzlichen Pensionsalters – EuGH 18.11.2011 (Rs Kleist)." *Europäische Zeitschrift für Arbeitsrecht* 3 (2011): 340-50. Print.

Ruppert, Stefan. *Alter im Recht. Rg* 9 (2006): 138-47. Print.

—. "Lebensalter und Recht." *Lebensalter und Recht.* Ed. Stefan Ruppert. Frankfurt am Main: Vittorio Klostermann, 2010. VII-XXXIII. Print.

Saake, Irmhild. "Lebensphase Alter." *Lebensphasen. Eine Einführung.* Ed. Heinz Abels, Michael-Sebastian Honig, Irmhild Saake, Ansgar Weymann. Wiesbaden: Verlag für Sozialwissenschaften, 2008. 235-79. Print.

Ucakar, Karl. *Demokratie und Wahlrecht in Österreich. Zur Entwicklung politischer Partizipation und staatlicher Legitimationspolitik.* Wien: Verlag für Gesellschaftskritik, 1985. Print.

Resch, Reinhard. *Sozialrecht.* Wien: Manz Verlag, 2011. Print.

Weymann, Ansgar. "Lebensphase Erwachsenenalter." *Lebensphasen. Eine Einführung.* Ed. Heinz Abels, Michael-Sebastian Honig, Irmhild Saake, Ansgar Weymann. Wiesbaden: Verlag für Sozialwissenschaften, 2008. 158-234. Print.

**Representations of Ages of Life
in Media and Art**

"The Journey into the Land of Forgetfulness"

Metaphors of Aging and Dementia in Media

Heinrich Grebe/Welf-Gerrit Otto/Harm-Peer Zimmermann

It is no longer unusual in affluent Western societies to regard old age as a positive opportunity to embark on a new life. The idea is that, freed from the pressures and constraints of work and family, this new life can be dedicated first and foremost to the project of self-realization. "Old at last! Now I can do what I want!"[1] (Oppermann and Tippelt). However, the notion of old age as a dividing line also becomes relevant in the context of age-related changes to a person's physical and cognitive constitution. In this case, a distinction is made between a person's former, unimpaired life and a fundamentally different life filled with limitations and impediments. Aging with dementia is currently emerging as a particular symbol of this kind of existential discontinuity. The following description of the situation in which Walter Jens, an emeritus professor of rhetoric and dementia sufferer[2], finds himself, offers an example of this:

---

1 | Book titles as well as quotations from media and research texts have been translated, where necessary, from German into English. The original German versions can be made available by the authors upon request.

2 | The authors are aware that formulations such as "people with dementia," "dementia sufferers," or "people affected by dementia" are a product of the discursive practice of labeling (Bond, Corner, and Graham). Since the issue of labeling cannot be addressed adequately in this paper, our use of these formulations is subject to certain reservations.

Walter Jens led his first life amidst the learned societies and literary circles of the scholarly community of Hamburg, Tübingen and Berlin. He is now leading his second life on a farm amongst cows, chickens, and children...Walter Jens and [his personal caretaker] Margit Hespeler would probably never have met if it had not been for this rupture in his life or for this illness which has attacked his brain and destroyed everything he once was, thought, and represented (*Schwäbisches Tagblatt* 2011/09/24).

This extract reveals a twofold metaphorical portrayal of dementia. First, the image of a *rupture*[3] conveys the view that dementia-related impairments lead to an existential transformation, it seems there is 'nothing left' of Walter Jens, the scholar, or of his life as it once had been. Second, the medical condition associated with these impairments is imagined as a destructive actor that has *brought about* said *rupture* by *attacking* Jens' brain.

Metaphorical representations of aging with dementia such as the one shown in the example above constitute the main subject of this article. Our discussion of this topic is divided into four sections. First, we present the theoretical arguments explaining why the analysis of metaphorical representations of age and aging is important. Principal among these are discourse analytic considerations such as those developed by Jürgen Link, drawing on the work of Michel Foucault. Second, we make use of the ideas contained in George Lakoff's and Mark Johnson's cognitive metaphor theory for the purpose of conducting a discourse analysis of media texts. Other theoretical approaches to metaphor such as those developed by Hans Blumenberg, for example, will not be considered here. Based on these considerations, we then, as our third point, analyze three types of metaphor relating to age and aging with dementia found in examples taken from various German print media. In the conclusion of the article, we examine the extent to which these metaphors and their associated cultural discursive contexts of interpretation suggest that growing old with dementia robs a person of key aspects regarding the quality of life. We also briefly discuss a number of countervailing representations pointing to the view that growing old with dementia does not threaten the lives of sufferers to the extent that media representations would often have us believe.

---

3 | The use of italics here and in the following serves to highlight a word's metaphorical usage.

(INTER-)DISCOURSES WE LIVE BY

The analysis presented here is part of a research project funded by the Volkswagen Foundation entitled *Living well in old age* which explores, among other things, mass media representations of age and aging.[4] Based on the approach by Jürgen Link, a scholar of discourse analysis, we regard mass media as an area of societal interdiscourse. Link takes Michel Foucault's theory of discourse further by distinguishing interdiscourse from academic special discourses on the one hand, and everyday knowledge, characterized as elementary discourse, on the other (Link, *Diskursanalyse*). One key function of interdiscourse consists in highlighting issues contained in special discourse and making them accessible for use in wider social debate. Media interdiscourse, for example, conveys gerontological and medical knowledge about age and aging to the general public by means of TV programs, magazine articles, and self-help books geared towards non-specialists.

Interdiscursive representations of age and aging do more than simply convey expert knowledge for information purposes; they serve to disseminate those interpretations of age and aging which are (assumed to be) especially relevant in society at a particular point in time. Even though these interpretations often claim to represent the undisguised nature of age and aging, they have to be seen as products of socio-historical relations of power and knowledge. By disseminating such interpretations of age and aging, mass media interdiscourse provides various blueprints (*Applikationsvorlagen*) for growing old that highlight certain actions and behaviors and seek to make them binding. This issue highlights two phenomena: "[...] on the one hand, the cultural malleability of images of aging, and on the other, the power to shape culture that is intrinsic to images of aging themselves" (BMFSFuJ 52).

With regard to everyday life impacts of interdiscursive interpretations and images of age and aging, we concur with Link in stressing certain

---

4 | The project's full title is *Living well in old age in the face of vulnerability and finality – an analysis of images of aging in public discourses and everyday practices* (Kruse, Rentsch, and Zimmermann; Otto and Grebe) with scholars participating from the fields of gerontology (University of Heidelberg), philosophy (Technical University of Dresden) and cultural studies (University of Marburg). The authors of this paper are part of the cultural studies working group.

limitations. It certainly cannot be said, for example, that the consumption of any one newspaper article, TV program, or radio feature will lead to an internalization of the image of aging conveyed in it. "What is crucial [...] is not the hermeneutics of isolated examples, such as individual caricatures, linguistic images, photographs, texts, films, but rather the constant repetitive impact of large numbers of blueprints [*Applikationsvorlagen*] and of their associated specific subjective applications [*Applikationsvorgänge*]" (Link, *Normalismus* 375).

Link also shows that linguistic imagery or 'collective symbols' widespread in society are an elementary component of the different discursive spheres (Link, *Diskursanalyse* 413). Collective symbols appear throughout special discourses, interdiscourses, and elementary discourses, helping to illustrate the phenomena and subject matters addressed. Collective symbols thus possess their own interdiscursivity (Link, *Diskursanalyse* 411). Metaphorical expressions are part of this system of collective symbols.[5]

For example, characterizing certain developments as problematic in scientific, political, media or indeed everyday life contexts is often done by using the collectively shared metaphor of a rising tide or an explosion. Particularly with regard to the demographic trend in affluent Western societies, there is frequent mentioning of a *rising tide of pensioners* or of an *explosion* in the numbers of elderly people. In both cases, the highly specific way the demographic trend is illustrated metaphorically leads to this phenomenon, and ultimately old people themselves, are being portrayed as a threat to society. These kinds of metaphors, together with their associated discourses, are of manifestly practical significance whenever it comes to legitimizing cutbacks in pension payments. Cutbacks are then portrayed as a strategy to help avert the threat of *floods* of pensioners causing an *explosion* in the welfare state system.

---

5 | The social system of collective symbols does not consist of metaphorical elements alone, however: "Referring to the railway as a symbol of progress is metaphorical; railway as a symbol of modern technology, however, is not metaphorical but rather synecdochic (pars pro toto)" (Link and Link-Heer 45). It should also be noted that not every metaphor is always also a collective symbol. Novel or original metaphorical usages, such as those invented in works of literature, often have no collective relevance (yet): "By contrast, the 'system of collective symbols' is much more widespread, more stereotypical and more long-lasting" (Link and Link-Heer 46).

METAPHORS WE LIVE BY

In their study *Metaphors We Live By*, linguists George Lakoff and Mark Johnson elaborate the idea that metaphors are the main means of creating and disseminating interpretations of social reality. Unlike Link, however, they do not place metaphors in a context of collective symbolic or discursive systems. The central thesis put forward by Lakoff and Johnson is that human thought and action is based on a system of cognitive models which in turn is structured by a large number of conceptual metaphors. Metaphors are conceptual to the extent that they arrange or order cognitive concepts using linguistic symbols. Ideas about what such complex situations (illness or aging) mean arise by comparing them to other situations. This is the case where, for example, illness is described as *a malfunctioning* of the *body-as-machine*[6] or age and aging as the *evening of life*: "The essence of metaphor is understanding and experiencing one kind of thing in terms of another" (Lakoff and Johnson 5). Lakoff und Johnson do not assume that the cognitive model of 'old age' is structured by just one metaphor (i.e. 'old age is the *evening of life*'). Rather, a range of metaphors reveals different aspects of a certain cognitive model.

Instead of speaking about cognitive models, from a discourse analysis perspective one might also speak of internalized interpretations of phenomena which inform everyday ways of life in the form of "orientational knowledge" (Link and Link-Heer 44). Unlike Lakoff and Johnson, this kind of approach emphasizes the fact that socially relevant interpretations of reality come about on the basis of various discursive formations and, in addition, that they cannot be formulated in isolation from constellations of social power. Collective symbolic expressions, such as socially relevant metaphors, are embedded in this context rather than seen as an exception. Indeed, they are "elements that support and reinforce discourse" (Jäger and Jäger 39). As such, it behooves us to pay close attention to them. "Due to their specific symbolic character, collective symbols generate knowledge shaped both by reason and emotion, because they simplify complex realities, make them plausible, and thus interpret them in a specific way" (Jäger and Jäger 39).

---

6 | In this context, Susan Sontag's publications on *Illness as Metaphor* and *AIDS and Its Metaphors* are also relevant.

Nevertheless, Lakoff and Johnson's study provides important hints for how to go about deconstructing metaphorical expressions. The following description of the field of interdiscursive metaphors of dementia therefore takes up the differentiation introduced by Lakoff and Johnson between structural metaphors, orientational metaphors and ontological metaphors. The analysis is rounded off by linking interdiscursive metaphors of dementia to a cultural discursive context of interpretation.

EMPIRICAL ANALYSIS: AGING AND DEMENTIA IN THE MEDIA

Dementia-related impairments, such as those that may arise as people grow older (particularly in old age), have in Germany become an issue of considerable interest in academia, politics, the media, the caring professions, and everyday life, largely as a result of increased life expectancies. In keeping with its interdiscursive character, media reporting engages with the issue in a special way. On the one hand, it provides the public with specialist (medical) knowledge about those conditions that are regarded as playing a causal role in the symptoms of dementia. On the other hand, media representations also take the everyday lives and the elementary discourses associated with people who suffer from dementia into account, trying to show what it is like to experience the symptoms of dementia in old age. Thus, media interdiscourse creates a specific image of age and aging.

Medical diagnostics regard the underlying condition of Alzheimer's disease as being the most common cause of dementia-related impairment in old age. Accordingly, Alzheimer's is the focus of media presentations concerning growing old with dementia. In many cases, it is apparent that despite the special discursive distinction between pathology and syndrome, Alzheimer's and dementia are treated as synonymous.

1. Data Base and Methods

A corpus consisting of representations found in German newspapers, illustrated periodicals, magazines, and self-help books for the elderly provides the source for our analysis of media reports about aging and dementia.[7] Some 250 articles in total were investigated, covering a period between 1990 and 2011. The source material was closely analyzed using MAXQDA software, which was useful among other things in identifying all the metaphorical expressions contained in the texts examined. Based on this computer-assisted work, it was possible to conduct a synoptic analysis providing a comprehensive view of the field of metaphors of dementia in print media. The metaphorical patterns that emerged in relation to aging with dementia are described in the following.

2. Structural Metaphors

The linguistic images subsumed within the term "structural metaphor" (Lakoff and Johnson 14) are apparent wherever a complex phenomenon such as aging is illustrated by reference to another complex phenomenon such as military withdrawal from a battle, 'Aging means withdrawal.'

In the context of media accounts of dementia, three different types of structural metaphor become apparent, as described in the following.

Aging with dementia is often described, first, as a journey or a path towards a place that is fundamentally different from the reality inhabited by the cognitively unimpaired, healthy people in the person's social environment. "For patients, the *journey into the land of forgetfulness* begins *slowly but inexorably*[8]" (*Neue Post* 5/2003, 56); "Consultants can now establish with a fair degree of certainty whether slip-ups in old age are normal or whether they are the precursors of those *phantoms* that will accompany the patient in future on their *way into no-man's land*" (*Frankfurter Allgemeine Zeitung*[9] 36/2004, 61); "*In a world of their own*[.] *The mind goes, feelings remain*. Not only with Alzheimer's. Confused old people live *in a reality of their own*" (*Reader's Digest* 8/2002, 71).

The symbolization of dementia occurs here by linking it with the concept of 'absence.' Those who set off on a journey, those who are on their way to somewhere else leave a certain place, and are consequently no lon-

---

7 | These include periodicals such as the *Frankfurter Allgemeine Zeitung*, *Bild*, *Apotheken-Umschau* (a free magazine available in local pharmacies), *Reader's Digest*, *Neue Post* and many others.

8 | The phrases highlighted in italics in the print media quotations are the authors' emphases.

9 | Henceforth abbreviated as *FAZ*.

ger where they used to be. The metaphorical expressions presented above reveal a perplexing ambiguity: the fact of physical (or indeed emotional) presence is juxtaposed with moving mentally ever further away from the socio-spatial order of the present. References to *phantoms* and the image of *no man's land* emphasize the notion that the absence triggered by dementia involves an existential threat; indeed, it is essentially a death threat. Metaphors of journeying and absence are also strongly linked to culturally influential metaphorical representations of serious illness and dying. It is often said that people who have died *have left us*. Accordingly, structural metaphors of this type shape the metaphorical model of 'dementia is absence,' in which absence is symbolically brought into the context of human dying.

Accounts that describe the notion of 'dementia' using the concept of 'loss' form a second pattern of structural metaphor, namely Alzheimer's disease as an insidious, mysterious illness. The victims slowly *lose their memory* and so *lose themselves* as well" (*Bild* 197/31 2001, 20); "Alzheimer's patients *lose themselves* in the here and now. When the *real world is lost*" (*Frankfurter Allgemeine Sonntagszeitung* 13/2005, R5); "Some 1.5 million people in Germany suffer from dementia, which begins with forgetfulness and leads to considerable memory problems and a *loss of personality*" (*Süddeutsche Zeitung* 2000/11/16, L3).

The analogy of losing an object serves as a basis for the statements presented above. Just as people with dementia lose certain things, such as their house keys, they also lose their memory. This loss of memory is seen in turn as the basis for a loss of self, of personality and of the real world. Metaphors of loss thus convey a very similar idea to that conveyed by metaphors of absence: something, indeed someone that used to be there has *gone*, has *been lost*. The losses caused by dementia could hardly be more serious, the relevant metaphors raising the question are more or less directly what remains when a person loses his or her personality. The metaphorical model underlying the statements presented above is thus 'dementia is loss.'

A third group of structural metaphors conveys the view that dementia-related impairments set in motion a process of transformation that turns the adults affected by dementia into infant children. "*It is just like after the birth of a child*, from their first cry to their first steps to their first intelligible word: the same sorts of things happen in the course of this insidious disease – *only the other way around*: a respected doctor, father of five children, forgets how to read, how to speak, how to dress himself, and even how to eat" (*FAZ* 228/1996, 43); "We like to think that a toddler senses every act of caring; this is much more difficult in the case of a *childlike elderly person.* And this is also what makes Alzheimer's so disturbing: it seems *to reverse rather than accelerate* the process of aging" (*FAZ* 159/1997, 32).

When considering metaphorical formulations such as those quoted above, it is necessary to take into account the discursively informed models of adulthood and childhood. In this context, a further dimension of ambiguity arises. On the one hand, childhood acts as a symbol for a life phase that is carefree and filled with spontaneous joie-de-vivre. This image contrasts with the idea of adulthood perceived as full of responsibilities, obligations and worries, and is therefore not very pleasant. On the other hand, widespread notions of maturing and development point to the fact that children are often regarded as unfinished adults and therefore as unfinished people per se. In this view adults embody characteristics that are valued positively, such as competence, independence, responsibility for oneself, and free will, whereas childhood is equated with precisely the lack of such characteristics. This latter mode of interpretation of adulthood and childhood, based on the positive value attached to development, is also brought to bear prominently in the metaphors of the kind described above. The corresponding metaphorical model is thus 'dementia is regression.'

3. Orientational Metaphors

Lakoff and Johnson make a distinction between structural metaphors and so-called orientational metaphors. "Orientational metaphors give a concept a spatial orientation; for example, HAPPY IS UP. The fact that the concept HAPPY is oriented UP leads to English expressions like 'I'm feeling *up* today'" (Lakoff and Johnson 14). As Lakoff and Johnson stress, this type of metaphor is based on certain physical and cultural experiences. The significance of the physical dimension of experience[10] is illustrated in the following extract: "HEALTH AND LIFE ARE UP; SICKNESS AND DEATH ARE DOWN[:] He's at the *peak* of health. [...] He came *down* with the flu.

---

10 | Lakoff and Johnson are not assuming here that there is any kind of 'naturalness' or 'originality' attached to the physical dimension of experience: "[...] [W]hat we call direct physical experience is never merely a matter of having a body of a certain sort; rather *every* experience takes place within a vast background of cultural presuppositions" (Lakoff and Johnson 57).

His health is *declining*. [...] Physical basis: Serious illness forces us to lie down physically. When you're dead, you are physically down" (Lakoff and Johnson 15).

Positioning related to a high-low scheme is an important component of the metaphorical representation of dementia, "Walter Jens – enlightened thinker *sinks* into the *darkness* of forgetfulness" (*Bild* 55/10 2008, 12); "Shocking *decline* of a human being: Götz George as an Alzheimer's patient with Klaus J. Behrendt in the TV drama 'My Father'" (*Neue Post* 5/2003, 56); "It is only at the start of their *free fall* that sufferers still notice their own biography leaving them (and, with it, that which had made their life what it was), their identity – in other words, their 'self' – slipping away in an inexorable *slide into nothingness*" (*FAZ* 220/2006, 35).

Just as adverse developments are characterized by formulations such as 'things are going downhill,' descriptions of dementia cast in terms of sinking, declining, or falling also express an unambiguously negative view. The 'light-dark' contrast, closely linked to the 'high-low' scheme, is influential here. The symbol for light and clarity is the sun, and the sun (as our everyday language emphasizes) is *high* in the sky. For the darkness of night to come, the sun has to *go down*. In Western cultures, brightness, light, and the sun are closely associated with mental activity and intellectual potential as illustrated by the term given to the historical era of Enlightenment. The above description of Walter Jens as having once been an *enlightened* thinker accords with this scheme. Interestingly enough, metaphors of light tend to appear in print media treatments of dementia whenever brief moments of *being able to remember again*, of temporary mental functioning, are being described, "Yet even if a person is already seriously ill, they are still able to comprehend their situation in *lucid* moments" (*FAZ* 275/2001, 10). Conversely, impaired mental capacity equates with *darkness*. The motif of a sunset or of darkness, for example, is also prominent in the context of Ronald Reagan's experience of Alzheimer's disease. "When Ronald Reagan became ill in the early 1990s, he wrote, "I now begin the journey that will lead me into the sunset of my life" (*Neue Post* 29/1998, 57). Reagan's use of the sunset metaphor almost certainly stems from his background as an actor in Western movies. Nonetheless, the sunset motif still accords with the light-dark scheme described here.

The second way darkness operates, along with declining, sinking, or falling, is by symbolizing disease and death, to which Lakoff and Johnson explicitly refer. If health and life are *up* in metaphorical terms and disease and death are *down*, then the metaphors of darkness and decline suggest that people with dementia are not simply suffering from a condition. What is simultaneously being suggested is that sufferers are in the process of dying, especially in mental terms, or even that in a certain sense they are mentally no longer alive. The accompanying metaphorical model here is 'dementia is darkness' or 'dementia is down.'

4. Ontological Metaphors

Ontological metaphors are said to be present whenever a phenomenon is illustrated by reference to an entity or substance, "[O]ur experiences with physical objects provide the basis for an extraordinarily wide variety of ontological metaphors, that is, ways of viewing events, activities, emotions, ideas, etc., as entities and substances" (Lakoff and Johnson 25).

In print media debate about dementia, ontological metaphors take among others the following form. "It is as if they had *holes* in their memory" (*Reader's Digest* 11/2006 142); "Alzheimer's. I'm so *empty*, I want to die" (*Bild* 172/30 2005, 16); "Dead nerve cells, *gravestones* to a lost past, turn the *brain's hard drive* into a graveyard" (*FAZ* 36/2004, 61). In these examples, the human memory is described using the metaphor of a container (Lakoff and Johnson 27-34), this *memory container* gathers together all of a person's memories and experiences and keeps them for present as well as future tasks. The neurodegenerative pathology of Alzheimer's disease creates *holes* in this *container*, causing it to *empty*. Very similar to this is the notion of the *brain as a hard drive* that has been *deleted* by neuropathological events. At the same time, there is no doubt that these *holes* and *empty hard drives* are highly problematic, as here again a symbolic association is made with the phenomenon of death. This is indicated by the death wish ("I want to die"), which is set in a causal relation to the empty memory container ("I'm so *empty*, I want to die"). The same is true of the description of dead nerve cells as *gravestones* and of the *empty hard drive memory* as a graveyard. Overall then, the emptying of the hard drive storage space or memory container is identified with an emptying of the human being concerned. Ontological metaphors of this kind, also present in widespread reports of the "empty gaze" (*FAZ* 223/2008, 35) of people with dementia, suggest an ongoing process of de-humanization. Last but not least, the metaphor of a rupture already mentioned at the start of this article is also an ontological one, as it refers to a defect, to something that is irretrievably broken, and as such has thoroughly changed. In the case discussed this 'something' was the life of the scholar Walter Jens, which along with his memory container has been *destroyed* by the changes brought about by dementia.

As also mentioned in the introductory section, dementia is often portrayed as if it were a human actor. In such cases, Lakoff and Johnson speak of ontological metaphors of personification. "Perhaps the most obvious ontological metaphors are those where the physical object is further specified as being a person. This allows us to comprehend a wide variety of experiences with nonhuman entities in terms of human motivations, characteristics, and activities" (Lakoff and Johnson 33). The following metaphorical personifications of dementia may serve as examples. "Dementia is a *thief; lurking* inside your head, ready to *grab hold of* bigger and bigger *pieces of your life*" (*Brigitte Woman* 4/2002, 114); "This disease is *brutal*. It *robs* you of the people you have loved. A little bit more every day" (*Bild* 212/37 2007, 14).

Thus, dementia, or rather the underlying condition of Alzheimer's disease in particular, appears in these extracts as a *thief* who symbolically speaking is guilty of the crime of theft and ultimately of murder. Pathology is described as a person who takes hold of *pieces* of another person's life, until not a single *piece* of his/her life remains, thus logically following the above stated metaphors. *Victims* of dementia are not only those directly affected, but also the people around them in their social environment, especially family. These people are faced with the growing absence and loss of a beloved person, a person whom the 'disease of old age' has stolen *piece* by *piece*. Considering the seriousness and the *brutality* of these *crimes,* it is apparent that dementia is personified here as evil in the guise of disease. The corresponding metaphorical model could be translated into the formula 'dementia is a murderous thief.'

LIVING WITH DEMENTIA – A CONTRADICTION IN TERMS?

An analysis of various metaphors of aging and dementia clearly shows their meaning making capability. Thanks to their illustrative character, they are able to persuasively convey a readily understandable answer to the question of what are the causes and the consequences of symptoms of dementia. The complexity of neuromedical research, for example, is reduced by using the metaphor of a container or a hard drive, thus making the related issues accessible to wider social debate.

However, orientational knowledge created by the metaphors of age, aging and dementia discussed here is limited to certain specific elements. Throughout all the texts and over a period spanning several years, these metaphorical models establish comparisons especially to phenomena and situations such as absence, loss, regression, darkness, emptying, and brutal attack. There is no doubt that people with dementia and those around them have experiences that can indeed be aptly described as absence or loss. In this sense, the reason for the conceptual limitation mentioned here may be that media accounts provide an especially fitting portrayal of age and aging with dementia.

A number of factors indicate, however, that this assumption is not warranted. First, there are interdiscursive representations showing that age and aging with dementia can mean something other than just loss, regression, or emptying (Otto). Not least among these are representations communicated by dementia-impaired people themselves (Zimmermann and Wißmann; Demenz Support Stuttgart). Second, scientific studies confirm that in many cases the experiences and sensitivities of people with dementia do not fit with the characteristics of aging with dementia that are suggested by the metaphorical representations (Kruse; Beard, Knauss, and Moyer).

It seems especially important to look at the influence of the cultural discursive context of interpretation. Lakoff and Johnson argue that the metaphorical structure of a culture's concepts is consistent with the values of this culture (Lakoff and Johnson 22). Good mental health constitutes a key value in Western culture. Societies such as Germany express this value orientation by describing themselves above all as 'knowledge-based-societies.' Accordingly, impaired cognitive potential constitutes an especially problematic situation in socio-cultural terms, which in turn renders the comparison of dementia with phenomena of loss and regression especially plausible.

As we have shown, accounts of dementia frequently contain metaphors that are also prevalent in figures of speech relating to human death. The idea that impaired mental potential or a neurodegenerative condition such as Alzheimer's represents a kind of dying that occurs prior to a person's biological death is also rooted in the context of cultural discursive orders of values and knowledge. This is the point at which an image of human being comes into play that is supported by both the philosophical distinction between mind and body and the neuroscientific reformulation of cognicentric dualism (Post; Lyman; Zimmermann). When the mind (or the brain) is damaged, it means that the human being has also come to serious harm. This is because the mind embodies the crucial quality of being human, just as the brain *saves* and *manages* the information and capabilities that make a person human.

If the consequence of the loss of character traits and bodily functions due to dementia is that people who suffer are actually treated as sub-human, when they express their desires (Scholl and Sabat), their 'mental death' quickly manifests itself in their 'social death' as well. An exploratory study undertaken by British sociologists Helen Sweeting and Mary Gilhooly suggests that this assumption is valid. Based on conversations with one hundred respondents who care for relatives with dementia, they come to the following conclusion: "In over one third of caregiving relatives there was evidence of both beliefs and behaviors, suggesting that a degree of social death had occurred before the sufferer's biological death" (Sweeting and Gilhooly 93). One interview extract in which a family caregiver speaks about her mother who suffers from dementia illustrates the extent to which the metaphor of absence can be associated with the phenomenon of social death: "We treat her mostly, unfortunately, as if she's not really in our world" (104).

Two caveats should be issued here: First, Sweeting and Gilhooly observe that "perceiving a sufferer in ways which could be characterized as socially dead was not necessarily combined with behaving as though they were" (93). Second, most of the texts in which the above-mentioned metaphors appear are explicit in calling for the social inclusion of people with dementia; any meanings conveying exclusion are in these cases undoubtedly unintentional.

Thus, processes of social exclusion of people with dementia are certainly not initiated solely by metaphors of absence, loss, or emptying. Rather, as we have shown, it is an overarching cultural discursive perspective which makes these metaphors appear as almost natural and necessary representations of dementia. What can be said is that the cultural discursive interpretive context influences people's perceptions and ways of dealing with dementia. If growing old with dementia were not a generally feared scenario, a society would not deploy scientific and material resources in the service of preventing it, such as administering drugs.

Nonetheless, analyzing media metaphors of dementia raises an awareness of the problematic aspects of the linguistic images discussed here. Metaphorical expressions are part of a society's system of interdiscursive collective symbols that create meaning and orientation, and therefore remain important and indispensable. Rather than arguing that dementia should no longer be portrayed using metaphors at all, we appeal instead for their modification. The form such modified metaphors might take can be demonstrated by reference to those representations that differ from the deficit-oriented perspective dominant in the media (Grebe), and are therefore based in a different interpretive context than the cognicentric one. One aspect especially clearly highlighted by the above-mentioned counter representations to the media's deficit narratives is that people with dementia (contrary to widespread assumptions) are not *beyond reach*: "The thing is to find the right *key* in order to make *contact* with the seemingly *closed-off* and *submerged world* in which people with dementia live. The more *keys* or *door openers* you can find the better" (*Menschen. Das Magazin* 4/2008, 100).

Although the metaphor of absence is still prominent here, its potentially excluding aspect is addressed in a particular way. The reference to *keys* and *door openers* underscores the fact that the supposed *absence* can be *broken down* if those in the social environment of people suffering from dementia deploy certain strategies. One everyday practical effect of establishing this idea would be to ensure that people with dementia enjoy greater social inclusion rather than being implicitly or explicitly excluded.

Social exclusion is often described as existing in society's *shadows*. This metaphor too can be modified for the purpose of demanding that people with dementia be socially included. *Stepping out of the shadows: Why I am fighting for our rights as people affected by dementia* is the title of a book by Helga Rohra, who has been diagnosed with Lewy body dementia. The formula 'stepping out of the shadows' is a metaphor that poignantly symbolizes the self-confident and emancipatory demand for self-confidence and independence by the activist.[11]

Thus, it is not a matter of substituting the public demonization of dementia with an idealized image of the condition. Instead, it is important to develop representations that take the breadth of experience of people living

---

11 | At a later stage of the research project *Living well in old age*, the authors will be studying, among other things, these kinds of (counter) metaphors developed by people affected by dementia.

with dementia and of those around them seriously, without automatically succumbing to the cultural reflex of denying the value of a life lived with the impairing symptoms of dementia. In this way, living and growing old with dementia might be reconciled rather than being seen as a contradiction in terms.

REFERENCES

Beard, Renée L., Jenny Knauss, and Don Moyer. "Managing disability and enjoying life: How we reframe dementia through personal narratives." *Journal of Aging Studies* 23 (2009): 227-335. Print.

Bild. Berlin: Axel Springer AG. Print.

BMFSFuJ (Bundesministerium für Familie, Senioren, Frauen und Jugend), ed. *Sechster Bericht zur Lage der älteren Generation in der Bundesrepublik Deutschland. Altersbilder in der Gesellschaft.* Berlin: BMFSFuJ, 2010. Print.

Bond, John, Lynne Corner, and Ruth Graham. "Social Science Theory on Dementia Research: Normal Ageing, Cultural Representation and Social Exclusion." *Dementia and Social Inclusion: Marginalised Groups and Marginalised Areas of Dementia Research, Care and Practice.* Ed. Anthea Innes, Carol Archibald, and Charlie Murphy. London/Philadelphia: Jessica Kingsley Publishers, 2004. 220-36. Print.

Brigitte Woman. Hamburg: Gruner & Jahr AG & Co KG. Print.

Demenz Support Stuttgart, ed. *'Ich spreche für mich selbst.' Menschen mit Demenz melden sich zu Wort.* Frankfurt am Main: Mabuse-Verlag, 2010. Print.

Frankfurter Allgemeine Zeitung. Frankfurt: Frankfurter Allgemeine Zeitung GmbH. Print.

Grebe, Heinrich. "Über der gewonnenen Zeit hängt eine Bedrohung ... Zur medialen Thematisierung von (hohem) Alter und Demenz: Inhalte, Strukturen, diskursive Grundlagen." *Gutes Leben im hohen Alter. Das Altern in seinen Entwicklungsmöglichkeiten und Entwicklungsgrenzen verstehen.* Ed. Andreas Kruse, Thomas Rentsch and Harm-Peer Zimmermann. Heidelberg: AKA Verlag, 2012. 97-107. Print.

Jäger, Margarete and Siegfried Jäger. *Deutungskämpfe. Theorie und Praxis Kritischer Diskursanalyse.* Wiesbaden: VS Verlag, 2007. Print.

Kruse, Andreas, ed. *Lebensqualität bei Demenz. Zum gesellschaftlichen und individuellen Umgang mit einer Grenzsituation im Alter.* Heidelberg: AKA Verlag, 2010. Print.

Kruse, Andreas, Thomas Rentsch, and Harm-Peer Zimmermann, eds. *Gutes Leben im hohen Alter. Das Altern in seinen Entwicklungsmöglichkeiten und Entwicklungsgrenzen verstehen.* Heidelberg: AKA Verlag, 2012. Print.

Lakoff, George and Mark Johnson. *Metaphors We live By.* Chicago/London: The University of Chicago Press, 2003. Print.

Link, Jürgen. "Diskursanalyse unter besonderer Berücksichtigung von Interdiskurs und Kollektivsymbolik." *Handbuch Sozialwissenschaftliche Diskursanalyse. Band 1: Theorien und Methoden.* Ed. Reiner Keller, Andreas Hirseland, Werner Schneider, and Willy Viehöfer. Wiesbaden: VS-Verlag, 2001. 408-30. Print.

—. *Versuch über den Normalismus. Wie Normalität produziert wird.* Göttingen: Vandenhoeck und Ruprecht, 2006. Print.

Link, Jürgen and Ursula Link-Heer. "Kollektivsymbolik und Orientierungswissen. Das Beispiel des 'Technisch-medizinischen Vehikel-Körpers.'" *Der Deutschunterricht* 4, 1994. 44-55. Print.

Lyman, Karen A. "Bringing the Social Back in: A Critique of the Biomedicalization of Dementia." *The Gerontologist* 29.5 (1989): 597-605. Print.

Menschen. Das Magazin. Kassel: Publikom Z Verlagsgesellschaft mbH. Print.

Neue Post. Hamburg: Heinrich Bauer Verlag KG. Print.

Oppermann, Jutta and Frank Tippelt. *Endlich alt! Jetzt mache ich, was ich will! Ein Lese- und Ideenbuch für und über Menschen in der zweiten Lebenshälfte.* Bielefeld: J. Kamphausen Verlag, 2005.

Otto, Welf-Gerrit. "Zugewinn im Defizit – Sinnfenster in der populären Rezeption von Demenzen." *Gutes Leben im hohen Alter. Das Altern in seinen Entwicklungsmöglichkeiten und Entwicklungsgrenzen verstehen.* Ed. Andreas Kruse, Thomas Rentsch and Harm-Peer Zimmermann. Heidelberg: AKA Verlag, 2012. 109-20. Print.

Otto, Welf-Gerrit and Heinrich Grebe. "Bilder von Elan und Elend – Das Forschungsprojekt Gutes Leben im hohen Alter." *Moderne. Kulturwissenschaftliches Jahrbuch, 6. Jg. Alter und Altern.* Ed. Helga Mitterbauer and Katharina Scherke. Innsbruck/Wien/Bozen: StudienVerlag, 2012. 204-10. Print.

Post, Stephen G. "The Concept of Alzheimer Disease in a Hypercognitive Society." *Concepts of Alzheimer Disease. Biological, Clinical, and Cultural*

Perspectives. Ed. Peter J. Whitehouse, Konrad Maurer, and Jesse F. Bal-
lenger. Baltimore: John Hopkins University Press, 1999. 245-56. Print.

Reader's Digest Deutschland. Stuttgart: Verlag Das Beste GmbH. Print.

Rohra, Helga. *Aus dem Schatten treten. Warum ich mich für unsere Rechte
als Demenzbetroffene einsetze.* Frankfurt am Main: Mabuse-Verlag, 2011.
Print.

Scholl, Jane M. and Steven R. Sabat. "Stereotypes, stereotype threat and
ageing: implications for the understanding and treatment of people
with Alzheimer's disease." *Ageing & Society* 28 (2008): 103-30. Print.

Sontag, Susan. *Illness as Metaphor.* New York: Farrar, Straus & Giroux, 1978.
Print.

—. *AIDS and Its Metaphors.* New York: Farrar, Straus & Giroux, 1989. Print.

Süddeutsche Zeitung. München: Süddeutscher Verlag. Print.

Sweeting, Helen and Mary Gilhooly. "Dementia and the phenomenon of
social death." *Sociology of Health & Illness* 19.1 (1997): 93-117. Print.

Zimmermann, Christian and Peter Wißmann. *Auf dem Weg mit Alzheimer.
Wie sich mit einer Demenz leben lässt.* Frankfurt am Main: Mabuse-Verlag, 2011. Print.

Zimmermann, Harm-Peer. "Über die Macht der Altersbilder. Kultur – Diskurs – Dispositiv." *Gutes Leben im hohen Alter. Das Altern in seinen Entwicklungsmöglichkeiten und Entwicklungsgrenzen verstehen.* Ed. Andreas
Kruse, Thomas Rentsch and Harm-Peer Zimmermann. Heidelberg:
AKA Verlag, 2012. 75-85. Print.

Representation of Old Age in Media
Fear of Aging or Cult of Youth?

Julian Wangler

'Cultural plasticity' has become a key word in research of old age. Social realities of age and aging are not primarily based on biological facts, but on social constructions of what it means to be and grow old. By 'doing age' we are defining social practices which change the treatment of age and create a framework of standards and conventions, as well as a course of action for old people themselves. In the center of social formability of old age, we find images of the elderly, which are culturally dependent and volatile in time. On the one hand, images of old age represent and reflect collective views on age, on the other hand, they generate, cause, and enforce interpretations of old age. Especially representations of age wide-spread through modern mass media have become important sources for such interpretations. Since media representations generate and concentrate public discussions and points of views concerning the old generation, age becomes a social construct which influences also individual notions of age and identification processes (Ehmer 40).

In this essay, I intend to discuss the relevance, specifics and potential of images of old age in media representations. In this context, I will focus on research devoted to the general image and its development in terms of old age that determines how to analyze and interpret images of the elderly shown in media. This article will discuss how age discourse in German speaking countries has changed over the past three decades. In addition, I will present first results of an ongoing dissertation project that explores representation of age in mass media news.

OLD AGE IN MEDIA: RELEVANCE AND SPECIFICS

One very recent development of modern society is the fact that old people are no longer seen determined by a singular life situation or lifestyle. Although the life course is marked by a continuing process of defining one lifestyle, descriptions or characterizations of age in media do not do justice to this (Filipp and Mayer 39). The term 'age image' itself simplifies influential metaphors and leads to an immense reduction of complexity. Today, mass media representations of age create and transport images of the old on a daily basis and take on a prominent role in defining intergenerational connections (Scherer et al. 333). Whether in advertising, film, television, or in news coverage, these images of age in addition to physical symbolizations are constituted by language and arguments. An essential feature of the media's image of being old is that they do not show only the current understanding of social notions concerning age, but they represent more general perceptual and evaluative categories. These representations then largely determine what we consider to be old age reality and influence actions performed with regard to old people. Public images of age have a great power of suggestion, because these images regardless of visual or textual components always refer to visual perceptions. These kinds of interpretative patterns arise from the regularities of media production. By selecting and emphasizing certain aspects of age in specific news contexts, the audience is provided with social guiding principles on how to construct age. As a public "supplier of social imaginations" (Merten 158), media are able to produce consensually shared knowledge and as a consequence make the portraits of old age "chronically available" (Filipp and Mayer 212).

POTENTIAL INFLUENCES

According to age image research, media representations of old age influence two important concepts of identity that are constantly interacting with each other: the external image and the self-image of age. While the external image is a kind of outside view concerning the old in more general terms (Mayer et al. 68), the self-image refers to the experience of personal aging (Rothermund 223). Usually, young people look at age as uninvolved bystanders, but with the increase of life expectancy the external image develops into an internal view. It is safe to assume that mass media take on an extremely important role in this transitional process. If the external view of age is affected by negative media representations of the elderly, one might no longer acknowledge that one is growing old and there is no possibility of a gradual acceptance of the aging process, as age images as suggested by the social context cannot be transformed into self-images. With the experience of physical changes of an aging body, it becomes increasingly difficult to ignore the fact of one's own aging, so that different forms of anxiety or old age depression can be the consequences (Schirrmacher 10). Internalized negative views of old age and aging have a negative impact on self-efficacy and well-being and pose a risk for successful development in age. Not only negative but also positive media representations of old age can result in the denial of one's aging process and create problems of self-acceptance and age confidence.

A different form of influence by media images of old age refers to everyday communication between the young and old. As gerontological research concerning communication patterns in nursing homes has shown, caretakers tend to overcompensate in order to avoid stereotypical age-related interaction, thus producing and maintaining the presumed deficits. Categories of an aging model based on language interaction (Ryan and Kwong) are therefore also relevant for an analysis of media images of old age. When a young person has internalized specific presentation patterns of age, this influences present and future encounters with an old person. The young person perceives certain external characteristics of old age (old age cues), which causes a priming effect, and media representations lead to certain expectations concerning the elderly. As a result, the younger person modifies his/her behavior and communicates with an old person on a very low intellectual and social level, which can affect the self-esteem and psychological well-being of the senior. Since old people are also influenced by a moral code of old age, they react by also altering their behavior. In the worst case, they confirm the stereotypical alien image they are confronted with (Munnichs 308). Thus, the external view of old age becomes a self-fulfilling prophecy and develops into a self-image.

APPROPRIATENESS OF AGE IMAGES AND THE CONSTRUCTIVIST TURN

As suggested, interdisciplinary research on age images can reveal how images are perceived and how they work. Central to this question is a paradigm shift of age image research leading to the recognition that age images are not a reflection of social reality, but these images are actively constructed creating cultural significance for young and old. This change in discourse is based on two key issues: the question of the appropriateness of age images and the influence of constructivism. Early on, gerontologists had expressed skepticism concerning the portrayal of old people. Butler, for example, warned about negative consequences that 'false' age images may have in terms of life expectancy and cohesion of generations. Age image research made use of a specific epistemological perspective by following the implicit assumption that representations of old age reflect social and aging reality (Kessler 147). It has been emphasized that only by using the 'right' indicators of old age in media representations the audience can draw the 'right' conclusion about the reality of the lives of old people. Relying on extensive gerontological data, it was believed that the plausibility of media portrayals of the elderly could be objectively checked and evaluated. Thus, media coverage and the contribution of the population of old people were compared. This traditional approach to age image research, however, has been overcome. First of all, the epistemological understanding of age images as patterns of aging reality led to inadequate and distorted media portrayals. Secondly, these findings were reinforced by a normative skepticism towards age images (Kruse and Schmitt 16). Finally, age image research was restricted to a content level. Instead of taking into account how age images operate and influence the recipient, gerontologists tended to accept and analyze the content of age images as the effects of media.

Since the 1990s, social constructivism has fundamentally changed the position of gerontologists. Based on this understanding, images of age are no longer analyzed as empirically experienced living conditions and are seen as constructed and incomplete in nature (Saake 145-46). Constructivism has replaced the question of authenticity of age images by questioning their social aspects and how they affect expectations and evaluations (Erlemeier 45). In short, it is about the creation of social reality and not its reflection (Kessler 147). The influence of constructivism also led to the realization that age images merely identified by content analysis have no automatic effect on the recipient since the construction of reality depends on a large number of (pre)conditions and influencing factors.[1]

MEDIA DISCOURSE ON AGE IN TRANSITION: FROM GENERATIONAL WAR TO NEW COMPLEXITY

In German speaking countries, media discourse on age and aging has dramatically changed over the past three decades. In the 1980s, according to a study by Thimm (156-57), old people were not a significant target group for media professionals, because they were merely associated with loss of status, physical and mental decline, social incompetence and inactivity. Several content analysis studies support this assumption, although one needs to keep in mind that some of these studies suffer from the previously mentioned epistemological circular reasoning. Eichele analyzed a series of German local newspapers and reported that the descriptions of the social and health situation of the elderly were very negative. Furthermore, he noted that although problems of an aging society would be discussed, old people would rarely appear. A less systematic but comprehensive content analysis was performed by Dierl. After analyzing all major German daily and weekly newspapers from November 1, 1985 to October 31, 1987, he concluded that news coverage mainly reported on old age care and aging as continuous decline, and no active and self-determined old person was shown. Studies on TV entertainment reported an obvious marginalization of the old. These studies have provided substantial evidence that old people are underrepresented in terms of their statistical share of the population (Flueren et al.; Gerbner et al.; Jürgens; Robinson and Skill). In addition, there is evidence that old people that look younger are portrayed more favorably. In addition, there is a gender bias, since women are less represented than men (Coltrane and Messineo).

In the late 1980s and early 1990s, the media discourse on age gradually shifted to a new phase from a portrayal of the needy and fragile senior to the parasitic old, who then became the focus of media interest (Thimm

---

1 | Psychological research has discovered that old age images do correspond with social comparison processes, so it is possible that under certain circumstances even negative portrayals are conductive to life satisfaction and self-esteem of older people (Kessler 152).

157). The discourse on age was now centered on an intense public debate about social transfer, pensions, and limits of the welfare state. This focus promoted age representations of greedy seniors who live at the expense of younger generations. Against the backdrop of an unprecedented demographic change, the media provoked an intergenerational conflict which related primarily to the struggle between old and young for welfare state resources. This new portrayal of the old started with a demand to end intergenerational solidarity and a call for a war against old people by the magazine *Wiener* (3/1989). The magazine accused the elderly of having lived their lives in disregard of the consequences for the next generations, who were now overburdened by the exorbitant claims for privileges from prosperous pensioners. The weekly newspaper *Die Woche* (Leggewie 1) joined the new hostile tone concerning age with the headline, "The senior avalanche buries the future – will the lost generation fight back?" This position was then taken up by the well-known news magazines *Focus* and *Spiegel*, who used the imagery of intergenerational war and looting the young (Feldenkirchen and Wisdorff). The image of the unproductive and parasitic old became more and more dominant in the media discourse on age. This campaign was accompanied by panic mongering concerning the demographic changes. Thus, the daily newspaper *die tageszeitung* (April 30, 1993) used the headline, "Help, we will all become senile!"

Starting with the beginning of the 21st century, a greater differentiation of age images in the media can be seen. Today, these representations do not only stigmatize the elderly, but exaggerate characteristics of old age in a positive way (Zhang et al.). Ochel analyzed news coverage on TV as well as in print media and recognized the fact that old people are shown in a more positive way than young people. A systematic analysis by Kessler et al. showed that the representation of old age in various TV programs differs positively from gerontological factors of aging reality, such as health and socio-economic status.

The image of a vital, eternally youthful senior in media has particularly been promoted by the promises of advertising. By staging old people as 'best agers' and encouraging them to adapt to the lifestyle, dress, and sexual activity of the younger generation, the consumer industry has repositioned itself towards old people and positively transfigured old age in public space (Hoffmann-Kramer). Several studies have already detected a substantial change in the presentation of old age in German print advertising. Röhr-Sendlmeier and Ueing conclude that advertising more and more tries to avoid drawing the attention to age deficits. Meta-term comparisons show that negative age stereotypes are declining, while at the same time seniors have become more attractive, active, and social. The essence of these findings is confirmed by Femers (211), who analyzed the use of language in advertisements; today many business fields prefer positive images of old people.

Although there are still stereotypes and behavioral differences in media representations of the elderly, a tendency in advertising is noticeable that is currently revising the image of old age. While these new forms of staging old people offer a chance to replace cultural imaginations of a frail and socially isolated old generation, it should not be ignored that the representation of a consistent young age can also pressure the elderly to comply with this new image. In this context, some age image researchers complain that media follow a cult of youth that has even been reinforced. On the basis of new social norms that require activity, vitality, and independence (Jäckel 131), old people are expected to mask their own age. As a consequence, successful aging, namely the realization of special limitations and opportunities in old age, might fail. Therefore, some authors conclude that nowadays no one can be old, but only young in different gradations and detect a strategy in our modern society to extinguish old age (BMFSFJ 48).

RECENT FINDINGS: AGE IMAGES IN THE NEWS GENRE

While there are several detailed studies analyzing the construction of the old in advertisements, the news genre is still an almost unnoticed research field (Thimm 156). This is surprising considering the fact that news are usually structured around everyday lives of many recipients and provide orientation in a world becoming more and more complex. Unlike advertising or entertainment, which offer guiding principles of desire and will (Zurstiege 299), the news sector claims to report objectively on social issues. Thus, the recipients' expectations towards journalistic coverage regarding age differ from other media genres, as it is based on an assumption of credibility emphasizing the importance of news-related media.

In order to bridge this research gap, I have conducted a study focused on textual representations of the old in the German news magazines *Stern*, *Spiegel,* and *Focus* from 1999 to 2010. This study is based on the framing approach used in communication research. Although the text corpus is analyzed in the context of a qualitative research design, the access criteria nonetheless ensure the identification of basic patterns of old age[2].

PATTERN ONE: OLD AGE AS HUMAN DECLINE

The first frame prototype creates old age as human decline, where demographic changes are viewed with horror and seniors are seen suffering from physical and mental deterioration. The articles using this pattern concentrate on two major aspects to present the old:

- *Old Age as Helplessness and Heteronomy:* Old people are presented due to physical limitations as incapable of acting. As a consequence their fate is determined by others. Since they cannot maintain their own independence they are unable to defend themselves against injustice and cannot escape humiliating situations. Many articles that use this pattern show old people as victims of old age care and social scandals, as well as of exploitation by racketeers and criminals. Old people are also shown as victims of natural disasters. By presenting old age as helplessness and heteronomy, moral arguments are made highlighting social coldness and cruelty in our society. Furthermore, this frame is often employed to illustrate the young generation's burden trying to cope with the physical decline of their parents and grandparents.
- *Old Age as Solitude:* The second staging aspect shows the loneliness of old people. It creates an age reality where the elderly have been left behind by their families and friends and have been socially excluded. In addition to physical and mental decline, this solitude is portrayed as punishment, since the lack of visibility leads simultaneously to a loss of social status.

---

2 | Formal access criteria: a) German opinion-leading news magazines, b) survey period 1999 to 2010 c) articles with at least 500 words. Additional access criterion: age as the article's main theme. Using these access criteria, 203 relevant articles were found.

PATTERN TWO: OLD AGE AS SUPERIORITY

In contrast to the first pattern, the second does not show passive and frail elderly people. Nonetheless it connotes old age very negatively. This scheme models old age as a social power factor that plays a more and more dominant political and economic role. Old age becomes a driving force which restructures the general composition of society. Taking a closer look, we can find two frame aspects:

- *Old Age as Political Predominance:* The first aspect includes old age as a political power. Seniors seem to be a well-organized group in the public sphere and ready to fight for their own interests. Old people can be understood as a dominant clientele gathering more and more political importance and influence. With demands for more welfare and pensions, they are threatening younger people whose financial capacities have already been exceeded.
- *Old Age as Aging Horror:* A second variation is the representation of old age as a personification of the demographic development. In this case, old people do not act, but instead age is symbolized as an inescapable, anonymous senescence invading society as a whole, robbing vitality and future potential. Examples would be articles which focus on the necessity of using robots in age care facilities, mourning the disappearance of children's playgrounds for the benefit of senior playgrounds, or outlining the risk of Germany's economic decline as a result of its demographic paralysis.

PATTERN THREE: OLD AGE AS A NEW BEGINNING

Unlike the first two old age patterns, the third scheme contains a positive image. Old Age is a happy, fulfilling, and promising phase of life providing specific opportunities and advantages. Old age appears as a new departure to late freedom and a secure life phase in which time and wealth can be used to make up for chances missed in life. There are three aspects of this frame, where media representations glorify the old:

- *Old Age as a Consumer Market:* Old people seem to be an independent, self-directed group preferring a high standard of living. From the viewpoint of the advertising, electronics, and health industry these seniors are highly competitive. Moreover, these articles are about highly skilled old workers being courted on the job market. The impression is made that a high standard of living is an essential prerequisite for a dignified life, and prosperity is described as a requirement for happiness.

- *Old Age as Mental Vitality and Zest for Life:* In the context of economically demanding old people, life-affirming people with great mental vitality and adaptability are shown. Especially 'young' agers are characterized by having a sophisticated sense of fashion, determined by wanderlust, and being culturally engaged and mentally active. Old people are portrayed imitating the behavior of their children and grandchildren by using the internet and playing computer games. Ideals of lifelong learning and the popular saying, 'you are as old as you feel' are undoubtedly reflected by this frame.

- *Old Age as Partnership Idyll:* Some articles focus on the aspect of growing old together. Based on the idea that the elderly tend to withdraw, old age is marked as a safe retreat where family and partnership values are held high. In times where lasting domestic happiness can no longer be taken for granted, journalistic news coverage seems to associate the myth of lifelong love with old people. However, such relationships are portrayed as sexless.

DISCUSSION

Looking at the results of the content analysis, it is striking that in media representations concerning old age there is a strong polarization, which Göckenjan considers to be the essential historic feature of the public discourse on age and aging. Today we find presentation patterns that have developed in the wake of current demographic changes in the Federal Republic of Germany. Besides the negative images of old people still to be found in news coverage, two further frames have been identified that suggest a new and different approach to age.

One pattern stages old age as second youth, where traditional ideas of old age are completely irrelevant. Euphoria for this new young old age is accompanied by distain for traditional values of becoming and being old. The other frame constitutes old age as a threat for intergenerational relations because of a dramatic increase of numbers of old people with growing claims for wealth and a high standard of living. Following Thimm's argument, this frame can be considered new in context with a change of discourse on age at the beginning of the new millennium. The discourse no longer concentrates on pension policy or conflicts connected with welfare state resources. In the face of accelerating demographic change, old age is now seen as an imminent power which occupies the last free space (Thimm 163).

Over the past decades, representations of age in German speaking media has changed and become more diverse. The results of the content analysis, however, have shown several basic and stable presentation patterns which can be found in similar forms in advertising, entertainment, and news coverage. Therefore, it will be important to further explore these constitutive patterns within the different media genres in order to make content analysis studies more comprehensive for a wider public. In addition, age image research should not restrict itself to an analysis of the portrayal of old people, but needs to expand its scope of research to the perception of these images and its effects in terms of attitudes and personal development both on a young and old audience.

REFERENCES

BMFSFJ [Bundesministerium für Familie, Senioren, Frauen und Jugend], ed. *Sechster Bericht zur Lage der älteren Generation in der Bundesrepublik Deutschland. Altersbilder in der Gesellschaft.* Berlin: BT-Drs., 2010. Print.

Butler, Robert. "Age-ism: Another Form of Bigotry." *The Gerontologist* 4 (1969): 243-46. Print.

Coltrane, Scott and Melinda Messineo. "The Perpetuation of Subtle Prejudice: Race and Gender Imagery in 1990s Television Advertising". *Sex Roles* 42 (2000): 363-89. Print.

Dierl, Reinhard. *Zwischen Altenpflegeheim und Seniorenstudium. Alter und Alte als Zeitungsthema.* Köln: Kuratorium Deutsche Altershilfe, 1989. Print.

Ehmer, Josef. *Sozialgeschichte des Alters.* Frankfurt a.M.: Suhrkamp, 1990. Print.

Eichele, Gert. "Das Bild des älteren Menschen in der lokalen Öffentlichkeit." *Freizeitverhalten älterer Menschen.* Ed. Dieter Blaschke and Joachim Franke. Stuttgart: Enke, 1982. 63-69. Print.

Erlemeier, Norbert. "Altersbilder in den Medien." *Zeit-Schnitte. Beiträge zum Verständnis kommunikativer Wirklichkeit*. Ed. Karl-Heinz Grohall and Hans Michatsch. Münster: Waxmann, 1998. 45-60. Print.

Feldenkirchen, Markus and Flora Wisdorff. "Alte konsumieren auf unsere Kosten." *Der Tagesspiegel* 5. Aug. 2003: 1. Print.

Femers, Susanne. *Die ergrauende Werbung. Altersbilder und werbesprachliche Inszenierungen*. Wiesbaden: Verlag für Sozialwissenschaften, 2007. Print.

Filipp, Sigrun-Heide, and Anne-Kathrin Mayer. *Bilder des Alters. Altersstereotype und die Beziehungen zwischen den Generationen*. Stuttgart: Kohlhammer, 1999. Print.

Flueren, Hanns, Marion Klein, and Heidrun Redetzki-Rodermann. "Das Altersbild der deutschen Daily Soaps. Ergebnisse einer quantitativ-qualitativen Untersuchung." *medien praktisch* 1 (2002): 23-27. Print.

Gerbner, George, Larry Gross, Nancy Signorielli, and Michael Morgan. "Aging with Television. Images on Television Drama and Conception of Social Reality." *Journal of Communication* 30 (1980): 37-49. Print.

Göckenjan, Gerd. *Das Alter würdigen. Altersbilder und Bedeutungswandel des Alters*. Frankfurt a.M.: Suhrkamp, 2000. Print.

Hoffmann-Kramer, Ursula. *Die verjüngten Alten. Lebensstile, Bedürfnisse, Konsumverhalten*. Saarbrücken: Dr. Müller, 2007. Print.

Jäckel, Michael. "Ältere Menschen in der Werbung." *Medien und höheres Lebensalter. Theorie – Forschung – Praxis*. Ed. Bernd Schorb, Anja Hartung, and Wolfgang Reißmann. Wiesbaden: Verlag für Sozialwissenschaften, 2009. 130-45. Print.

Jürgens, Hans. *Untersuchung zum Bild der älteren Menschen in den elektronischen Medien. Themen – Thesen – Theorien*. Kiel: ULR, 1994. Schriftenreihe der Unabhängigen Landesanstalt für das Rundfunkwesen 4. Print.

Kessler, Eva-Marie. "Altersbilder in den Medien: Wirklichkeit oder Illusion?" *Medien und höheres Lebensalter. Theorie – Forschung – Praxis*. Ed. Bernd Schorb, Anja Hartung, and Wolfgang Reißmann. Wiesbaden: Verlag für Sozialwissenschaften, 2009. 146-50. Print.

Kessler, Eva-Marie, Katrin Rakoczy, and Ursula Staudinger. "The Portrayal of Old People in Prime Time Television Series: The Match with Gerontological Evidence." *Ageing and Society* 4 (2004): 531-52. Print.

Kruse, Andreas, and Eric Schmitt. "Zur Veränderung des Altersbildes in Deutschland." *Aus Politik und Zeitgeschichte* 49-50 (2005): 9-17. Print.

Leggewie, Claus. "Kampf der Generationen, Krieg den Alten." *Die Woche* 43/1995, 1. Print.

Mayer, Anne-Kathrin, Christina Lukas, and Klaus Rothermund. "Vermittelte und individuelle Vorstellungen vom Alter – Altersstereotype." *SPIEL* 1 (2005): 67-99. Print.

Merten, Klaus. "Evolution der Kommunikation." *Die Wirklichkeit der Medien. Eine Einführung in die Kommunikationswissenschaft.* Ed. Klaus Merten, Siegfried J. Schmidt, and Siegfried Weischenberg. Opladen: Verlag für Sozialwissenschaften, 1994. 141-62. Print.

Munnichs, Joep M. A. "Intervention: Eine notwendige Strategie für die Bewältigung des Alterns." *Erfolgreiches Altern: Bedingungen und Variationen.* Ed. Margret M. Baltes. Stuttgart: Enke, 1989. 308-13. Print.

Ochel, Jens. "Senioren spielen in den Medien keine Rolle." *Medien-Tenor-Forschungsbericht* 129 (2003): 26-27. Print.

Robinson, James D., and Tom Skill. "Media Usage Patterns and Portrayals of the Elderly." *Handbook of Communication and Aging Research.* Ed. Jon F. Nussbaum and Justine Coupland. Mahwah: Lawrence Erlbaum Associates, 1995. 359-91. Print.

Röhr-Sendlmeier, Una M., and Sarah Ueing. "Das Altersbild in der Anzeigenwerbung im zeitlichen Wandel." *Zeitschrift für Gerontologie und Geriatrie* 1 (2004): 57-62. Print.

Rothermund, Klaus. "Effects of Age Stereotypes on Self-Views and Adaptation." *The Adaptive Self: Personal Continuity and Intentional Self-Development.* Ed. Werner Greve, Klaus Rothermund, and Dirk Wentura. Göttingen: Hogrefe, 2005. 223-42. Print.

Ryan, Ellen B., and Sheree T Kwong See. "Sprache, Kommunikation und Altern." *Sprache und Kommunikation im Alter.* Ed. Caja Thimm and Reinhard Fiehler. Radolfzell: Verlag für Gesprächsforschung, 2003. 57-71. Print.

Saake, Ingrid. *Die Konstruktion des Alters. Eine gesellschaftstheoretische Einführung in die Alternsforschung.* Wiesbaden: Verlag für Sozialwissenschaften, 2006. Hagener Studientexte zur Soziologie. Print.

Scherer, Helmut, Beate Schneider, and Nicole Gonser. "Am Tage schaue ich nicht fern! Determinanten der Mediennutzung älterer Menschen." *Publizistik* 3 (2006): 333-48. Print.

Schirrmacher, Frank. *Das Methusalem-Komplott.* München: Karl Blessing, 2004. Print.

Thimm, Caja. "Altersbilder in den Medien – Zwischen medialem Zerrbild und Zukunftsprojektionen." *Bilder des Alterns im Wandel. Historische, interkulturelle, theoretische und aktuelle Perspektiven.* Ed. Josef Ehmer and Otfried Höffe. Stuttgart: Wissenschaftliche Verlagsgesellschaft Stuttgart, 2009, 153-65. Akademiengruppe Altern in Deutschland 1. Print.

Wiener. "Krieg den Alten." *Wiener* 3/1989, 6. Print.

Zhang, Yan Bing, Jake Harwood, Angie Williams, Virpi Ylänne-McEwen, and Caja Thimm. "Old Adults in Advertising. Multi-national Perspectives." *Journal of Language and Social Psychology* 25 (2006): 264-82. Print.

Zurstiege, Guido. *Zwischen Kritik und Faszination. Was wir beobachten, wenn wir die Werbung beobachten, wie sie die Gesellschaft beobachtet.* Köln: Herbert von Halem, 2005. Print.

Age Images in Advertising

An Art-Historical Analysis of Advertisement Images in the Austrian Province of Styria

Eva Klein

As early as 1508, the Italian painter Giorgione visualized age in "Three Philosophers" as different phases of life by presenting three men in three distinctive stages. Around 1900, Edvard Munch also addressed the issue of aging in a three-part phase model on the basis of three females in his "Dance of Life." Representing age in this form has been the dominant motive in advertising practiced in Styria. An analysis of the visual components of the advertising media can offer valuable insights concerning the question of age both in terms of aesthetic representation as well as visual communication. Age in this context is to be understood as a term referring to all phases of life.

New technical achievements, such as lithography as a new printing technology, were a reason for the increased use of images in advertisements (Kugler 860; Wagner 1). These new techniques made the production of posters at reduced costs and in larger numbers possible and made printing pictures cost-effective. As the poster quickly developed into a popular advertising medium, it was now produced in greater quantities than before industrialization. The consequence was not only a high appearance of posters in Graz, the capital of Styria, but more importantly led to a competition with rival advertisers. Advertising agencies had to develop up-to-date solutions in order to avoid their posters being one among many unrecognizable in the mass of other advertisements. In order to meet this challenge, advertising businesses contracted artists to design illustrated posters in a contemporary style relying on the fact that art had established a sophisticated understanding of images throughout the centuries. The term contemporary style refers to all stylistic novelties that were developed as a reaction to the historicized language of shape and used in contemporary magazines of the time, such as *Ver Sacrum* and *Grazer Kunst*. Around 1900, concepts of the secession style, art nouveau, Vienna style, and Vienna new style were very individually applied within the German-speaking language area. Therefore, a conceptual differentiation is not possible (Klein 36-39). The strong connection between advertisement and art, however, is especially noticeable in the early 20th century, where advertisements appropriated the style of the visual arts (Denscher 21-75; Klein 67-123).

Fig. 1 & Fig. 2: Poster Grazer Herbstmesse, 1912

In the early 20th century, age-specific distinctions were prominent in advertising illustrations in Styria. In the two posters of the fall trade fair in 1911 and 1912, the advertising protagonists are, on the one hand, two men of advanced age who point to the fall trade fair using trumpets on the Schlossberg, a castle hill in the center of the city of Graz (Fig.1), and on the other hand, two children (Fig. 2), a boy and a girl, who are only separated by a fence from the temptations of the amusement park that was part of the fair.

These illustrations already point to an imbalance between the representation of women and men in the early 20th century. In aesthetic terms according to art historical style categories, the poster is committed to the Styrian tradition of historical design. These two posters advertising the traditional trade fair *Grazer Messe* are stylistic models for the advertisement of the early 20th century. Design options in advertising prior to World War I were limited and therefore committed to traditional styles used in Styria, which made it extremely difficult for young and cosmopolitan artists to establish new and modern trends in Styria. As an exception, a poster produced in 1901 from the Styrian art association *Steiermärkischer Kunstverein Graz* (Fig. 3) provides an example of a turn towards modernity.

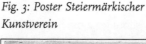

Fig. 3: Poster Steiermärkischer Kunstverein

It refers to the artistic avant-garde around 1900 by presenting a reduced, distinct and strong language of color and design. The poster is experienced as an intentionally designed unit of text and illustration, which once again emphasizes its modernity. The black color application presented in precise streaks is very close to xylography; nonetheless this graphic art is lithography. An iconological analysis provides information about the struggle of the visual arts between tradition and innovation in Styria. Concerning content, Wilhelm Gurlitt, the artist of the Styrian *Kunstverein*, uses a mythological topic common around the turn of the 20th century. It is Athena, the goddess of war and wisdom, apparent by the representation of a helmet and spear as well as the distinctive and striking facial features (Zuffi 57; Roscher 687). Wilhelm Gurlitt was professor of classical archaeology at the University of Graz. In the course of his research at the Theseion in Athens, he was intensely concerned with the interpretation of mythological representations. From 1900 onwards, he assumed the leadership of the Styrian *Kunstverein* in his role as president, which resulted in an essential reorientation, and with great dedication he attempted to establish new art movements in Graz. Wilhelm Gurlitt, next to Otto Benndorf and Josef Strzygowski, was also considerably involved in the introduction of a new art history at the University Graz (Klein 75-76). In the here shown illustration, Athena, patron saint of science, art, and war, puts her hand gently on the young man's shoulder crouching down on the ground and leaning against a step. With this visual motif there are two possible interpretations: Firstly, the one of Theseus who is symbolically fighting a battle for the modern mind, and secondly, the one of Heracles who is standing at crossroads. Both interpretations, however, rely on the image of youth to represent new art and a demand to use contemporary art in terms of style and content in advertising. In accordance with current illustrations of mythological characters, the two protagonists are presented as athletic and vital human beings at a young age. Following the role model of the *Galeries Lafayette* in Paris, the department store *Kastner & Öhler* presented itself around 1900 as particularly modern by being open to the public regardless of social class or age. By using Ferdinand Wüst's commercial art for the company's advertisements, the store strongly encouraged a development towards modernity. Influenced by exhibitions of contemporary artists in Graz in 1900, Ferdinand Wüst incorporated modern, decorative artistic forms in his work and consistently included these in his concepts from then on. One of the examples is the millinery spring and summer catalog 1901 (Fig. 4).

Fig. 4 & Fig. 5: Catalog Kastner & Öhler

Similar to the example from the Styrian *Kunstverein* published the same year, the choice of theme is mythological in accordance with the orientation towards mythology around 1900 due to influences of the Vienna and Munich Secession. The floral, tiara-like headdress and the peacock are classic attributes of the most important Olympic goddess Hera, who is considered the protector of women (Zuffi 126). Conforming to mythological representations, the woman floating in the center of the image is pictured as young and attractive. On her left shoulder, a putto is standing on its left foot, turning to the right, holding a millinery catalogue. In the picture, the woman holds her dress with her lavishly decorated right hand and it falls in wide arcs downwards alongside her body without touching the ground. On her left side, a peacock is sitting on floral elements. The peacock is strongly reminiscent of the peacock display of James McNeill Whistler in his installation *Harmony in Blue and Gold: The Peacock Room*. Interesting here to note is that Ferdinand Wüst studied in Vienna under Ferdinand Laufberger, and was therefore exposed to influences of the Vienna *Kunstgewerbeschule*, which today is the University for the Applied Arts. Viennese artists, especially the artists of the Vienna Secession and Vienna Workshop, were themselves strongly influenced by the art movements originating in England (Klein 155). The pictured putto conforms to the motif of a child, mostly appearing naked or lightly dressed as often used in art history. The fact that the young woman depicted on the cover of the millinery catalog is wearing a reform dress without a corset is striking. This image seems to suggest that wearing a corset was passé in Graz, however, when investigating the catalogue, the dress presented on the cover was not for sale. Instead, dresses with the characteristically traditional 'sans vetre' silhouette and fitting corsets were offered. Hence, the cover design was not an indication of the merchandise offered, but represented the image of a modern department store in tune with current fashion trends from France. However, demand dictates supply and therefore in terms of fashion design the profit-oriented company was dependent on the purchasing power of the conservative and strongly traditional customers of Graz.

While the style of advertisement developed considerably in the course of the 20th century, the visual concepts of age remained the same. Females in advertisement always were depicted as young and adhering to the ideals of the beauty concepts of the time (Femers).

Fig. 6: Poster Osterverkauf Kastner & Öhler

The millinery catalogue of the company *Kastner & Öhler* by Heinz Reichenfelser of 1928 (Fig. 5) shows the aesthetic development from art noveau to new sobriety by presenting a female image according to the style of the

1920s as a tall, slender woman with long limbs, whose height was additionally emphasized by the choice of the image section.

The same perception of women was used by Ernst Wendling in his poster promoting the Easter sale (Fig. 6). In another poster by Ernst Wendling advertising wax cloth (Fig. 7), the influence of geometrical purism, which can be attributed to the same form of language of the De Stijl movement, is already foreshadowed. The figure is dissected into its basic elements and therefore presented in an areal reduction. Even though age is not really indicated due to the level of abstraction, it is still another presentation of a youthful ideal of beauty.

Fig. 7: Poster Waschstoffe Kastner & Öhler

Fig. 8: Poster Alles für die Schule bei Kastner & Öhler

Fashion is consistently promoted by images of young, slender females, supporting the illusion that the buyer of the merchandise could slip into the skin of the propagated medial presenter. Children were also highly popular motifs for advertisement in Styria, as the already mentioned example of the trade fair in Graz indicates (Fig. 2). Ernst Wendling promoting school products (Fig. 8) presented a school-age girl befitting the advertising message. Fritz Kainz uses the image of a boy and a girl hand in hand walking down a path on an advertisement poster for the company Humanic (Fig. 9).

Fig. 9: Poster Kinder gehen weit! Humanic

In contrast to the presentation of women as conforming to a female ideal and keeping up appearances, the company Leitner (Fig. 10) presents in a poster by Fritz Krainz a male figure, who is obviously attributed more freedom of action and tolerance, as he is shown celebrating with many bottles of champagne.

The male protagonist obviously pursues the printed motto, "Drink without sorrows." The protagonist is presented as an old and big man, whose age is indicated by a white moustache and allegorically saved from his sinking ship by the wine wholesale company Leitner, and now allowed to indulge in cravings for alcohol "without sorrows." The design vocabulary of the Styrian advertisements of the interwar period and the early post-war era is strongly reduced and stylized at the same time. As a result of the simplification of forms, space is the dominant element, with the result of a direct boldness in the foreground of the composition.

Fig. 10: Poster Sauf ohne Sorgen, Leitner Weingroßhandel

The advertisements are clear and objective and in the draft there is usually an almost childlike banality in the conception. While women are shown in accordance to the beauty ideals of the time, men are represented as much more individual and are depicted with clear-cut facial features and more realistic body physiques. The discrepancy which appears in Styrian advertisement regarding gender-relevant aspects cannot be missed. Additionally, it should be noted that men are met with a more tolerant attitude regarding their age, as they are also depicted at a more advanced age, whereas women are subject to a strong fixation on youth.

Advertising in Styria with its strong emphasis of presenting young women was consistent with international trends of presenting age groups biased towards the young. Illustrations shaped by youthfulness thus superimpose social reality (Kühne 253). In the visual arts in Austria, artist Maria Lassnig sets a different example by visualizing bodies of advanced age, and therefore counter-acting the taboo of presenting advanced age (Drechsler). Only recently increasing efforts have been made to break new ground in advertisement by addressing the predominant discrepancies, as well as critically reflecting upon them (Meyer 81-131).

The advertisement campaign *Caritas & Ich* (Fig. 11 and Fig. 12) for the Austrian *Caritas* by the advertisement agency *CCP Heye* is a current example for a poster campaign which purposely constitutes the elderly as an advertisement subject, and tries to emphasize the advantages of aging.

Fig. 11 & Fig. 12: Poster Caritas & Ich

The people pictured are presented as fun-loving, energetic people who impress with their life experience. The Austrian wide campaign diverged immensely from the norm of the imagery of public space due to the age of the people presented. It advocates for care-giving and care-taking by the organization *Caritas*, which is presented as a desirable cooperation partner for both care-givers and those in the need of care.

To summarize, it can be said that images used in advertisements in Styria have consistently shown age-specific distinctions. These distinctions also demonstrate a high discrepancy along the lines of gender. In 1900 and today, women conform to a constructed ideal stereotype. Therefore, the young, attractive, and seductive female does not only represent an ideal type according to marketing guidelines, but has also since the beginning of illustrated advertisement been used as a leitmotif. Currently, the attempt of critically facing youth fixation and its medial staging is being made in order to counteract this development by consciously developing targeted advertisement campaigns. At this point it must be noted that these efforts are only exceptions aiming at a conscious counter-setting to the norm. The norm, however, still corresponds to those advertising illustrations which have dominated the public space in Styria for more than a century.

LIST OF FIGURES

Fig. 1: Poster *Grazer Herbstmesse*, artist unknown, 1911, © Kunstgewerbe-sammlung, Universalmuseum Joanneum

Fig. 2: Poster *Grazer Herbstmesse*, artist unknown, 1912, © Kunstgewer-besammlung, Universalmuseum Joanneum

Fig. 3: Poster *Steiermärkischer Kunstverein*, artist unknown, 1901, © Plakat-sammlung, Landesarchiv Steiermark

Fig. 4: Catalog *Kastner & Öhler*, Ferdinand Wüst, 1901, © Kastner & Öhler

Fig. 5: Catalog *Kastner & Öhler*, Heinz Reichenfelser, 1928, © Kastner & Öhler

Fig. 6: Poster *Osterverkauf Kastner & Öhler*, Ernst Wendling, ca. 1930s, © Kastner & Öhler

Fig. 7: Poster *Waschstoffe Kastner & Öhler*, Ernst Wendling, ca. *f*1930s, © Kastner & Öhler

Fig. 8: Poster *Alles für die Schule bei Kastner & Öhler*, Ernst Wendling, ca.1930s, © Kastner & Öhler

Fig. 9: Poster *Kinder gehen weit! Humanic*, Fritz Krainz, ca. 1930s, © Stadt-museum Graz

Fig. 10: Poster *Sauf ohne Sorgen, Leitner Weingroßhandel*, Fritz Krainz, ca. 1930s, © Stadtmuseum Graz

Fig. 11: Poster *Caritas & Ich*, CCP Heye, Foto Darius Ramazani, 2010 © Caritas Österreich

Fig. 12: Poster *Caritas & Ich*, CCP Heye, Foto Darius Ramazani, 2010 © Caritas Österreich

REFERENCES

Denscher, Bernhard. *Österreichische Plakatkunst 1898-1938.* Wien: Brand-stätter, 1992. Print.

Drechsler, Wolfgang, ed. *Lassnig. Das neunte Jahrzehnt.* Wien: Walter König Verlag, 2009. Print.

Femers, Susanne. *Die ergrauende Werbung. Altersbilder und werbesprachliche Inszenierungen von Alter und Altern.* Wiesbaden: VS Verlag für Sozial-wissenschaften, 2007. Print.

Klein, Eva. "Das Plakat in der Moderne. Der Beginn des Grafikdesigns in der Steiermark im Kontext internationaler soziokultureller Entwicklungen." Diss. University of Graz, 2011. Print.

Kugler, Franz. *Handbuch der Kunstgeschichte.* Stuttgart: Ebner & Seubert, 1842. Print.

Kühne, Bärbel. "Wrinkled ... Wonderful? Eine semiotische Erkundung neuer Altersbilder in der Werbung." *Alter und Geschlecht. Repräsentationen, Geschichten und Theorien des Alter(n)s.* Ed. Heike Hartung. Bielefeld: transcript, 2005. 253-276. Print.

Meyer, Sönke. *Alter(n) in der Werbung. Von der Entdeckung und Inszenierung einer vergessenen Zielgruppe.* Saarbrücken: Verlag Dr. Müller, 2010. Print.

Roscher, Wilhelm H., ed. *Ausführliches Lexikon der griechischen und römischen Mythologie.* Vol. 1. Leipzig: B. G. Teubner, 1884. Print.

Wagner, Carl. *Alois Senefelder. Sein Leben und Werk.* Leipzig: Giesecke & Devrient, 1914. Print.

Zuffi, Stefano, ed. *Götter und Helden der Antike.* Berlin: Parthas, 2003. Print. Vol. 1 of *Bildlexikon der Kunst.*

Of Mimicry and Age

Fashion Ambivalences of the Young-Old

Thomas Küpper

INTRODUCTION

It is often said that fashion has a life cycle of its own. Margaret Morganroth Gullette has attested that common beliefs about age(ing) can be analyzed in terms of fashion discourse. Gullette considers the so-called life cycle of fashion objects as "a practice through which American culture constructs our age identity and our sense of the meaning of 'ageing'" (35-36). She suggests "that going through any market cycle affects our experience of the life cycle" (36), and points out that in the fashion world the use of the metaphor 'life cycle' privileges the beginning, quasi the youth part of the object's life, and implies an ideology of decline. "The known life of an object moves from purchase, through consumption (public display of possession), to the 'decline' (going out of fashion) necessary to start up the cycle again" (35). At the same time, however, fashion discourse is reciprocally influenced by changes in perception of age(ing), and this has implications for the fashion industry. As an example, I will be discussing fashion as an essential topic for the young-old, who claim to be up-to-date and to some degree youthful. At first glance, the young-old might be seen as merely affirming the norm of youthfulness by appropriating so-called youthful fashion. However, I will show that affirmation of the norm is not as clear-cut as might be assumed. Adaption of youthful fashion rather proves to be ambivalent as it supports and at the same time undermines the norm. This ambivalence comes into sharp relief when consulting Homi Bhabha's term of mimicry and transferring it onto the fashion context.

FASHION AND YOUTH

Generally, fashion is closely connected to youth, as Roland Barthes has argued:

[I]t is age which is important, not sex ; [...] the model's youth is constantly asserted, defended, we might say, because it is naturally threatened by time [...], and it must constantly be recalled that youth is the standard for all measurements of age (*still young, forever young*): its fragility creates its prestige [...] (258).

When applying Margaret Morganroth Gullette's approach to my topic of research, it is important to keep in mind that in the fashion context youth is equated with the starting point of a product's life-cycle. Moreover, youth is usually associated with innovation in modern society. Society that is focused on an open future, on change and novelty values youth as a representative of what is to come (Oesterle 9). Fashion in particular idealizes the young, because it is a field where rapid change expresses modernity in a tangible way. Furthermore, since around the 1920s youth has often been equated with attractiveness and therefore fashion is usually (re)presented by young models (Vincent 359). In view of this close connection between fashion and youth, it is not surprising that fashion is very relevant for the young-old. Dressing fashionably expresses the young-old's participation in current affairs and being up-to-date. Julia Twigg has pointed out:

In general, being correctly dressed is an element of engaging successfully with the social world. [...] But in relation to older people, these strictures operate in a harsher way, pointing to new and threatening meanings. Lapses of dress [...] do not just offend against the performance norms of the social space, but signal a social and moral decline that may threaten a person's capacity to remain part of mainstream society. (295)

On top of that, keeping up with fashions means keeping up with the times and participating intensely in society. Furthermore, fashionable clothes are a means of presenting one's body, and in doing so the young-old express their desire to not only be viewed as spiritual or transcending the sensual body in accordance with common stereotypes of wisdom and passivity in old age, but to present themselves as sensual beings with sexual desires participating in activities seemingly reserved for the young. This participa-tion of the young-old has been the subject of controversy. In Europe and in the US for example, the young-old are usually defined as being active, thus contesting stereotypes of old age. A popular website advertising 'clear answers for common questions' provides the following definition of the young-old (to quote a customary description):

The term "young-old" is sometimes used to describe older adults who are retired, but still active. The activity level of the young-old often defies stereotypes about normal behavior for older people, as many people are under the impression that retired people become inactive and detached from society, when in fact the op-posite can be just as true. (Smith)

Social and active participation of the young-old is accredited to medical progress:

Thanks to advances in medical care, many retired people enjoy active lives long after retirement, and their activity level actually keeps them healthier. [...] [The young-old] are robust, healthy, engaged individuals who may choose to be active in their communities in addition to engaging in athletic activity which can include cycling, skiing, running, horseriding, rock climbing, rafting, and a variety of other activities. (Smith)

As the young-old attach importance to not being detached from society, fashion plays a major role in presenting the body in accordance with com-mon beauty norms, and in displaying activity and participation. However, Barbara Pichler, for example, has pointed to the downside of celebrating the active age. Doesn't highly valuing an active life style, including, not least, fashion consciousness, simultaneously mean undervaluing a life marked by inactivity and detachment? (74-75) If fitness, sprightliness, sen-suality, and sexuality are signified as positive values by keywords such as 'young-old,' are those who don't fulfill the norm encouraged to judge their own lives as worthless? Pichler and others might have a point in question-ing the norm of activity, but it seems worthwhile to ask if this norm itself doesn't deliver the power to destabilize itself. It might be rewarding to in-quire more deeply into the secondary effects of this norm: Isn't it possible that the norm is disrupted at the same time when being adopted by the 'young-old'? In that way, the norm of activity could include the capacity for its own dissolution.[1]

"Mutton Dressed as Lamb"

Currently, not only the young are present in the fashion world, but increasingly older models are requested and the young-old are employed on catwalks (Femers 17). The musician Bryan Ferry is an example of this new trend. In 2006, the 60-year-old Ferry modeled a menswear collection for the retailer Marks & Spencer, and in 2011/12, he appeared together with his son Tara on an advertising campaign of the retail-clothing company Hennes & Mauritz (H&M). Referring to this campaign, the weekly German newspaper *Die Zeit* remarked, "When looking at the billboards of H&M that are now posted everywhere, two thoughts come to mind: 1. Bryan Ferry got old. 2. But he seems more laid-back than all the young people around him" (Kemper).[2] The columnist found that the greyish-white strands of hair at Ferry's temples let him appear easygoing, and that he looked like a 66-year-old proud of his age (Kemper). In this case, grey hair did not signify absence of youth, but marked an independent position in the fashion world.

Along these lines, fashion designer Wolfgang Joop detects a 'new older age-chic' when agencies specialize in placing older models at fashion shows and in advertisements (132). Joop explains this new trend as a promise of eternal agelessness (133), and emphasizes the many possibilities that exist to appear young: miracle cures that turn grey hair back to its original color and let hair grow on almost bald heads or stimulate the growth of biceps. Soon, biochemical solutions will make implants made from one's own body available (132). The fashion industry is aware of the fact that the 'new ageless generation' does not feel represented by teenage models. Teenagers

---

1 | There are parallels to my approach in Silke van Dyck's proposed agenda: "Theorizing the unnoticed subversive potential of the active-ageing-paradigm" (S. van Dyck: "Theorizing the re-negotiation of Old Age in Germany. The Active-ageing-paradigm as a Challenge to Critical Gerontology." Speech given at the conference Theorizing Age: Challenging the Disciplines, Maastricht, Oct 7th, 2011).

2 | All translations from the German texts are mine.

"are still provided by nature with desirable qualities, firm skin and youthful freshness, for free. For the others everlasting youthfulness can only be reached by hard work or a lot of money" (134). The beauty industry was the first to develop anti-aging products, and now the fashion industry closes the gap, "Myriads of push up fabrics lifts buttocks and breasts. The eyeglass industry produces lenses that make crow's feet appear invisible" (134).

Joop's description of the ideal of 'agelessness,' however, is ambivalent. On the one hand, he explains that older fashion models as representatives of a 'new ageless generation' cannot be replaced by teenage models, thus ascribing specific significance to the 'ageless.' On the other hand, he defines 'everlasting youthfulness' as the goal, thus defining youth as the desirable but not fully achievable ideal. Older models merely demonstrate that they are able to approximate it to a reasonable degree (134). Joop alludes to the naturalization of age, allegedly naturally firm skin and youthful freshness of teenagers, whereas the old are forced to invest effort and money in order to acquire these qualities. From this point of view, the 'youthful freshness' of teenagers appears as something original, whereas the old have to be satisfied with mere substitutes. Joop talks of age boundaries as natural with a clear dividing line between young and old, and defines 'ageless' as exceeding teenage years. Thus, the style of the 'ageless' becomes age-specific.

How strictly the 'border to youth' is being monitored becomes evident in the fact that the 'ageless,' especially the young-old, are often urged not to dress too youthfully (Lewis, Medvedev, and Seponski 102). The fashion style guide *Ageless Beauty* explains that many aging women "want to look young, and think that wearing the latest fashion trends will help them achieve that youthful look. [...] [S]ome women fall into the trap of wearing clothing that is entirely too 'young' for them" (*Ageless Beauty*). Such behavior is ridiculed by a phrase:

The British have an expression that I like: "Mutton dressed as lamb" which refers to someone older (usually a woman) dressed far too youthfully. The result, instead of making her appear more youthful, is that the woman emphasizes her age. Just imagine, say, Sharon Stone dressed the same as Brittany Spears or Jessica Simpson. (*Ageless Beauty*)

This passage makes ageism visible, paradoxically despite the ideal of 'agelessness.' If beauty is supposedly 'ageless,' age should not be noticeable (Andrews). Thus, in the context of this fashion guide, the construction of 'agelessness' is closely linked to a construction of age. By recommending an 'ageless' style as age-appropriate for older women, age is considered natural and needs to be concealed.

If at least a hint of youth is to be retained, so the fashion guide, an 'ageless' style should not be completely unrelated to fashion trends:

The truth is, in order to look young you do need to keep your wardrobe current. Fabrics, colors, patterns and shapes change from year to year and all serve to date the wardrobe and the person wearing it alike. But keeping your wardrobe current doesn't mean you should go for the trendy or hip looks. Instead, you should look for classic styles and shapes that flatter your figure in the colors and fabrics that are up to date. As a woman ages, she must pay attention to these details. (*Ageless Beauty*)

From this perspective, 'agelessness' is a mere approximation of youth as a goal that can never be fully achieved. However, the concept of 'agelessness' does not generally imply that age limits have to be drawn. In economic terms, 'ageless marketing' is a strategy for addressing a broader target group by avoiding exclusion by age (PricewaterhouseCoopers 33-39). The Boston footwear company New Balance, for example, uses 'ageless marketing' very successfully on the sneaker market. Central to the campaign are seemingly universal values that are not bound to any specific age. The worth of an individual is, for instance, not measured by being superior to others or aspiring to a different social self, but by appreciating one's true inner self. The fashion models in the ads are depicted in such a way that their age cannot be estimated (Wolfe and Snyder 106-09; PricewaterhouseCoopers 34-35). Accordingly, 'ageless fashion' moves between erasing age differences on the one hand, and concealing age by idealizing youth on the other.

The marketing campaign of 'Chuck Taylor All Star' shoes by the company Converse is a good example for these different notions of 'age(lessness)' used in the fashion world. The shoes are frequently associated with sports but also with rebellion, and have played a role in different youth cultures (Gerhard; van Rooijen). The use of 'Chuck Taylor All Star' shoes in the video *young at heart* by Maike Kusche, the winning clip of the contest *What does it mean to be old?* (*Was heißt schon alt?*) initiated by the German Federal Ministry for Family Affairs, Senior Citizens, Women and Youth is accordingly provocative. The video shows an almost 80-year-old woman tying red

'All Star' shoes while explaining that age is not the number of years lived but an attitude. On the website of the federal ministry a viewer criticizes this shoe-tying scene as utterly staged, "What kind of grandma would ever wear Converse shoes?" (Bundesministerium). The portrayals of 'being young at old age,' respectively of 'active aging,' were seen as staged and the way the shoes were placed in the clip as exaggeration.

Internet forums have discussed the age appropriateness of Converse 'All Star' shoes, and have asked whether old people may wear them, "Is there an age limit for Converse shoes?" (Dik Dik) or "Am I too old for the brands 'Bench' and 'Converse'?" (EquusCaballus). The approaches already discussed concerning the concept of 'age(lessness)' are also evident in this context. Some postings defend those who wear Converse shoes past their teenage years by referring to values that are taken for age-independent and emphasizing the importance of personal identity and loyalty to one's own personal style, "I know people in their 50's and 60's who wear [Converse shoes]. It just has to suit your [...] personality" (Dik Dik). Another post referring to the same thread states, "Everyone has their own style." These arguments agree with a concept of 'agelessness' that erases age differences. Other statements, however, emphasize the fact that only an approximation and slight appropriation of fashion targeted at teenagers are possible. Referring to a question of a 34-year-old woman about whether she is too old for the brands Bench and Converse, she was given the advice to buy these brands in age-appropriate colors, Converse shoes with a black toe cap and not the bright green Bench jacket (EquusCaballus; Twigg 293-94). Such postings obviously take age boundaries for granted, as do postings that strongly restrict wearing Converse shoes to a certain age. Age boundaries are put into perspective by some posts that point out that Converse 'All-Star' shoes were already en vogue in the days when the old people were young, "chuck taylors are as old as those seniors you speak of!!! What's wrong with them wearing the shoes they grew up with?" (Dik Dik). Other postings, however, clearly define an age limit, "The age limit for converse is 45 when your 45 I say no way with converse" (Dik Dik). This corresponds to Robert Johnston, a 44-year-old associate editor of the magazine *GQ*, being quoted as follows, "I was recently told I was too old to wear Converse. I was devastated. I'll still wear them but with far less enjoyment" (Chilvers).

Such positioning corresponds to the saying 'mutton dressed as lamb' (Fairhurst 261-65). People run the risk of appearing ludicrous because of age-inappropriate ways of dressing. However, it is worthwhile to consider this aspect of age-inappropriateness from another angle. Doesn't the transgression of age-limits bear a potential of subversion? Might not the image of lamb be just as influenced by such an act of defiance as the image of mutton? Using Bhabha's term of mimicry in this context, the ambivalence of 'mutton dressed as lamb' becomes evident.

FASHION AND AGE MIMICRY

Bhabha (1994) relates his theoretical concept of mimicry to colonialized people who imitate their colonial rulers and their culture, yet are supposedly not able to fully copy them. The colonialized are almost like the colonializing, but 'not quite,' 'not white:' "[C]olonial mimicry is the desire for a reformed, recognizable Other, as a subject of a difference that is almost the same, but not quite" (Bhabha 86). Although the colonialized have the alleged benefaction of adapting to a large extent to their colonial rulers, difference still remains and is ontologically assured, so that the supremacy of the colonial rulers prevails: "Almost the same but not white: the visibility of mimicry is always produced at the site of interdiction" (Bhabha 89). At first it seems that Bhabha's concept only works in the context of colonialism, and a comparison to age-groups in terms of fashion seems far-fetched. However, on an abstract level structural similarities between both fields can be established.

According to some commentators, the relation between the fashion of the young and the fashion of the young-old, respectively the 'ageless,' is based on the fact that the older may imitate the younger, yet only to a certain degree and only when respecting the allegedly natural boundaries between age-groups. In this respect, the young-old appear almost like the young, although 'not quite.' The effort of imitating youth ultimately has to fail and seemingly only reaffirms the ideals of youth. This approach ignores the fact that youth as an ideal and fashion for the young are also affected by the young-old's failing attempts to copy. The act of imitation creates a form of distortion and thus initiates change. Bhabha shows how the self-perception of the colonial rulers is challenged if the colonized transform into a distorted picture of the former:

[...] a discursive process by which the excess or slippage produced by the *ambivalence* of mimicry (almost the same, *but not quite*) [...] becomes transformed into an uncertainty which fixes the colonial subject as a 'partial' presence. By 'partial' I mean both 'incomplete' and 'virtual.' It is as if the very emergence of the 'colonial' is dependent for its representation upon some strategic limitation or prohibition *within* the authoritative discourse itself. The success of colonial appropriation depends on proliferation of inappropriate objects that ensure its strategic failure, so that mimicry is at once resemblance and menace. (Bhabha 86)

In the context of fashion discourse, Bhabha's definition of mimicry shows that by presenting a distorted appropriation this failed attempt to imitate youth undermines the ideal itself. The 'true' or 'genuine' fashion for the young is questioned by the 'old' appropriation of youth and turns it into a floating signifier. Authenticity of youth and of fashion for the young is thus contested. The term 'mimicry' is of imminent value for these considerations as it can describe unintentional subversive practices. These effects (intended or not) constitute the ambivalences that are characteristic for the fashion of the young-old.

ACKNOWLEDGEMENTS

I would like to thank the editors and the European Network in Aging Studies (ENAS) for inspiring discussions on my topic.

REFERENCES

"Ageless Beauty. Clothing and Fashion for Older Women." *Greatest Look. Fashion, Hairstyles & Beauty*. Web. 15 Jan. 2012.

Andrews, Molly. "The seductiveness of agelessness." *Ageing and Society* 19 (1999): 301-18. Print.

Barthes, Roland. *The Fashion System*. Translated from the French by Matthew Ward and Richard Howard. London: Vintage Books, 2010. Print.

Bhabha, Homi K. "Of mimicry and man: The ambivalence of colonial discourse." *The Location of Culture*. London: Routledge, 1994. 85-92. Print.

Bundesministerium für Familie, Senioren, Frauen und Jugend. Wettbewerb "Was heißt schon alt?" Web. 15 Jan. 2012.

Chilvers, Simon. "Are you dressing inappropriately for your age?" *theguardian* 1 June 2010. Web. 15 Jan. 2012.

Dik Dik. "Is there an age limit for converse shoes?" *Yahoo! Answers*. Web. 15 January 2012.

EquusCaballus. "Bin ich zu alt für die Marken Bench und Converse?" *gutefrage.net*. 11 March 2011. Web. 15 January 2012.

Fairhurst, Eileen. "'Growing old gracefully' as opposed to 'mutton dressed as lamb.' The social construction of recognising older women." *The Body in Everyday Life*. Ed. Sarah Nettleton and Jonathan Watson. London: Routledge, 1998. 258-75. Print.

Femers, Susanne. *Die ergrauende Werbung*. Wiesbaden: VS, 2007. Print.

Gerhard, Serjoscha. "'Chucks' – zwischen Subkultur und Mainstream." *Kulturgemein.de*. 4 August 2010. Web. 15 January 2012.

Gullette, Margaret Morganroth. "The Other End of the Fashion Cycle: Practicing Loss, Learning Decline." *Figuring Age. Women, Bodies, Generations*. Ed. Kathleen M. Woodward. Bloomington: Indiana University Press, 1999. 34-58. Print.

Joop, Wolfgang. "Falten als Schmuckstück." *Der Spiegel* 16/1999: 132-36. Print.

Kemper, Anna. "Über Männerhaar." *Zeit Magazin* 52/2011 22 Dec. 2011: 11. Print.

Lewis, Denise C., Katalin Medvedev, and Desiree M. Seponski. "Awakening to the desires of older women: Deconstructing ageism within fashion magazines." *Journal of Aging Studies* 25 (2011): 101-09. Print.

Oesterle, Günter. "Einleitung." *Jugend – ein romantisches Konzept?* Ed. Günter Oesterle. Würzburg: K&N 1997. 9-22. Print.

Pichler, Barbara. "Autonomes Alter(n). Zwischen widerständigem Potential, neoliberaler Verführung und illusionärer Notwendigkeit." *Die neuen Alten – Retter des Sozialen?* Ed. Kirsten Aner, Fred Karl, and Leopold Rosenmayr. Wiesbaden: VS, 2007. 67-84. Print.

PricewaterhouseCoopers and Institut für Marketing und Handel, Universität St. Gallen. "'Generation 55+.' Chancen für Handel und Konsumgüterindustrie." Web. 15 Jan. 2012.

van Rooijen, Jeroen. "Zerlegt - Ein zäher Dauerläufer." *NZZ Folio* 4/2009. Web. 15 Jan. 2012.

Vincent, Susan J. "Fashioning the Body Today." *The Fashion Reader*. Ed. Linda Welters and Abby Lillethun. 2nd edition. Oxford and New York: Berg, 2011. 358-61. Print.

Smith, S.E. "Who are the Young-Old?" *wiseGEEK. clear answers for common questions.* Web. 15 Jan. 2012.

Twigg, Julia. "Clothing, age and the body: a critical review." *Ageing & Society* 27 (2007): 285-305. Print.

Wolfe, David B. and Robert E. Snyder. *Ageless Marketing: Strategies for Reaching the Hearts and Minds of the New Customer Majority.* New York: Kaplan Publishing, 2003. Print.

Representation of Ages of Life
in Literature

The Irony of the Ages of Life

Etienne Pasquier's *Les Jeus Poetiques* (1610)

Cynthia Skenazi

"One man in his time plays many parts" Jaques says in Shakespeare's *As You Like It*. He then describes seven parts of life in the theater of the world, from the mewling and puking infant to the decrepit old man (2.7.138-65). From antiquity on, the number of these life course stages varied from three to seven, and the scheme to divide the life course into various stages according to one's biological age is reflective of the temporal nature of human existence. Jaques is prompted to this reflection by spectacles of suffering and injustice:

> And so from hour to hour we ripe, and ripe,
> And then from hour to hour we rot, and rot;
> And thereby hangs a tale.
> (Shakespeare II, 7.I.26-28)

This essay is about an ironic tale on the ages of life. In *Les Jeus Poetiques* (1610), the 81-year-old French poet Etienne Pasquier playfully questions abstract accounts of the life cycle as a repetitive and timeless sequence of ages. Social games on refined and witty expressions of desire were among the favorite pastimes of the French literary circles at the beginning of the seventeenth century. Pasquier's presentation of his *éducation sentimentale* from youth to old age fully complies with the salons' mode of civility. Throughout his collection, age is not only thought of as simply a measure of time between birth and death, but as the way people perceive themselves and the way others see them. It is, in fact, considered a predominant factor in social and in love affairs that one's age permits access to certain experi-

ences, denies access to others, and embraces numerous implicit expectations about manners and behavior. For centuries, Western philosophers
and moralists have stressed the weaknesses, moral and physical, to which
the various phases of life are prone. They have scorned youth's concupis-
cence, condemned adulthood's ambition, and poked fun at the lustful old
man. In contrast to these negative views of sentimental development, others have argued that as years go by young men's attraction to love's sensual
pleasures is balanced by opportunities for emotional growth, which culmi-
nate in the wisdom traditionally granted to old age.

Such is the schematic perspective that Pasquier imposes upon the representation of his amorous behavior from youth to decrepitude. From the
start, his address to the reader calls the value of any division of the life
course into specific age groups with a common set of fixed features into
question by challenging the reader to view the octogenarian author as an
old man (106). *Les Jeus Poetiques* presents life as a story of commonplaces,
yet, as the author's own case makes it clear, chronological age explains
nothing, and is nothing but an arbitrary index. Aging as applied to human existence implies a multiplicity of perspectives, such as biological,
medical, or psychological. No overview can take stock of all these levels. In
Pasquier's collection, the recourse to the concept of aging through life to
locate people's identities only becomes meaningful in terms of individual
responses to them. *Les Jeus Poetiques*, in this respect, goes even further than
Jaques' remark in *As You Like It*. The 'tale' of one's life is the product of a
montage insofar as the octogenarian writer recycled some of his earlier
poems, revisions were effected, new poems were added, and others were
deleted. A coherent narrative was carved out of a set of previous texts to account retrospectively for clearly delineated stages of the life cycle.

Les Jeus Poetiques blurs the distinction between the practice of a literary
style and the shaping of one's identity through time. The collection is, in
many ways, an anthology of the rhetorical trends that dominated French
love poetry during the second half of the sixteenth century. It provides an
ironic review of the postures of the poet as a lover who inspired Pasquier
during his long career. The author knew very well that he was dipping into
material that any member of his literary and social circle would recognize
and would enjoy catching the allusions. Stereotypes of old people describe
them as fully absorbed in the contemplation of their past and not interested in the present, but this was not Pasquier's case at all. The 81-year-old au-

thor adapted his verses, some of which had been published as early as 1555, to the audience contemporary with *Les Jeus Poetiques*'s publication in 1610.

We may, of course, distinguish between the poetics of each of the five sections of his collection and their representations of the poet's various amorous behaviors at specific ages of life, but in doing so we begin to lose the sense of the complex interactions between the 'self' and literature in a given culture. *Les Jeus Poetiques* playfully stresses that, as Clifford Geertz writes, "there is no such thing as a human nature independent of culture," if by culture we mean "not primarily complexes of concrete behavior patterns (customs, usages, traditions, habit clusters), but rather a set of control mechanisms (plans, recipes, rules, instructions) for the governing of behavior" (51). The overall poetic quality of each section therefore becomes a moot point since Pasquier's collection engages its readers with an experience of the instability of the canon as a product of shifting tastes.

What marks this project is the enduring imprint of Pierre de Ronsard on Pasquier's successive self-definitions as both poet and lover. As the most versatile poet of his time, Ronsard had excelled in every form and possible expression of desire, tirelessly drawing his inspiration from Italian, Greek, and Latin sources to enrich the French literary repertoire. Pasquier's acknowledgement of Ronsard's influence on his career was a means of sharing the glory of a famed poet, and praising his lasting influence. The old writer proudly showed his 1610 audience that he had been an active member of the famous Pléiade, which under Ronsard's leadership gave France a renewed cultural prestige. This claim reappears in Book 7, Chapter 6 of the Recherches de la France, which Pasquier was writing at the same time as the Jeus Poetiques (Oeuvres II, 231). In a similar way, in a letter dated between 1589 and 1605, Pasquier said to his friend, the poet Pontus de Tyard, "Si je ne m'abuse, vous et moy restons presque seuls en cette France de cette belle brigade, que produisit le regne du Roy Henry II," which translates into "If I am not mistaken, you and I are about the only ones left in France in this beautiful 'brigade' [the first 'incarnation' of the Pléiade] of Henri II's reign"[1] (Oeuvres II, 520).

Pasquier's own medal (which was engraved in 1605, five years before the publication of *Les Jeus Poetiques*) represents him as a Gallic Hercules dragging people by his tongue. The medal praised Pasquier's rhetorical gift

---

1 | Translations from the French original into English are done by the author. All following translations are by Skenazi, unless otherwise noted.

as a brilliant lawyer, but any educated contemporary would have caught the allusion to the cultural propaganda of artists from the beginning of Henri II's reign. The Gallic Hercules had been staged during the king's royal entry in Paris in 1548, and a year later it reappeared as a symbol of eloquence at the end of Du Bellay's *La Deffence et illustration de la langue françoyse* (1549), the 'manifesto' of the future *Pléiade* (180).

When preparing his collection, Pasquier certainly had the example of the aged Ronsard in mind, given that he was gathering his earlier publications in successive editions of his complete works. Ronsard's *Oeuvres* were conceived as an immortal poetic monument; likewise, Pasquier's *Les Jeus Poetiques* is the product of a theatrical culture. Both authors act as the stage-managers of their poems, carefully revising their previous texts and organizing them in meaningful ways. Both of them proceed by way of assimilation, distance, appreciation, and alternative castings of poetic and affective postures of the lover. In addition, Pasquier reevaluated the legacy of fifty years of love poetry dominated by Ronsard's powerful presence. His dialogue with his own literary production capitalized on his capacities to make and remake himself, to resist the social constraints and imperatives imposed upon old age.

YOUTH AND ADULTHOOD: "LOYALTY, LIBERTY, AND AMBITION"

In the address to the reader prefacing his collection, Pasquier claims to present his own love affairs, but in reality, each section of *Les Jeus Poetiques* creates the effect of a collective discourse on love and elaborates on depersonalized, stereotyped amorous behaviors at different ages. The first section, "Loyauté," presents the poet lover as a "young man in the age of innocence" (106), in the author's words. Since this part contains the higher proportion of the author's earliest verses, it is not surprising to find a significant number of conventional Petrarchan conceits and imagery. The lover finds himself at once a prisoner of a beautiful and cruel lady. After love's fatal glance comes the standard description of the physical and moral perfections of the beloved. The young lover worships his lady but his efforts to seduce her remain vain; his obsessive passion becomes a source of frustration and torture. The Petrarchan paradoxes which were so fashionable in love poetry of the 1550s (the icy fire, the darkness of light) express his contradictory feelings. Half a century later, Pasquier was fully aware that many aspects of such rhetoric seemed outdated. He reassessed the tone of his youthful verses in *Les Jeus Poetiques*; from the outset, he stressed the ridiculous figure cut by the young poet lover of "Loyauté." These verses, the old poet now declares in his prefatory address to his reader, were written with tongue in cheek and should be read accordingly: "En un mot je laisse au grand Petrarque pour closture de ses amours, un long repentir," "In a word, I leave to the great Petrarch a long repentance in conclusion to his love" (106). He also mocks the poet Tasso for becoming mad because of his unrequited love for the Princesses of Ferrara (106).

Already in 1553, the fashion had begun to run swiftly against the representation of the faithful poet lover. Ronsard sarcastically accused Petrarch of playing the transfixed lover (I, 168-69). Intent as ever to inscribe his own career into the poetic record of his time, Pasquier reacted in a similar way in 1555 and also questioned the sincerity of Petrarch's and his numerous imitators' passionate love (*Oeuvres* I, 145). "Liberté," the second section of *Les Jeus Poetiques*, makes use of a substantial repertoire of situations and words inspired by the posture of the inconstant lover championed by Ronsard. Once again, this section, which incorporates poems by Pasquier published in 1555 and 1578, is a hallmark of commonplaces on youthful lovers who turn women into objects they long to possess. Once again also, this amorous behavior is expressed through a blending of lyrical voices, in addition to the Ronsardian model, the poems of "Liberté" openly mention Du Bellay and Tyard (Sonnet 13), poets who were both members of the *Pléiade*.

Yet, *Les Jeus Poetiques* is not the work of a dilatory and servile imitator but rather of a lawyer well equipped to give rhetoric a central place in the creation of his *roman d'amour*. Each section of the collection contains the seeds of the next ones and demonstrates Pasquier's versatility in his self-casting as a lover. "Loyauté" focuses on the young and inexperienced lover's obsessive passion for a single woman. "Liberté," in contrast, depicts a more mature protagonist who is determined to enjoy every opportunity for love affairs because nothing is permanent. "Loyauté" elaborates on images of entrapment into the labyrinth of love, whereas "Liberté" focuses on instability as a general principle governing human behavior and the world as a whole. The third section, "Ambition," complements Pasquier's catalogue of amorous behaviors by playfully adding a new character to the repertoire of French love poetry. The protagonist, who is now in the middle of his life and a married man, forms the identity of a successful lawyer. He climbs the social ladder and concentrates his energy on a professional career, which leads him away from love. His lust for money, glory, and fame, echo many of Ronsard's poetic concerns, but these motives strike an ironic note for they appear as part of the bourgeois and pragmatic ideal of adulthood. The section concludes with an elegy spelling out a husband's and a wife's respective duties for living peacefully, and expresses concern for the couple's future children (314-16).

OLD AGE

Throughout *Les Jeus Poetiques,* metamorphosis renders a poetic and an amorous experience. As he reaches old age, the protagonist falls in love again in the fourth section entitled "La Vieillesse Amoureuse" ("Old Age in Love"). This new development challenges the idea that individuals do not revert back to earlier stages insofar as the aged lover is wounded by one of Cupid's arrows and shows every sign of the youthful passion he sung in "Loyauté." The lover whose passion is inappropriate to his advanced age, according to the early seventeenth-century norms, is a comic figure *per se,* and is readily related to a stereotypical figure with a long theatrical history and much present in the French comedy of the period, and Pasquier's own *Pastorale du Vieillard Amoureux (Pastoral of the Old Man in Love)* published in 1592 was a witty contribution to this genre (*Oeuvres* II, 897-912). Yet, to limit the interest of "La Vieillesse Amoureuse" to its comic potential would be to give too little credit to its creative energy.

In his *Sonnets pour Hélène* (1578), Ronsard elaborated on the perceived incongruity of the poet adopting the lover's role in his advancing age, and occasionally detailed his physical limitations as suitor (I, 341-423). In a similar way, "La Vieillesse Amoureuse" offered a renewed response to the Petrarchan model, which had informed Pasquier's and Ronsard's careers as a whole. Both of them imitate themselves, or rather sound out new resonances from their earlier poems. Ronsard emphasized the willful choice of Hélène's aged lover, thereby distancing himself from the rhetorical model of his previous love collections. Pasquier, on the other hand, reinforced the fated nature of his protagonist's last passion to offer a parody of the first section of his *Les Jeus Poetiques.* Both sonnets I and II, to cite but two examples, are so largely a composite from poems of "Loyauté" as to echo the young and inexperienced lover's *innamorento.* Ardent in his desire, heedless of the consequences of his passion, the aged lover shows no sign at all of the stereotypical prudence and wisdom of old age. Equally fundamental is the failure of his reason to resist the attraction to sensual pleasure. Circling back to second youth, he puts his beloved on a pedestal, yet he is old enough to appreciate what is so absurd about aged men falling in love. Absurd as the process may be, it is also a process of discovery, a whole reassessment of the aged lover's own sense of identity.

A number of elements of his story ironically echo Petrarch's passion for Laura in his *Canzoniere* to which Ronsard also referred in his *Sonnets pour Hélène*. The enumeration of losses to time and death, for instance, includes the many attributes beloved in the lady: the lady falls ill, ages faster than the old lover, and becomes a repulsive carcass (Sonnet 16). A lawyer by profession, Pasquier adds a smiling judiciary touch to this satirical portrait of her on her deathbed, the lady makes her will and donates her wealth to the poet (Sonnet 17). The section ends with a game about words: two songs present arguments, respectively, against and in favor of a love relationship between an old man and a young lady. The aged lover concludes by saying that he does not tell the truth either when he claims to love the young lady or when he pretends not to love her. His statement immediately prompts a response from the young lady, who pokes fun at his rhetorical subtleties, and says that when it comes to love, no old man can be taken seriously because of his age (337-42).

By and large, the poems gathered in the two sections on old age had not been published previously but were written by an octogenarian author who had firsthand experience of this stage. In "La Vieillesse Rechignée" ("Grumpy Old Age"), the final section of the collection, Pasquier elaborated on yet another set of commonplaces on old age, which Ronsard had also explored to meditate on time and immortality. As he reaches the stage of decrepitude, the protagonist of *Les Jeus Poetiques* becomes disillusioned about love. He is now an unattractive, impaired, and socially dysfunctional person. In short, he has become a narcissistic and selfish man whose age has rendered everything in the world displeasing. He hates everyone, including himself, and longs for death to deliver him from his wretched life (364). Yet, discouragement and despair are far from being the final words of his *éducation sentimentale* along the life cycle. Instead, the 81-year-old author concludes his collection by playfully praising the pleasures of illusions, and admiring his own wit:

De l'Amour je me mocque, et encores de moy, [...],
Et voiant que ce Tout n'est rien que vanité,
Bien vivre, et m'esjouir c'est ma Philosophie.

I make fun of love, and also of myself,
And seeing that everything is but vanity,
Living well and rejoicing is my Philosophy. (370)

This is not to say that he is only, or even chiefly, an ironist. His final claim
is less a process of disengagement than a transition to another valued role,
that of the *senex puer* (the childish old man), who enjoys a bearable present,
by delighting in trifles. As Pasquier physically ages, his mind rejuvenates,
and like his friend Michel de Montaigne, he represents himself fully absorbed in apparently useless pastimes which keep him from kicking and
grumbling against the woes of old age (Skenazi 589-93). "Je veux à face
descouverte qu'on sçache que je fais le fol," "I want to make it clear that I
openly am playing the fool," Pasquier wrote in a letter to his friend Airault
about another of his work, *La Pastorale du Vieillard Amoureux* II, (899-
900). Eighteen years prior to *Les Jeus Poetiques* being published on January
15, 1592, he already observed similar things and shared them in a letter to
the lawyer Pierre Pithou:

Puisque la vieillesse apporte mille incommoditez de corps et d'esprit quant et
soy, je me veux chatoüiller pour rire, malgré la malice du temps, et de mon aage,
et en ce faisant, bannir le chagrin au moins mal qu'il me sera possible, et me
resjoüyr sans pecher. A la charge que si je desplais à quelques-uns, je veux qu'ils
sçachent qu'aussi me desplaisent-ils, et si voulez que je passe plus outre, leur
desplaisir est mon plaisir.

Since old age brings on a thousand inconveniences to the body and the mind,
I want to tickle myself and laugh despite the evil of time and old age, thereby
chasing sadness in the least possible harmful way, and rejoicing with no remorse. Now if I displease a few, I want them to know that they displease me too,
and if you want me to go further, that their displeasure is my pleasure. (*Oeuvres*
II, 911–12)

As he watches himself grow old, he learns, in other words, to enjoy what
he has without clinging to it. This, in turn, means that he can not only in-

crease his chances of experiencing joy but increase the chance that the joy he experiences will survive changes in a world where everything is short-lived and perishable.

In words attributed to George Bernard Shaw, "We don't stop playing because we grow old, we grow old because we stop playing." Old age puts more wrinkles on Pasquier's body than in his mind; play was the very sign of the wisdom he acquired during his long life. Aging wisely, then, is less about having certain ends in mind rather than coming to terms with new beginnings. This issue needs to be addressed in terms of practices of everyday life rather than of compliance with a set of coded behaviors. What Pasquier also acquired as years went by was frankness; indeed, he is quick to point out that old people are traditionally granted more freedom of speech than young ones. His experience enlightened him to the value of things and the intrinsic worth of pleasures while dispelling illusions and prejudices about old age. He confronted stereotypes concerning age, but did not challenge social decorum and *convenances*, for throughout *Les Jeus Poetiques*, love is a poetic experience.

If love is a game, poetry is another, but ultimately more serious. *Les Jeus Poetiques* was conceived as a social entertainment for the learned guests of the French salons, but its playful tone did not prevent its author from dreaming of literary fame. No author is able to predict which one of his works will survive the ravages of time, Pasquier notes in his address to the reader. Sometimes, posterity gives a stamp of approval on a few lines that were written just for fun whereas, in contrast, the text that his author most values immediately goes unnoticed and then sinks into oblivion. He then adds: "Quel sera le hazard de mes *Jeus Poëtiques* (ainsi me plaist-il les nommer) je ne m'en donne pas grande peine;" "What will be the fate of my *Jeus Poetiques* (so I like to call them), I don't really care" (105). One may, however, question the sincerity of such a statement, for in a letter to his friend Antoine Loisel, Pasquier wrote: "et peut-estre adviendra-t-il que celles [mes oeuvres] dont je fais moins de compte seront les mieux recueillies," "and maybe it will happen that those of my works I value the least will be best received" (*Oeuvres* II, 282). It is true that this observation was made several years before the publication of *Les Jeus Poetiques*, but Pasquier obviously kept thinking of the immortality of Giovanni Boccaccio's *Decameron*, a work that its author did not consider seriously (*Oeuvres* II, 282).

In reentering the social stage with yet another collection of love poetry at the age of 81, Pasquier was aware of the gamble. The writing of these verses was itself a part of an *aventure galante,* insofar as he overtly postured as postulant for the attention of ladies who were no less well versed in half a century of rhetorical fashions in French poetry. He showed them how a man who looks old in the eyes of another can be the most youthful and convivial author. By gracefully adapting to a process whose effects are beyond human control 'growing old,' Pasquier stressed the value of his age without being pretentious or offensive. He revealed himself to be more sensitive to the intrinsic worth of pleasures as time passed, and this posture was a way to remain a key player at table conversations despite, and ultimately because of the physiological changes taking place in his body. His smiling defense of old age, with its emphasis on politeness, grace, and elegance in social behavior, was a key aspect of the social identity of the cultural elite gathered in French salons toward the beginning of the seventeenth century. Pasquier was at pains to please his lively circle of learned friends, for nothing makes a love story more jovial than laughter and trust. As Linda Hutcheon observed, "irony is a relational strategy in the sense that it operates not only between meaning (said, unsaid) but between people (ironists, interpreters, targets)" (58). By adding a note of self-mockery to his self-portraits, Pasquier was seeking confirmation and affection from his audience, he wanted to be esteemed for what and who he was; for his honesty, his wit, his old age. His collection was an elegant demonstration of an old man's superiority when it comes to speak of love.

As he reached the final stage of his life, he who was ahead of his time as an active member of the *Pléiade* in the 1550s fell back as a witness who passed something on to new generations of poets. There were two lines of life he wanted to hand on to his successors: the art of detachment and the art of discernment. Both lines had poetic implications. When confronted with the mutability of human existence and rhetorical fashions, Pasquier offered neither resignation nor acceptance, but rather the ability to respond imaginatively to the passage of time, with an ironic smile.

What are the broader implications of this acute and compassionate observation of the human comedy? If we consider the idea that our age is integral to our identity, then we need to recognize that it is also frequently in potential tension with it. We subjectively cling to an image of ourselves as forever young. While the inside of the body supports this phenomenological sense of coherence and continuity, its external appearance continuously disrupts this self-consciousness. Pasquier used stereotyped and abstract accounts of the stages of the life cycle to promote a much more varied notion of aging as a social and literary process.

References

Du Bellay, Joachim. *La Deffence et Illustration de la langue françoyse*. Ed. Jean-Charles Monferran. Geneva: Droz, 2001. Print.

Geertz, Clifford. *The Interpretation of Culture*. New York: Basic Books, 1973. Print.

Hutcheon, Linda. *The Theory and Politics of Irony*. London: Routledge, 1994. Print.

Pasquier, Etienne. *Les Jeus Poetiques*. Ed. Jean-Pierre Dupouy. Paris: Champion, 2001. Print.

—. *Oeuvres complètes*. 2vols. Geneva: Slatkine Reprints, 1971. Print.

Petrarch. *Lyric Poems. The Rime Sparse and Other Lyrics*. Ed. and transl. Robert M. Durling. Cambridge, Mass.: Harvard University Press, 1976. Print.

Ronsard, Pierre de. *Oeuvres*. Eds. Jean Céard, Daniel Menager, Michel Simonin. Paris: Gallimard, 1993. Print.

Shakespeare, William. *As You Like It*. Ed. J. H. Walter. London: Heinemann Educational Books, 1965. Print.

Skenazi, Cynthia. "The Art of Aging Gracefully: Castiglione's *Book of the Courtier* and Montaigne's 'On Some Verses of Virgil' (*Essays*, III, 5)." *Bibliothèque d'Humanisme et Renaissance* LXX, 3 (2008): 579-93. Print.

Past the Mirror of Victorian Aging and Beyond

Recurring Transatlantic Archetypes of the Aged

Marta Miquel-Baldellou

According to Kathleen Woodward, discourses of aging can be perceived as a sign of difference and, like other markers of social difference, it is socially constructed. With others concepts which contribute to shaping identity such as gender, nation, or race, our perceptions of aging are essentially culturally constructed (Gullette, *Declining* 4). The ways we perceive aging are both determined and influenced by the culture from which they arise. In this respect, Margaret Morganroth Gullette refers to cultural constructs of age and the need to change and reconceptualize age culture. To this end, she coined the term age identity (Gullette, *Aged by Culture*) as a fluid rather than the fixed concept traditionally envisioned.

However, the process of aging has often been evaluated in relation to dominant culture, suggesting there is one and only one life course which necessarily involves a period of progress and a resulting time of decline. Consequently, aging has frequently been associated with a time of accepted decline in a dominant culture, and individuals in acceptance of this notion perceive aging as a time of loss rather than an enriching stage in life. Cultural manifestations such as in the arts and literature have often reflected this perception of aging and contributed to this archetypal representation of the aged.

Perceptions of age are dependent on culture, and Teresa Mangum has argued that it was during the Victorian period that old age was invented. The aging population at the time received more attention due to major social, cultural, and scientific changes. Prior to the nineteenth century, age was based on function rather than chronology, and people were usually deemed old on the basis of their physical constitution or their mental abilities. The Victorian mindset, with its preference for dichotomies and systematic categories, encouraged the passing of legal acts that specified the age at which citizens should be termed old. As a case in point, in 1908, the Old Age Pensions Act was passed, establishing the basis of social welfare in England.

More recently, Karen Chase has analyzed Victorians' deep concern about aging as a set of intersecting problems. Chase referred to the indeterminacy of old age as a central place of institutions, problematic cross-generational relationships, the creation of 'the elderly subject' as a category in medical research, and the beginning of public provision for old age. The prevalence old age acquired at the time was thus necessarily reflected in its cultural manifestations. As Helen Small argues, literature has shown a prominent tradition of engagement with old age, even though novelists at the time represented an aesthetic perspective of aging from the outside, rather than a socially committed one, which is now the case in contemporary narratives of aging. Thus, literary works in the Victorian period significantly contributed to prevalent attitudes towards aging as well as reflecting cultural perceptions of old age at the time.

When these cultural perceptions of aging are repeatedly taken up in literary and audiovisual manifestations, they turn into symbolic images or stereotypical representations of the aged. The way aging is perceived is shaped within a culturally determined framework, thus constructing archetypal representations of aged characters. According to Jane Garry and Hasan El-Shamy, the concept of the archetype was appropriated from the work of psychoanalyst C.G. Jung and subsequently applied to literary theory. The concept of the archetype is linked to Jung's analysis of the collective unconscious and refers to primordial types and "universal images that have existed since the remotest times" (Jung 5). Even though his interest was mainly psychological, Jung also looked into manifestations of the archetype in myths and fairy tales. Both Maud Bodkin, who was the first to apply Jung's ideas to literature, and Northrop Frye did much to establish Jung's ideas of the archetype as a method of literary criticism.

According to Herbert Covey, these recurring symbolic images of aged people in the arts are usually endowed with both positive and negative associations. Old age traditionally associated with values such as contemplation, spiritual restoration, repentance, or wisdom is also perceived as a period of decay, lust, foolishness, childishness, and poor health. Hence, it is by means of these cultural precepts (references) and their direct association with the elderly (referents) that stereotypical representations of age (archetypes) are constructed and perpetuated through time. In this respect, many literary renderings, and especially popular culture manifestations, have often portrayed aged characters playing the role of religious figures, sages, misers, pursuers of youth, fools, witches, spinsters, widows, preservers of status and hierarchies, lustful individuals, invalids, vampires, time embodiments, and even living reminders of death.

Even though these archetypes pertaining to the aged have been pervasive in Western culture, some of these stereotypical representations became especially recurrent during the Victorian period. According to John Morris, this fact is linked to the age of industrialism and commerce that "systematised people into objects and machines" (2). Similarly, critics such as Mircea Eliade and Harry Levin have argued that the nineteenth-century novel can be considered the great repository of degraded myths (Garry and El-Shamy xv). Stereotypical portraits of the aged are still prevalent in current cultural manifestations. Robert Butler defined "ageism" as "a process of systematic stereotyping, and discrimination against people because they are old, just as racism and sexism accomplish this for skin color and gender" (22-23). Prevailing limits of our perception of aging are still strongly rooted in concepts of the nineteenth century. In addition, the same archetypes can be found in different cultures with different meanings making cross-cultural studies necessary. Aged characters very often give way to archetypal representations in narratives at different times and in different cultures acquiring different connotations depending on the cultural and historical frameworks analyzed.

Discourses of aging vary from culture to culture and perceptions are significantly shaped by historical, scientific, and political issues which contribute to definitions of national identities. In the nineteenth century, Great Britain and the United States of America faced very different situations. After the War of Independence and the Declaration of Independence in 1776, the separating divide between Great Britain and its former colony grew significantly wider. National identities on both sides of the Atlantic emerged through the engagement with a transatlantic imaginary defining both similarities and differences of the two nations. Paul Giles claims that "one reason for focusing upon British and American cultures in the eighteenth and nineteenth centuries is to show how the emergence of autonomous and separate political identities during the era can be seen as intertwined with a play of opposites" (3). This apparently binary opposition underlines "the radical proclivities of American culture with what the authors took to be the more genteel liberal humanism of the English tradition" (Giles 4). It is, therefore, during this period when Anglo-American identities began to reify through the virtual perception of one another. Differences in the approach to cultural aging expressed this increasing cultural divide. David Hackett Fischer's *Growing Old in America* (1978) and Thomas Cole's *The Journey of Life: A Cultural History of Aging in America* (1992), for example, focus on historical perceptions of age in America, while Pat Thane's more recent volume *Old Age in English History: Past Experience, Present Issues* (2000) analyzes aging and its cultural perceptions in Great Britain.

The Declaration of Independence brought about significant cultural changes in terms of national perceptions and established a national allegory of a young nation independent of the old mother country. This national allegory also exerted an important influence on the cultural perceptions of aging held at the time. In this respect, David Hackett Fischer argues that nineteenth-century America developed a gerontophobic attitude towards the elderly owing to the historical and political circumstances at the time. In contrast, David Hackett Fischer alludes to the cult of youth that characterized the nineteenth-century transcendentalist America. Independence from England made Americans reject any representation of their past subjection to the old world (113).

By contrast, the Victorian period in England became mainly symbolized by the length of Queen Victoria's reign stretching from 1837 to 1901 and the longevity of the monarch. This in turn reflected the long-lasting splendor of the British Empire with its climax during the Victorian era. As a result of the widening historical and political divide between both nations, America rejected old values in favor of new ones. The English committed to traditional values saw age in a more positive light, whereas in America, youth was claimed as a symbolic value characterizing the emerging nation.

In addition to influences of national identity, old age representations were also gender-determined. At the beginning of the nineteenth century, aging was characterized by behavioral infirmity and physical deterioration rather than by chronological age. However, criteria differed in terms of gender. According to Teresa Mangum, the age of men was usually determined by their ability to work in the public domain, while women were often deemed old in relation to their reproductive capacity. Women were considered aged once they reached menopause, while men, provided they enjoyed good health, could continue to work until late in their lives. Nonetheless, once men were unable to work, they were also deprived of their social and public worth. As aged individuals, their infirmity confined them to the household domain, and consequently, aged men underwent a lapse into a state characterized by helplessness and dependence, both values being falsely but traditionally associated with women and children at the time (Mangum 99). In this respect, according to Kay Heath's assessment, old age was usually figured in gender neutral terms. Sexual roles clearly differentiated in youth and mid-life, now adapted to each in old age, aged men and women were treated as if they were all the same (Mangum 98-99). Likewise, Teresa Mangum also argues that in the Victorian period, men underwent a process of pseudo-feminization and their dependence led them to what is traditionally regarded as an assumed second childhood (100).

Nonetheless, these ideas were counteracted by the myth known as the Golden Age fantasy, usually applied to men rather than women. The Golden age fantasy came from ancient times and was based on the premise that the aged should be venerated due to the wisdom they had accumulated through life. A well-known literary archetype of the time was representing old men as transcendent sages or patriarchs. According to Elizabeth Abel et al., in narratives of development male growth is marked by social maturity and public resonance, whereas women are presented as developing later in life after fulfilling conventional expectations of marriage and motherhood. Contrary to male development narratives, fictional accounts of female development are presented with values which place importance on community and empathy rather than achievement and autonomy (Abel et al. 10).

In nineteenth-century narratives, the presence of aged characters is recurrent, and even though they hardly ever acquire a central role, their influence is often decisive to the development of the story. Both in Great Britain and the U.S., the elderly are depicted as secondary characters that either propel or hamper the protagonist's process of growth in order to attain maturity. Some of them are presented as embodiments of authority, social class or ethics pertaining to former times which protagonists try to subvert or rather aspire to acquire in order to accomplish their own process of maturation.

However, other representations of the aged in literature present them in rather a bleak way. Nineteenth-century narratives often portray wealthy aged males unwilling to hand over their fortune to their young inheritors, while aged women are often associated with gloomy witches, comic spinsters, wicked widows or even tyrannical queens who endeavor to persist in time, often resembling Queen Victoria. The unusual longevity of the elderly was also a topic for gothic narratives depicting individuals crossing the boundaries between life and death. As a case in point, the popularity of the vampire as a literary character mainly originated in the nineteenth century as the embodiment of a contemptuous aged figure who gained life at the expense of imbibing the fresh blood of the young. Even though these literary archetypes of aged individuals were recurrent in both American and English nineteenth-century narratives, these conceptualizations of old age differed culturally and with regard to gender portrayal. Therefore, a comparative analysis is necessary to determine the differences of approaches to aging in terms of cultural and historical background of the two countries.

SPINSTERS, WIDOWS AND WOMEN VAMPIRES: LITERARY ARCHETYPES OF THE FEMALE AGED

Elderly female characters in nineteenth-century narratives were often portrayed as aging spinsters, distant aunts, doting mothers, wealthy relatives, and even cunning or deceitful ladies endowed with some special power resembling the archetypal witch in medieval times. All these aged female characters acquired importance inasmuch as they exerted some control or influence on the female or male protagonist of the story. These literary archetypes are commonly found in both American and English narratives of the time, even though their portrayal acquires different connotations in both nations, as they are depicted through humor or scorn in some cases, and awe or even fear in others.

Miss Havisham is probably one of the most popular aging female characters in nineteenth-century English literature. In Charles Dickens' novel *Great Expectations*, Miss Havisham is described as a wealthy aging spinster who lives in a mansion with her adopted daughter Estella. Even though she is her mid-fifties, it is implied that a long life of seclusion has aged her before her time. On her wedding day, Miss Havisham is informed that the man she was to marry intended to deceive her. In her grief and humiliation, Miss Havisham decides to remain in her mansion, stopping all clocks and refusing to take off her wedding dress. Miss Havisham raises her adopted daughter Estella to deceive men in order to take revenge. However, Estella manages to cause the same feeling of grief and humiliation in Pip, whom Miss Havisham favors, when Estella leaves to marry Pip's rival, Bentley. Miss Havisham realizes that she has only managed to cause Pip the same grief she had suffered in youth and ultimately asks Pip for forgiveness. Even if at first Miss Havisham is presented as a sort of sorceress or witch, she becomes a tragic figure as a victim of her own circumstances and thus ultimately gains Pip's understanding and sympathy. Miss Havisham can be read as an archetype of the aging spinster, feared but also highly respected as a lonely lady presiding over her decaying mansion.

Two decades later, in his novel *Washington Square* Henry James casts the figure of Lavinia Penniman as an eccentric and overly melodramatic widow of a penniless clergy who moves in with his brother, Doctor Austin Sloper, and his daughter Catherine. Lavinia acts as Catherine's companion, and not unlike Miss Havisham she entertains the notion of Catherine meeting a young man and initiating some sort of romantic liaison. Once the handsome but selfish Morris becomes interested in Catherine, Lavinia hopefully persists in bringing them together, despite Morris' evident deceitful intentions. Lavinia's romantic hopes remain unfulfilled when Morris leaves and only returns when Catherine has turned into a middle-aged spinster who then rejects his renewed advances. Miss Havisham and Lavinia Penniman are both aging women who try to arrange marriages - which all end in failure. Nonetheless, if Miss Havisham is able to notice her mistake and correspondingly make amends, Lavinia makes Catherine's situation worse and her even more miserable. Lavinia's romanticized nature is often scorned and ridiculed in Henry James' novel, while it is Catherine, as she grows older, who is described with dignity and resolution, thus ultimately resembling Miss Havisham.

In Charlotte Brontë's novel *Jane Eyre*, Mrs. Reed is presented as another example of the archetype of the aging aunt. Mrs. Reed is Jane's cruel aunt, who favors her own spoiled children and constantly scorns Jane, even to the extent of locking her up in a red room. However, on her deathbed, embodying an early Victorian stereotypical archetype of the aging female invalid, Mrs. Reed confesses concealing a letter in which a distant uncle of Jane's proclaimed her niece as the sole heiress of his fortune. Despite the fact that Mrs. Reed is portrayed as a wicked aging aunt, Jane finally decides to forgive her. Mrs. Reed's imposing ways and her long-lasting influence on Jane's development as a character seem to be in sharp contrast with well-known portraits of other aging aunts in American narratives of the time. Aunt Polly, for example, in Mark Twain's *The Adventures of Tom Saw-yer* is depicted as a grumpy but inherently good aging aunt. Since Tom is an orphan, Aunt Polly is mainly responsible for Tom's upbringing and is repeatedly shown as exasperated with Tom's naughty behavior. Even though Aunt Polly is presented in a significantly more positive light than Jane's aunt in Charlotte Brontë's novel, Aunt Polly never develops as a character and her role mainly seems to be aimed at keeping Tom's naughtiness in check before he escapes with Huck in search of adventure and excitement. Moreover, Aunt Polly lacks the social and authoritarian power which characterizes Mrs. Reed in Charlotte Brontë's novel. In this sense, while Jane despite her inherent cruel manners feels awe and respect for her aunt, Tom Sawyer is mostly able to trick and deceive Aunt Polly so as to have his own way. Aunt Polly strives to teach Tom good manners through morals, religion, and discipline so that he becomes a respectable individual.

In Edward Bulwer-Lytton's very successful silver-fork novel *Pelham*, typically for the English novel, more emphasis is placed on social class. Henry Pelham's coming-of-age takes place through social interaction at the balls where the upper-classes gather. Henry Pelham is constantly advised by his mother Frances Pelham how to be liked and praised in his social interactions. Even if Frances Pelham is described in a rather sarcastic way, full of pretense and social aspirations, she constantly supports Henry as a doting mother and guides him in his process towards adulthood. In sharp contrast with this archetype of the English mother who is very aware of the importance of social class and the need to behave according to one's social category, in Henry James' novella *Daisy Miller*, Daisy's aging mother like Daisy herself arises as an eminently innocent character, but it is precisely her ingenuousness which leads Daisy to be too exposed to the European ways. As a result of Mrs. Miller's careless ways, Daisy's innocence succumbs to the ways of traditional Italian society where the narrative is set, and then eventually dies of a fever she contracts in her visit to the Roman Coliseum.

As opposed to Mrs. Miller and her failure to understand the importance social manners acquire, aging ladies who are very aware of social status frequently populate English narratives during this time period. An archetypal character in this respect is Lady Catherine de Bourgh in Jane Austen's classic novel *Pride and Prejudice*. Lady Catherine is deeply conscious of class differences. As a character, she is highly-opinionated and usually advises people how to conduct their lives, however, she is also endowed with authority and respect as a member of the English aristocracy. Moreover, Lady Catherine is also Mr. Darcy's aunt, as well as Mr. Collins' benefactress, and as such, she tries to prevent Darcy from proposing to Elizabeth, even though her intentions ultimately prove to be of no avail. It is through Lady Catherine's admonitions that Elizabeth becomes aware of her own feelings towards Darcy and thus eventually decides to accept his proposal of marriage. Even if Lady Catherine is an aging lady who lives alone with her daughter, she exerts an important influence. Mr. Collins constantly praises her ways, and Mr. Darcy respects her authority. Even if Elizabeth is reluctant to accept Lady Catherine's warnings not to marry her nephew, she is aware of the social divide separating classes as her mother constantly reminds her of the necessity to marry well. Lady Catherine takes great care to ruin any prospects Mrs. Bennet has envisioned for her daughters, and yet it is through Lady Catherine that Elizabeth mostly gains insight into her true feelings with regard to Darcy.

An American counterpart to Lady Catherine de Bourgh is Aunt March in Louisa May Alcott's popular novel *Little Women*. Aunt March is presented as a preserver of social standards and domestic values. Given Aunt March's high social status and strict nature, she reprobates any opposition to social conventions. Aunt March finds Jo's tomboy manners totally inappropriate for a girl and she also cautions Meg to marry well, especially after her father leaves to fight in the American Civil War. Likewise, Aunt March does not hesitate to reprimand Meg in a very harsh manner when she decides to marry John Brooke, Laurie's private tutor, instead of a more appropriate suitor that would have helped the family with their economic constraints. Aunt March also resembles other aging widows and distant relatives in English narratives of the time. This resemblance becomes more evident when she decides to ask Amy to be her companion on her trip to Europe, thus initiating her in the ways of society, which will ultimately lead her to become Laurie's wife in the sequence *Good Wives*, and acquire a remarkable social position. In Louisa May Alcott's novel, the two main aging characters, Mr. Laurence, Laurie's grandfather, and Aunt March, even if endowed with wealth and social status, are often scorned by the younger members of the family, and are also generally depicted as self-important, bad-tempered, and distant with regard to their own relatives. In the case of Aunt March, she is also perceived as significantly Europeanized in her ways, especially given her frequent journeys to Europe.

Traditionally, aging women have been stereotypically portrayed as witches, or endowed with evil powers often owing to their extraordinary longevity. In gothic narratives, such as Joseph Sheridan Le Fanu's novella *Carmilla*, the middle-aged and apparently languid protagonist soon gets acquainted with Laura, becoming her guardian as well as her intimate friend. Laura is a young and innocent girl who seems to have met Carmilla for the first time in early dreams in her childhood, and precisely due to these latent memories, Carmilla manages to exert a permanently haunting influence on Laura. As the plot unfolds, Carmilla's reasonably young appearance becomes prematurely aged at certain points, thus physically embodying her dual nature as a female vampire. Carmilla's intercourse with Laura also initiates the latter into sexuality while as a vampire, she nurtures on her protégée to remain perpetually young, despite actually being outstandingly aged. Sheridan Le Fanu's vampire novella gives a significant centrality to an aging female character. Carmilla, however, is clearly stigmatized not only because she is a vampire, but also because she is an aged woman who pretends to be young, ultimately rejecting to act her true age.

The blurring boundaries between youth and age were also explored in Edgar Allan Poe's humorous piece entitled "The Spectacles." Poe's tale focuses on Simpson, a conceited young man who becomes infatuated with Madame Lalande, an apparently beautiful young girl he meets at the theater. Due to the pride he takes in his good looks, Simpson refuses to wear spectacles in spite of his short-sightedness, and even if his close friends seem to disapprove of Simpson's attraction towards Madame Lalande, the young man feels so sure about his feelings that he decides to propose to her. Aware of the young man's injudiciousness, Madame Lalande decides to teach him a lesson and accept his proposal of marriage under the condition he should start wearing eye-glasses. When Simpson sees his fiancée with his glasses on, he is astonished at Madame Lalande's extraordinarily aged appearance, ultimately learning she is truly a distant relative who tried to punish him for his conceit and his poor judgment. If in Sheridan Le Fanu's novella Carmilla's youthful appearance deceives people about her true age, in Poe's tale, it is Simpson's defective vision which makes him unable to perceive Madame Lalande's aged appearance. If Carmilla arises as a dangerous and lethal female vampire able to defy aging, Madame Lalande is scorned by the man who had praised her good looks when he believed her to be a young woman.

SAGES, PATRIARCHS AND LONERS: LITERARY ARCHETYPES OF THE MALE AGED

Likewise, portrayals of aging male characters are also recurrent in nine-teenth-century Anglo-American narratives, even though these characters are often presented from a slightly different perspective depending on the culture from which they arise. Through history, aging men have traditional-ly been presented as sages as well as religious patriarchs. As a case in point in Edward Bulwer-Lytton's domestic novel *The Caxtons*, Austin Caxton, the protagonist's father, is depicted as an aging scholar who instructs his son Pisistratus. Austin Caxton is often presented as a recluse who spends most of his days in the pursuit of knowledge so as to write a philosophical trea-tise. However, even though he is depicted as an individual far removed from the hectic everyday life due to his constant dedication to learning, he is held in high respect by the rest of his relatives, and Pisistratus frequently listens to his father's advice.

If Austin Caxton exemplifies the archetype of the aging sage in Victo-rian society, some contemporary American narratives also feature aging patriarchs associated with religion and especially with Puritanism. In this respect, the religious aging archetype becomes a prevalent character in Na-thaniel Hawthorne's narratives, even though this portrayal is significantly bleaker than the way Austin Caxton is depicted in Bulwer-Lytton's novel. In his tale "The Minister's Black Veil," set in a Puritan community during the seventeenth century, Reverend Hooper appears to be a highly-esteemed pa-triarch within the community. However, all of a sudden he begins to wear a black veil which covers his entire face. His concern about concealing his face has often been interpreted as a blatant sign of having committed an unknown but terrible sin. Thus, from being considered a highly respected individual, he necessarily becomes an outcast, even though his need to cover his face has also been interpreted as a symbol of collective sin. Both Austin Caxton and Reverend Hooper are depicted as separated from the community. Nonetheless, if Austin Caxton voluntarily becomes a recluse to work on his philosophical treatise, Reverend Hooper gradually loses his authority in the community, becoming an outcast despite his previously acknowledged authority as a priest.

In addition to sages and religious patriarchs, aging male characters often play the role of eccentric individuals that are even perceived as de-mented or mean men. As a result of an extraordinarily long lifetime, these aging individuals are necessarily set apart from the rest, and because of the ideas and beliefs they hold in relation to the present times, they are often scorned or considered odd and peculiar in their ways. As a result of their longevity, these aging characters are also presented as living embodiments of old-fashioned values blending ideas from former times with present-day beliefs. In this respect, Scrooge in Charles Dickens' *A Christmas Carol* is portrayed as a cold, utterly selfish, and miserly creditor who finally transforms as a result of being haunted by the ghosts of the past, the present, and the future. Even though he is at first presented as an old miser, detached and mean, he eventually repents and becomes a kind-hearted master who sympathizes with his workers.

In Washington Irving's well-known tale "Rip Van Winkle," the passage of time and aging are central. Rip goes to the forest and falls asleep during the days prior to the American War of Independence. Once he awakes and goes back to town, he gradually realizes that the United States of America have emerged as an entirely newly-established independent nation. For Rip, the transition of America from its subjection to England to an independent nation has literally taken place overnight. When Rip goes back to town, he realizes that he has aged remarkably in just one night, and many changes have occurred in what he perceives to be a very short span of time. The former King George III is no longer revered in town, and his neighbors and relatives look strikingly more aged than they did the last time he saw them. Likewise, due to his long beard and scruffy clothes, the neighbors in town firmly believe him a crazy old man. Most of his former neighbors are dead and no one can identify Rip Van Winkle, as he was presumed to have died many years ago. In this respect, in the young emerging American nation, Rip embodies history and memory and is deemed to be a remnant from the past. As a result of his appearance and the strange stories he tells, he is soon considered to be an eccentric and crazy old man whose stories are widely heard and enjoyed, but hardly ever believed.

In nineteenth-century narratives, aging male characters are often portrayed as father figures, even if endowed with different idiosyncratic features, either through sarcasm, reverence, or even awe. Although noticeably distant from his wife and his daughters, Mr. Bennet in Jane Austen's *Pride and Prejudice* arises as one of the most popular father figures in the Regency Period. In sharp contrast with his wife, Mrs. Bennet, who is dramatically concerned about her daughters' need to marry well, Mr. Bennet's witty and skeptical remarks prove a necessary counterpart to his wife's continuous migraines and passionate outbursts. Moreover, Mr. Bennet plays an important role to prevent his daughter Elizabeth from marrying Mr. Collins despite Mrs. Bennet's insistence. Thus, Mr. Bennet stands for common sense and skepticism in contrast to his wife's and daughters' exaggerated concern about marriage.

A similar situation unfolds in Henry James' novella *Washington Square*, as Catherine Sloper's prospective marriage to Morris Townsend causes an upheaval, as well as numerous discrepancies between Doctor Austin Sloper, Catherine's father, and his single sister, Lavinia Penniman. Even if both Austin Sloper and Mr. Bennet share common sense and rigorousness pertaining to father figure archetypes, the former lacks Mr. Bennet's witticism as well as his apparent nonchalance. Austin Sloper's critical opinion of Morris and his fraudulent intention to marry Catherine once he knows she is an heiress let down Lavinia and especially his daughter Catherine profoundly. Although Austin Sloper's suspicions eventually prove well-founded, his behavior towards his daughter is often heartless and cruel. His concern about not being swindled takes precedence over Catherine's chance of happiness. Austin's strictness and rigidity contrasts with the ironic father figure archetype exemplified by Mr. Bennet who despite his apparent indifference is presented as a devoted father, particularly with regard to his daughter Elizabeth.

In Nathaniel Hawthorne's short story "Rappaccini's Daughter," the sternness characterizing some aged male characters becomes more acute and even distinctly malicious. Rappaccini is depicted as an unethical scientist who experiments with the medicinal properties of plants and lives with his only daughter, Beatrice. His methods have been repeatedly questioned and he lives in isolation from the external world. The inherent connection between Beatrice and the scientist's venomous plant prevents her from moving beyond the garden surrounding their house. In an attempt to protect his daughter, Rappaccini made her poisonous like the plants he grows in his garden. Despite Rappaccini's love for his daughter, he is a tyrannical father who deprives his own daughter of her liberty as a result of his endeavors to protect her. Rappaccini also exemplifies the archetype of the aging scientist who trespasses the blurry lines separating science from ethics. In his unlimited and selfish attempt to gain insight into the forbidden, he makes use of unethical methods which have endowed him with power but have also turned him into an unscrupulous individual.

As another archetypal example, Robert Louis Stevenson's novella *The Strange Case of Doctor Jekyll and Mister Hyde* presents an aging scientist who manages to split his dual personality, acquiring a different appearance when he gives free vent to his basest instincts. In the Victorian society of the time, the highly-respected aging philanthropist scientist Henry Jekyll transforms into the nasty but younger Edward Hyde in order to release his instincts without putting his good name in jeopardy. As Edward Hyde, he expresses his evil side and acquires animalistic traits as a younger man full of energy and strength. This transformation presents different values concerning youth and age. The young Edward Hyde is fond of indulging in pleasures and dubious habits, while the older Henry Jekyll is a respectable member of the scientific community and of his social class. Although both Henry Jekyll and Edward Hyde respond to both sides of the same mirror, good and evil, they cannot exist without their apparent opposites. Both stages in the process of aging acquire different connotations.

This personal struggle between body and mind demands a separate existence. The moral dilemma between public and private that Jekyll and Hyde face in Victorian society is portrayed in American narratives as the individual's struggle to survive in a dangerous environment. Aging male characters have often been depicted as the last remnants of a particular type. In Edgar Allan Poe's tale "The Fall of the House of Usher," both Roderick and Madeline Usher struggle to survive even if they know their end is close. In a last attempt to hold on to life, Roderick Usher writes a letter to a friend from his youth to ask him for help. Roderick, prematurely aged and afflicted with an unusual state of nervousness, and Madeline, suffering from catalepsy, personify the aging of both body and mind. Both twins are the last of their kind living as invalids in their family's manor house. In this respect, the Ushers represent English traits and are doomed to disappear as a result of the political and social changes.

In the struggle of opposing forces in gothic narratives of the Victorian period, however, permanence of the old order is reinforced. In these narratives, wise and experienced aging characters represent the old order struggling to survive, even though their strength is rapidly declining. In Bram Stoker's seminal novel *Dracula*, Van Helsing leads a group of men struggling to overcome the evil power of the vampire as a personification of external forces disrupting the established order. Even if aged and tired, Van Helsing's experience and knowledge about the vampire's nature proves crucial in order to defeat the revenant. Van Helsing thus becomes an invaluable figure and Dracula's evident nemesis, eventually arising as the only remaining individual capable of annihilating the vampire before he dies. Van Helsing's mission is finally successful and thus order is reestablished and reinforced. In Poe's tale, however, the last survivors of the old order die.

CONCLUSION

In American and British nineteenth-century narratives, aging and aged characters are not given a central role, but they contribute significantly to the protagonist's coming-of-age. Consequently, they are depicted as secondary characters and do not develop – with some exceptions – within the narrative. Such an exception is Mr. Scrooge, who develops and transforms all through the narrative. Aged characters are also often associated with particular values, thus giving shape to particular archetypes developing in a recurrent pattern in the narratives.

Aged female characters are often presented as spinsters, strict aunts, opinionated mothers, high-class widows, or perfidious and wicked ladies. Likewise, aged male characters often play the role of sages, religious patriarchs, scientists, grumpy aristocrats, or eccentric outcasts. It is often the case that aging female characters exert their influence over members of their households, while the presence of aged male characters resonates and becomes more noticeable within the community.

Thus, male and female aging archetypes in nineteenth-century English and American narratives bear some resemblance, although the perceptions of these aging characters usually differ because of their historical, political and cultural differences. In Victorian England, aging characters are often associated with social class, authority, family and domestic values, experience, knowledge, hierarchy, and security. Consequently, old age, especially due to the economic and social power it often implied, was generally perceived in a more positive way. In America, especially in the years after gaining independence, aged characters in the narratives of the time were often perceived as personifications of the past subjection to the Old World, symbolizing an old order that had to be left behind. Thus, aging characters often represented the past and were at odds with the new and young emerging nation. Aging archetypes were thus depicted with more ambivalence, even on occasion as indifferent.

REFERENCES

Abel, Elizabeth, Marianne Hirsch, and Elizabeth Langland, eds. *The Voyage In: Fictions of Female Development*. Hannover and London: University Press of New England, 1983. Print.

Austen, Jane. *Pride and Prejudice*. London, 1813. Print.

Beauvoir, Simone de. *The Coming of Age*. Trans. Patrick O'Brian. New York: Warner Paperback Library, 1973. Print.

Brontë, Charlotte. *Jane Eyre*. London, 1847. Print.

Bulwer-Lytton, Edward. *Pelham; or, The Adventures of a Gentleman*. London, 1828. Print.

—. *The Caxtons: A Family Picture*. London, 1849. Print.

Butler, Robert N. "Ageism." *The Encyclopedia of Aging*. New York: Springer, 1987. 22-23. Print.

Chase, Karen. *The Victorians and Old Age*. Oxford: Oxford University Press, 2009. Print.

Cole, Thomas. *The Journey of Life: A Cultural History of Aging in America*. Cambridge: Cambridge University Press, 1992. Print.

Covey, Herbert C. *Older People in Western Art and Society*. New York: Praeger, 1991. Print.

Dickens, Charles. *A Christmas Carol*. London, 1843. Print.

—. *Great Expectations*. London, 1861. Print.

Garry, Jane, and Hasan El-Shamy, eds. *Archetypes and Motifs in Folklore and Literature: A Handbook*. London: M.E. Sharpe, 2005. Print.

Giles, Paul. *Transatlantic Insurrections: British Culture and the Formation of American Literature, 1730-1860*. Philadelphia: University of Pennsylvania Press, 2001. Print.

—. *Virtual Americas: Transnational Fictions and the Transatlantic Imaginary*. Durham: Duke University Press, 2002. Print.

Gullette, Margaret Morganroth. *Aged by Culture*. Chicago: University of Chicago Press, 2004. Print.

—. *Declining to Decline: Cultural Combat and the Politics of the Midlife*. Charlottesville, VA: University Press of Virginia, 1997. Print.

Hackett Fischer, David. *Growing Old in America*. Oxford: Oxford University Press, 1978. Print.

Hawthorne, Nathaniel. "The Minister's Black Veil." *The Token and Atlantic Souvenir*. Ed. Samuel Goodrich. Boston, 1836. Print.

—. "Rappaccini's Daughter." *Mosses from an Old Manse*. London, 1844. Print.

Heath, Kay. "In the Eye of the Beholder: Victorian Age Construction and the Specular Self." *Victorian Literature and Culture* 34.1 (2006): 27-45. Print.

Irving, Washington. "Rip Van Winkle." *The Sketch Book of Geoffrey Crayon*. New York, 1819. Print.

James, Henry. "Daisy Miller." *Cornhill Magazine*. London, 1879. Print

—. "Washington Square." *Cornhill Magazine*. London, 1880. Print.

Jung, Carl G. *Collected Works of C. G. Jung. Archetypes and the Collective Unconscious*. Ed. and Trans. by Gerhard Adler and R.F.C. Hull. Vol. 9.1. Princeton: Princeton University Press, 1969. Print.

Mangum, Teresa. "Growing Old: Age." *A Companion to Victorian Literature and Culture*. London: Blackwell, 2005. 97-109. Print.

May Alcott, Louisa. *Little Women*. Boston, 1868. Print.

Morris, John, ed. *Exploring Stereotyped Images in Victorian and Twentieth-Century Literature and Society*. New York: The Edwin Mellen Press, 1993. Print.

Poe, Edgar Allan. "The Fall of the House of Usher." *Burton's Gentleman's Magazine*, 1839. Print.

—. "The Spectacles." *Philadelphia Dollar Newspaper* 27 Mar. 1844, Philadelphia. Print.

Sheridan Le Fanu, Joseph. "Carmilla." *In A Glass Darkly*. London, 1872. Print.

Small, Helen. *The Long Life*. Oxford: Oxford University Press, 2007. Print.

Stevenson, Robert Louis. *The Strange Case of Dr. Jekyll and Mr. Hyde*. New York, 1886. Print.

Stoker, Bram. *Dracula*. London, 1897. Print.

Thane, Pat. *Old Age in English History. Past Experiences, Present Issues*. Oxford: Oxford University Press, 2000. Print.

Twain, Mark. *The Adventures of Tom Sawyer*. Hartford, 1876. Print.

Woodward, Kathleen. "Instant Repulsion: Decrepitude, the Mirror Stage, and the Literary Imagination." *Kenyon Review* 5.4 (1983): 43-66. Print.

Beyond *Dis*-Ease

Positive Female Aging against the Cult of Invalidism

in Ellen Glasgow's Last Two Novels

Emma Domínguez-Rué

The 'Angelas' of Miss Glasgow's later novels would more fully illustrate the causal connections between the moribund chivalric tradition (especially in its Victorian southern form), evasive idealism, the sheltered life, feminine invalidism, and commonplace feminine tyranny through the solicitation of sympathy. (Raper, *Without Shelter* 224-25)

In *Without Shelter: the Early Career of Ellen Glasgow*, Julius Rowan Raper aptly reflects upon the potential source of power that the icon of female invalidism provided in the fiction of the Virginia writer Ellen Glasgow (1873-1945). Glasgow's literary gallery of tyrannical invalids clearly illustrates the fact that feigning sickness or actually becoming sick constituted a socially accepted strategy to achieve a considerable degree of influence in the domestic sphere, which women rarely attained if healthy. At the same time, her novels are also evidence of self-victimization that women's adherence to the ideal of femininity entails, and it condemns them to constant weakness (real or imagined) while it perpetuates their dependence and their utter disempowerment within the constraints of patriarchy.

This article examines the relationship between illness (both as a real condition and as a metaphor) and invalidism as seen in Glasgow's last two novels, *In This Our Life* (1941) and its short sequel *Beyond Defeat: An Epilogue to an Era*, published posthumously in 1966. The pervasive presence of illness in both novels, mainly embodied by the invalid character of Lavinia Timberlake, and the author's own struggle with frail health have lead both readers and critics to regard them as evidence of Glasgow's decline in creative energy. Even though Glasgow's heart condition was indeed serious during her final years, this essay contends that these two novels served Glasgow to reassess her complex and sometimes contradictory relationship with illness and invalidism, while she reaffirmed her identity both as a woman and an artist.

Glasgow began writing *In This Our Life* in 1937, but its development was frequently interrupted. The writing process was often curtailed by the author's frail condition because her health was becoming increasingly poor. Many of her letters are evidence of Glasgow's prolonged periods of illness during those years. As she wrote to H. L. Mencken in January 1939, her weak heart forced her to lead "the life of an invalid" (Glasgow, *Letters* 248). Despite those difficulties, she still hoped to finish the last novel she would live to see published, stating, "if only my capacity for work will last as long as I do, I shall feel that I am satisfied" (Glasgow, *Letters* 249). According to biographer Susan Goodman, Glasgow's first heart attack occurred in December 1939, and she experienced a second one on August 9, 1940. In the summer of 1940, Glasgow spent a month in hospital in New York, where "the cardiologist told her that she might live six weeks or six months" (Goodman 228).

Despite her feeble health, Glasgow's later years were extremely productive. In 1942, *In This Our Life* was awarded the Pulitzer Prize for Fiction for the year 1941, although, as Goodman asserts, it was more a recognition of her whole literary career than a specific acknowledgement of the novel's quality (236). According to some Glasgow scholars, she had been deeply disappointed when T. S. Stribling won the Pulitzer for *The Store* in 1933 even though Glasgow's *The Sheltered Life* (1932) was a clear favorite to the award (Thiebaux xi; Wagner 91). Therefore, Glasgow probably regarded the success of *In This Our Life* and the subsequent award of the Pulitzer Prize as both a literal and literary recovery, especially after her heart condition had seriously threatened her life. Precisely due to the author's painful experiences during the long period of her convalescence, and despite the fact that illness physically hindered her writing process, the novels are evidence that this experience was the source of her creativity, helping her develop her view of the tyrannical invalids she had since so stalwartly criticized.

In This Our Life[1] is set in the town of Queenborough, a fictionalized version of Richmond. The novel starts in 1938 and ends in 1939, on the eve of World War II. As Thiebaux among other critics observes, this novel concludes Glasgow's social history of Virginia which had started in the Civil War with *The Battle-Ground* (1902) and thus exceeds her fifty years of literary production and even her own lifetime (163). The opening scene presents Asa Timberlake, a fifty-nine-year-old man who observes the changes taking place in an increasingly industrialized Queenborough, while he reflects upon the evolution of his own life. For more than forty-five years, he has been a menial worker with a scant salary in the tobacco factory that had once belonged to his grandfather. After a short period of infatuation, his marriage to Lavinia proves miserable although he feels morally responsible for his invalid wife who is completely dependent on him.

Lavinia Timberlake is the last and one of the best of Glasgow's despotic invalids: her constant complaints, her medicine and doctors as well as her hypochondria absolutely pervade the novel. Lacking beauty or charm as a young woman, she managed to induce Asa into marriage and since then tyrannized him and the rest of the family by pretending to be ill. In *Ellen Glasgow*, Blair Rouse defines Lavinia as "one of the most insufferably repulsive creations ever encountered in the pages of fiction. She is selfish, soft, sentimental and cruel – but she is by no means a fool" (124-25). Rouse's final remark probably refers to Asa's acknowledgement of his wife's intelligence, "after all, Lavinia might be a fraud, but she was nobody's fool" (Glasgow, *ITOL* 38). In *The End of a Legend: Ellen Glasgow's History of Southern Women*, Barbro Ekman also comments on this point in her description of Lavinia as one of Glasgow's "victimizers" (Ekman 97-98). She contends that while Angela Gay in *The Miller of Old Church* (1911) and Angelica Blackburn in *The Builders* (1919) control their families through affected weakness but never openly admit to it, Lavinia consciously decides to become a chronic invalid (Ekman 97-98). Like her predecessors in Glasgow's earlier works of fiction, Lavinia is aware of the empowering possibilities of feigning invalidism and has voluntarily embraced the tradition of female self-immolation in order to use it as a weapon.

As Julius Rowan Raper states in *Without Shelter: the Early Career of Ellen Glasgow*, "Lavinia [...] is one of the grotesque invalids the sheltered life makes of women" (247). Critics have abundantly discussed Lavinia's char-

---

acter as the personification of everything that is malicious and disgusting. In my opinion, however, her cruelty ultimately inspires more pity than contempt since her self-centeredness paradoxically reveals a total lack of self. Raper's analysis of the novel in *From the Sunken Garden: the Fiction of Ellen Glasgow, 1916-1945* defines Lavinia's control over Asa as "matriarchal tyranny" (Raper 173), disregarding the fact that the cult of invalidism is actually a male construct. What he terms as "the tyranny of Lavinia's tradition" (Raper 185) is not a female tradition but a patriarchal invention whose first victim is Lavinia herself. Upon reflection, her perverse pleasure in tormenting her husband seems to be proof of her miserable life and her emptiness as a person. In *Disorderly Conduct: Visions of Gender in Victorian America*, historian Carroll Smith-Rosenberg pertinently notes that the invalid, like the hysteric, has "purchased her escape from the emotional [...] demands of her life only at the cost of pain, disability, and an intensification of women's traditional passivity and dependence" (197-217). Lavinia's internalization of the cult of invalidism and its adjoining values of dependence, selflessness, and extreme delicacy has indeed turned her into a monster. Nonetheless, it is worth remembering that she is a pathetic example of the atrocious beings that male-defined ideals make of women, which have above all destroyed the woman Lavinia could have been.

Biographer Susan Goodman posits that Glasgow wanted this novel "to communicate whatever wisdom she had gained from suffering and joy" (232). Aside from Glasgow's own delicate health, the author's mother Ann Gholson had left a debilitating legacy of invalidism and disempowerment that had always been present in the author's life. As late as 1942, Glasgow still recalled her mother's breakdown in a letter to her friend Bessie Zaban Jones (July 20, 1942) and remembered how, as a child, she had pictured her as "a beautiful shadow" (Glasgow, *Letters* 303-04). After giving birth to ten children and coping with an unsympathetic and unfaithful husband, Mrs. Glasgow developed serious uterine problems and had several nervous breakdowns, which progressively turned her into an invalid. The bittersweet knowledge Glasgow had gained from a lifetime of love, friendship, ill health, and loss, as well as the severe heart condition she was suffering at the time, is plausibly the reason why illness (especially illness as *dis*-ease) is present in *In This Our Life* more than in any other of her novels. Rather than being proof of an inferior quality, this process demonstrates the author's capacity to use her life experience (however painful) as a catalyst to creativity.

In a quite tangible way, Lavinia's condition seems to serve as a visible emblem for the complete disempowerment that adherence to this code entails. There is an all-encompassing sense of sickness that seems to affect almost every character in the novel. Lavinia's pernicious influence is perceived most effectively in the unambiguous contrast Glasgow establishes between the two Timberlake sisters, Roy and Stanley. The younger Stanley represents the fashionable and superficial beauty who looks modern in appearance but who is still defined according to traditional male standards. Thiebaux argues that Glasgow pictures Stanley as a newer version of the Victorian Southern lady, "who inherited the evasive idealism of her forebears but not their self-restraint" (164). Roy, in contrast, as her father reflects, has "all the qualities that men have missed and wanted in women: courage, truthfulness, a tolerant sense of humor, loyalty to impersonal ends" (Glasgow, *ITOL* 18-19).

Roy Timberlake is one of Glasgow's well-known courageous heroines, and the reader immediately identifies Roy with her father and his moral qualities; she is sensible, intelligent, hard-working, and conscious of Lavinia's deceptiveness. Apart from Asa's friend Kate Oliver, Roy is the only character who understands and sympathizes with Asa's miserable and unfulfilling life while the rest of the family tends to regard him as ruined because of his family's decline in wealth and social status. Roy is a modern and thoroughly independent woman who has successfully combined marriage with professional life – or so she thinks. While she works in an interior decorating shop, she is passionately in love with her surgeon husband Peter Kingsmill. However, as she tells her father, "he knows I'd never hold him" and both are "perfectly free to change if we wish" (Glasgow, *ITOL* 31-32).

Her beautiful, selfish, and spoilt sister Stanley is engaged to the lawyer Craig Fleming, but instead she fancies her attractive brother-in-law and elopes with him just before her wedding with Craig. Roy is of course devastated but refuses to be defeated by her husband's betrayal. She grants Peter a divorce so that he and Stanley can get married, and carries on with her own life. In contrast, after Stanley deserts him, Craig Fleming shows his weakness by indulging in self-pity and abusing alcohol.

Apart from her mother, Stanley Timberlake is one of the most powerful protagonists of the novel representing the omnipresent atmosphere of illness as *dis*-ease. She embodies the prototype of the stunningly beautiful blonde who lives only for her appearance and who believes that her beauty entitles her to everything. Her marriage to her former brother-in-law Peter Kingsmill soon proves a disaster as Stanley spends money beyond their means, goes out with other men, and aborts their baby. From the beginning, Peter is portrayed as shallow and lacking in moral strength. As early as chapter V, Asa prophetically observes that he "has the hands, but not the temperament, of a surgeon" (Glasgow, *ITOL* 41). When he cannot cope with his life with Stanley anymore, he surrenders to excessive drinking and finally commits suicide. Stanley comes back to Queenborough in a wrecked state of mind and, predictably, is pitied and sheltered by her family. Her loveliness and her long 'convalescence,' which clearly emulate her mother's façade of illness and suffering, enable her to escape her share of guilt for breaking her sister's marriage and providing the stimulus to Peter's suicide.

Besides providing an impulse to her literary creativity, Glasgow's later years also seem to reveal an evolution in her view of women who learn to feign helplessness to gain more control over their families. Her last two novels seem to be evidence of a development in her attitude towards tyrannical invalids. While her previous works openly condemn their behavior, maturity, and experience, *In This Our Life* and *Beyond Defeat* seem to have given her a wider sense of perspective and a greater awareness of the invalids' plight. Glasgow censures the family's obvious predilection for Stanley mainly because it reveals, as Marcelle Thiebaux posits, that "males esteem female sexuality, turpitude, and weakness over intelligence and independence" (170). Taking Lavinia as a role model, Stanley soon learns that an appearance of frailty and helplessness is a powerful weapon she can use to her own advantage. Like her mother, she also ignores the fact that her acquiescence to that tradition implies a complete loss of identity that is ultimately self-destructive. In Stanley, Glasgow typifies the conventional woman who, as late as 1939, has been debilitated by her own power to lure men. Since her power resides in her acceptance of patriarchal standards, it necessarily requires her entrapment within those conventions. As a result of her internalization of that stereotype she can only define her existence as a mirror of the male gaze, that is, in terms of the effect her hyper-feminine charm elicits in men.

Blair Rouse argues that Stanley embodies "the evils of sham, of happiness-hunters, and of dangerous selfishness." Stanley's loveliness enables her "to twist men and sentimental women about her finger", while her apparent innocence and sweetness conceal "an insidious evil quality more dangerous than poison. She is completely amoral. [...] If she wants something, then she must have it [...], she knows no remorse, only fear of punishment" (Rouse124-26). Raper similarly defines Stanley as "an irresponsible innocent" (Raper, *From the Sunken Garden* 174). In their description, both Rouse and Raper focus on Stanley's childish behavior, motivated only by desire, but they overlook the fact that the same system that grants her immunity also disempowers her. She eludes responsibility for her actions precisely because, in a male-defined society, she does not hold the status of a mature, independent and autonomous human being. In *A Certain Measure*, Glasgow reflects that Stanley is not consciously wicked, but simply driven by her childish whims and her appeal to others, "she is not evil; she is insufficient. She is not hard; she is, on the contrary, so soft in fiber that she is ruled or swayed by sensation. She embodies the perverse life of unreason [...] which destroys its own happiness" (259).

After her period of convalescence following Peter's suicide, Stanley goes back to her former thoughtless and irresponsible conduct. In the attempt to escape the emptiness and meaninglessness of her life, she turns to reckless driving in the expensive sports car her mother's uncle William Fitzroy has bought her. One night, she accidentally runs over a woman and her young daughter, killing the child. Unsurprisingly, instead of admitting to the crime, she runs away from the scene and leaves her car in the area of town of the black community. When the police arrive to make inquiries about the car, she indirectly accuses the worthy mulatto chauffeur Parry Clay, and Parry is immediately arrested and imprisoned. Stanley's family believes her story without question, except for her father, who notices the incongruities in her version of the events and makes her confess. Asa, however, finds himself alone in his struggle to act ethically. His family tries to convince him that it is not advisable to tell the authorities the truth. Of course, Stanley succeeds in appearing as an innocent victim by resorting to hysterical weeping and appealing to the protection of her mother, William Fitzroy, and Craig Fleming:

'You're cruel to me. You never loved me . . . It's only you. The others wouldn't be cruel [...]. Oh, Mother, oh, Uncle William, he wants to make me go to court! He wants to send me to prison! Oh, Uncle William, don't let him!' [...] It was Charlotte who, at last and too abruptly, shattered the silence. 'She ought to have bromide or something. You'd better send for the doctor.' 'She isn't herself,' Lavinia whispered. 'Asa has nearly killed her.' (Glasgow, *ITOL* 267-70)

Fitzroy insists on concealing the truth by arguing that "that's no way to treat a child" and that "she couldn't stand anything more." Craig, who is mesmerized by Stanley's performance of helplessness, betrays his principles and agrees with Fitzroy that "we'll do the best we can for the boy." Charlotte Fitzroy similarly argues that it is best to let Parry be sentenced on the grounds that "colored people don't feel things the way we do [...] not as a young girl would" (Glasgow, *ITOL* 270-71). Remarkably, Charlotte defends conventional femininity when she is precisely another of its victims. While Asa points to Charlotte's apparent simplicity, he remembers that "when William was absent one day, he had seen her display actual intelligence and a firm hand with an emergency" (Glasgow, *ITOL* 41). After her marriage to Fitzroy, the reader presumes, Charlotte's qualities have been progressively eclipsed by her husband's power and wealth, and she has been forced to assume a more convenient mask of docility.

As happened after Peter's suicide, the Timberlakes appeal to Stanley's "truly feminine" sweetness and delicacy to spare her from facing her responsibility. On the surface, they lie in order to protect women from the implacability of justice, although such acts reveal the moral codes that Glasgow continuously denounces in most of her novels. In Dorothy M. Scura's edition of Glasgow scholarship, Helen Fiddyment Levy notices that Stanley is repeatedly defined as a baby, a doll, and a child: as she remarks, she is a mere "mannequin [...] created by male desire and feminine weakness" (227). Fitzroy and Lavinia, the representatives of tradition, have encouraged her immature behavior by consistently indulging her, thereby preventing her development into adulthood. Under the pretense of 'sheltering' women from the unpleasant aspects of life, these standards perpetuate their powerlessness through the denial of their status as mature human beings.

In This Our Life seems to unveil the pernicious consequences that the code of genteel behavior produces in people of both sexes by replicating female imprisonment in the conventions of domesticity. Asa is trapped by his marriage to Lavinia and his duty to provide for the family. As Wagner notes, "even the fact that his father – faced with incurable illness – committed suicide under the old willow is a positive image when set against the mean invalidism of Asa's wife" (112). Rouse significantly argues that

Asa "has been hurt by circumstance and has sustained a psychic or spiritual wound which has permanently changed him." He describes him as "genuine" in the sense that he "refuses to pretend to himself any longer," becoming "more an observer than a participant" (105). Thiebaux holds a similar view and defines him as "an insensitive observer of what happens to the rest of the family" and as "the irritable mouthpiece of an aging, invalid author who found much to dislike in the world" (169). However, Asa's role in the novel is remarkable precisely because of his capacity for observation, and his participation in the plot is indeed crucial with regards to the events connected to the car accident. His decision to take action against the injustice of blaming Parry for the crime is certainly courageous and clearly defies conventions, as his fatherly duty would have been to protect his daughter. As *Beyond Defeat* will disclose, Glasgow did not view Asa's mature years as a further decline into misery and despair, but as a resolute move towards happiness and fulfillment.

Although he might appear dejected, Asa is not without hope. His occasional Sunday afternoon walks with Kate Oliver give him happiness and peace of mind. Her farm, "Hunter's Fare," is the haven where he longs to escape from Lavinia's sick and sickening influence. Upon William Fitzroy's death, Asa expects that his wife will inherit enough money to be economically independent so that he will be able to leave her and live with Kate. Fitzroy is truly ill with cancer, although he refuses to acknowledge the reality of his condition until it is too late. Fitzroy is regarded as the most prominent man in Queenborough because he has amassed a fortune in business. He is one of Glasgow's "great men" of the New South who are respected because of their wealth; however he embodies everything that is mean and abhorrent. Blair Rouse describes him as "a wonderfully repulsive portrait of an avaricious, ruthless, insensitive, yet sentimental Southern man of affairs." As he ironically comments, Fitzroy "might keep platinum blonde mistresses in New York, but he is a faithful worshipper at the Episcopal Church in Queenborough." Fitzroy is obviously partial to Stanley, "because of his lecherous, more than avuncular interest in his full-lipped, bright-haired niece." While Stanley has learned how to use her flirtatious charm to obtain money and expensive presents from him, Roy refuses "to prostitute herself to his attentions" (125).

During Stanley's absence, Craig and Roy establish a bond of friendship that turns into affection. Craig's attachment to her, as Rouse remarks, is grounded on his belief that Roy "has rescued him from himself and despair." Similarly, his attempts to convince her into marriage are mainly motivated by the fact that "he needs her" (126). Despite his liberal ideas and his apparent modernity, Craig's affection for Roy reproduces the patriarchal assumption that women are responsible for uplifting men spiritually and saving them from their weak nature. As is the case with Peter Kingsmill, Glasgow plainly depicts Craig Fleming as a flawed partner for Roy. Both Peter and Craig claim to admire her intelligence and her moral qualities but, although they belong to a new generation of men, both desert her for the more appealing (and less threatening) standard of womanhood that Stanley represents. Again, the incongruity of Southern moral standards is made patent: while women are expected to provide an example of ethical values to both husband and family, men do not choose women with greater intelligence or a strong personality as their partners, but conveniently prefer those who have been brought up in superficial values, ignorance, and moral shallowness. Again recalling Stanley's comparison with a baby and a doll, women like her are not thought to gain in intelligence or wisdom as they age. Although they are expected to reign in the domestic as proper 'angels in the house,' to use Virginia Woolf's term (Woolf 286), they are never regarded as proper adults and thus remain holding the status of children.

Roy's suspicions about Craig's lack of moral stance are finally confirmed, when he loyally supports Stanley after the car accident, and afterwards when he compromises his integrity as a lawyer by betraying Parry. Roy realizes that Craig never got over his fascination with her sister's beauty, so she breaks up her engagement and leaves the house. While walking the streets of Queenborough in the rainy night, absorbed in her disillusionment, she meets a young Englishman who is about to join the army in Europe, and spends the night with him. The following morning she goes back home, but only to pack her belongings, since she has decided to leave Queenborough. One of her last sentences in the novel attests to her moral strength, as she still retains hopes of a better future, "I want something to hold by! I want something good!" (Glasgow, *ITOL* 302). Predictably, only her father truly grieves over her departure and understands her words. Throughout the novel, his reflections have uncovered conventional family life as the cause of physical, psychological and emotional *dis*-ease: in her study of *In This Our Life*, Thiebaux also describes the institution of family as "a hotbed of ills" (170). Asa is conscious of the fact that, like him, Roy needs a more fulfilling existence, which she will not find amidst the suffocating atmosphere that surrounds her life in Queenborough.

In her book of prefaces *A Certain Measure*, Glasgow stated that "there is a shock at the discovery that, in print, one must be brutally obvious if one wishes not to be misconstrued" (249). According to several Glasgow scholars, the author was dissatisfied with many of the reviewers' and the readers' approach to the novel which regarded Roy and, above all, Asa, as failed and dispirited characters (Wagner 111-113; Raper, *From the Sunken Garden* 177; Rouse 129-30). This simplistic reading was probably further encouraged by the Hollywood film version released in 1942, starring Olivia de Havilland as Roy and Bette Davis as Stanley. Glasgow sold the rights to Warner Brothers for $40,000 but, as she feared, the film emphasized the romance plot and the rivalry between the two sisters. Although she finally decided not to publish it, Glasgow felt compelled to write a short sequel to the novel, which she entitled *Beyond Defeat: An Epilogue to an Era*.

On December 31, 1942, Glasgow had another heart attack. As Goodman states, "during the next two years, she did what conceivably kept her alive [...]. In August [1944], Glasgow physically could not write [...] she could type with just one finger. Even walking proved beyond her" (237-38). During those final years, she remained confined to her bedroom and (when her condition allowed her to move from her bed or the sofa) the adjoining room. Goodman mentions that one of Glasgow's intimate friends, Bessie Zaban Jones, remembered visiting her and visualizing her bedroom as "a place steeped in the atmosphere of Victorian ill-health" (239).

Critics have often regarded *Beyond Defeat* as a minor work. However, as Helen Fiddyment Levy posits, the sequel helped Glasgow "to resolve the perceived conflict between her own literary art and her gender [...]. Glasgow at last found a faith in the future that merged female identity and independent creativity" (220). In contrast to arguments that regard aging as a process towards loss of identity, Maierhofer considers "female aging as a paradigm of American culture, as aging [...] does not bring a loss of identity, but emphasizes difference instead of communality [...] and expresses individualism more prominently than in youth" (24). Glasgow's experience seems to substantiate Fiddyment Levy's and Maierhofer's views, as her weakening health offered her increasing inspiration. The quality of her writing certainly attests to this, since most scholars agree that Glasgow wrote her most celebrated masterpieces from age fifty onwards. As Glasgow recalls in her autobiography, at the time she wrote *Barren Ground*, "my imagination was more vital and urgent than it had ever been [...] I felt younger at sixty than I had felt at twenty" (Glasgow, *The Woman Within* 270-72).

Beyond Defeat describes a day in the life of Roy and Asa Timberlake in 1942, three years after the end of *In This Our Life*. William Fitzroy has died, bequeathing a considerable amount of money to his niece Lavinia, allowing Asa to finally work happily on Kate Oliver's farm. Stanley has moved to Hollywood (ironically, the place of appearances and artificiality) with her new lover, a cinema producer. The sequel also reveals that, as a consequence of her one-night stand with the unknown Englishman, Roy has given birth to a boy she calls Timothy. Critics disagree on the significance of Timothy seemingly personifying Roy's (and, by extension, all women's) liberation from the limitations of patriarchal control. Roy conceives a child outside the traditional family structure and hence fulfills an important aspect of her womanhood without the constraints of a conventional heterosexual relationship. Interestingly, Louis Auchincloss complains about Glasgow's insistence upon the victimization of "fallen women" when he comments on the character of Millie Burden in *They Stooped to Folly* (1929): "Why then, in 1929, did the author keep flogging so dead a horse? Is it possible that she was beginning to feel that the age of prejudices at least had standards? That one could only have ladies if one burned witches?" (79). Apparently, as late as 1944, the author felt there was still much to say (and much more to do) about the plight of single mothers.

Roy seriously ill with pneumonia and on the verge of death echoes Glasgow's recovery after the serious heart attacks she had suffered. Scholars like Helen Fiddyment Levy and Marcelle Thiebaux have commented on Roy's recovery as the literary expression of the author's regained health (Fiddyment Levy 221; Thiebaux 172). Roy returns to Queenborough because she needs someone to take care of her son while she goes to the Adirondacks to regain her lost strength. Charlotte Fitzroy, now a well-provided widow, is enjoying a comfortable old age after the long torment of her married life and does not wish to be troubled with the responsibility of caring for the child. Charlotte's newly acquired economic position seems to have given her the social status and respect that aged males traditionally enjoy in the South as the possessors of wisdom. Predictably, Lavinia refuses to acknowledge an illegitimate child, and only accepts to look after Timothy, if Roy can convince Asa to return. In clear contrast to Charlotte, Lavinia has also become wealthier but has remained an ailing child-woman. Besides perpetuating her disempowerment, years have not given Lavinia any wisdom or intelligence, but have instead increased her bitterness and prevented her development towards adulthood and self-realization. Lavinia's tragic story represents the most unpleasant image of mature womanhood, which Glasgow consistently denounced both in fiction and in life. Beneath the evident anger distilled through Glasgow's portrayal of Lavinia, however, the author was perhaps reflecting on her own life experience and the kind of woman she herself might have been, had she succumbed to the pressures of patriarchal constraints.

Kate Oliver generously welcomes the boy to Hunter's Fare and invites Roy to live with them once she recovers. According to Helen Fiddyment Levy, the creation of Kate responds to the author's lifelong search for some of the women's voices that had been suffocated by culture in an attempt to "reproduce the communal feelings of the woman-centered homeland." Kate is portrayed as an image of female self-fulfillment that implies, as Fiddyment Levy asserts, "that womanliness is an active force for enrichment of both nature and culture" (221, 230). In contrast, Kathryn Lee Seidl argues that "Glasgow's strong protagonists are singularly alone" and contends that her female characters generally do not have the support of other women. She states that "since their mothers destroy the feeling that home is a safe haven and since men are disappointing at best, one might think Glasgow would have had her heroines turn to friends for comfort and support. Such is not the case" (292). To my mind, *In This Our Life* and *Beyond Defeat* clearly show a brighter future for Glasgow's strong heroines Roy Timberlake and Kate Oliver. Kate's farm, for example, attests to Glasgow's endeavor to portray an alternative female world of nurturance. Her self-made home, the product of her physical work as well as of her intuition and imagination, provides a haven for all those who have been enfeebled and almost destroyed by the sickening influence of patriarchal conventions. As opposed to the Victorian cult of female invalidism and the patriarchal view of woman as an idealized object of the male gaze, this obviously relegates mature women to invisibility and a feeling of uselessness. Scholars such as Germaine Greer argue that women's middle years and especially menopause can bring about a quest for identity unhindered by reproductive aspects and a path towards real autonomy and an authentic self (367-68). Similar to how Roy can now approach middle age with hope of a fulfilling life, Kate seems to represent Glasgow's image of the mature woman whose experience and insight have allowed her to face old age as a promise, not as an end, but rather as a new beginning.

Raper also points to Glasgow's view of the traditional family as a source of *dis*-ease when he comments on Kate's alternative concept of home, stating that "the false families which our past and our facile emotions have imposed upon us may be replaced by better families, families to be created out of the core of our own being" (*From the Sunken Garden* 191-92). Like other strong heroines in Glasgow's novels, Kate is childless, but she provides the fertile soil of warmth and understanding that Glasgow envisions as the ideal home of shared female affection. In contrast, literal mothers like Lavinia, as Fiddyment Levy argues, merely engender psychological and emotional barrenness, and ultimately self-destruction, and "the calculating relationships of Fitzroy, Lavinia, and Stanley produce only death, heartache, and sterility" (227). The novel ends with Lavinia's death, the promise of Roy's return to Hunter's Fare, and a renewal of the relationship between Roy and Craig, who offers to marry her and adopt Timothy after he returns from the war. In her last work of fiction, as Fiddyment Levy states, "Glasgow transcends the victimization that threatens her strongest female protagonists" (225), finally exorcising the shadow of illness and invalidism that had haunted both her life and her fiction.

As Wyatt-Brown notes in her introduction to *Aging & Gender in Literature: Studies in Creativity*, some of the best-known novels from the turn of the century up to the 1930s include middle-aged characters who "appear and simultaneously decay [...]. T.S. Eliot's "Love Song of J. Alfred Prufrock" (1915), F. Scott Fitzgerald's *Tender Is the Night* (1934) [...] and Evelyn Waugh's *Brideshead Revisited* (1944) [...] supported the tendency to think of aging-into-the-midlife as a traverse to loss, disaster, or possibly death" (27). This seems not to be the case of female authors who, like Glasgow, did not experience middle or old age as crippling, but felt at their creative best as they approached maturity.

Women work long years and wait for success, and if it ever comes, success then enriches their middle and later years. [...] surviving years of disappointment or neglect, they received the greatest gift of all from age, the sense of increasing powers. (Wyatt-Brown 38)

As Glasgow explains in her autobiography *The Woman Within*, "my physical weakness, after the heartbreaking strain of a divided life, appeared to lend light and warmth to my imagination. Pain had not defeated me. It had made me defiant and more confident in my inner powers" (270). Glasgow was thus capable of using her literary creativity as therapy to break free from her fears of illness, old age and death by imagining a fictional home-land in which both men and women could overcome sickness and *dis*-ease. Similarly, as Will Brantley writes while commenting on Glasgow's auto-biography, Glasgow understood that "the autobiographical impulse is of necessity a shaping impulse – that ultimately one defines the self by writing the self" (93). The sequel that Glasgow wrote, while thoughts of an impending death most probably troubled her mind, denotes, as Thiebaux states, "not only a homecoming [...] but astonishingly [...] a return from the grave. The main character, having passed through death's sickly shadow, seems to rise again to a new paradisal world" (172).

REFERENCES

Auchincloss, Louis. *Pioneers and Caretakers: A Study of 9 American Women Novelists*. Minneapolis: University of Minnesota Press, 1965. Print.

Brantley, Will. *Feminine Sense in Southern Memoir: Smith, Glasgow, Welty, Hellmann, Porter, and Hurston*. Jackson: University Press of Mississippi, 1993. Print.

Ekman, Barbro. *The End of a Legend: Ellen Glasgow's History of Southern Women*. Stockholm and Uppsala: Almqvist & Wiksell, 1979. Print.

Fiddyment Levy, Helen. "Coming Home: Glasgow's Last Two Novels." *Ellen Glasgow: New Perspectives*. Ed. Dorothy M. Scura. Knoxville: University of Tennessee Press, 1995. 220-34. Print.

Gore, Luther Y. "'Literary Realism or Nominalism' by Ellen Glasgow." *American Literature* 34.1 (1962): 72-79. Print.

Glasgow, Ellen. *A Certain Measure: An Interpretation of Prose Fiction*. New York: Harcourt Brace, 1943. Print.

—. *Barren Ground*. New York: Hill and Wang, 1957. Print.

—. *Beyond Defeat: An Epilogue to an Era*. Ed. Luther Y. Gore. Charlottesville: University Press of Virginia, 1966. Print.

—. *In This Our Life*. New York: Harcourt, Brace and Company, 1941. Print.

—. *Letters of Ellen Glasgow*. Ed. Blair Rouse. New York: Harcourt Brace and Company, 1958. Print.

—. *The Builders*. Garden City, New York: Doubleday, Page and Company, 1919. Print.

—. *The Miller of Old Church*. Garden City, New York: Doubleday, Page and Company, 1911. Print.

—. *The Sheltered Life.* New York: Harvest/HBJ, 1985. Print.

—. *The Woman Within.* New York: Hill and Wang, 1980. Print.

Goodman, Susan. *Ellen Glasgow: A Biography.* Baltimore and London: Johns Hopkins University Press, 1998. Print.

Greer, Germaine. *The Change: Women, Aging and the Menopause.* New York: Knopf, 1992. Print.

Maierhofer, Roberta. "An Anocritical Reading of American Culture: The Old Woman as the New American Hero." *Journal of Aging, Humanities, and the Arts* 1.1 (2007): 23-33. Print.

Raper, Julius Rowan. *From the Sunken Garden: the Fiction of Ellen Glasgow, 1916-1945.* Baton Rouge: Louisiana State University Press, 1980. Print.

—. *Without Shelter: the Early Career of Ellen Glasgow.* Baton Rouge: Louisiana State University Press, 1971. Print.

Rouse, Blair. *Ellen Glasgow.* New York: Twayne Publishers, 1962. Print.

Seidl, Kathryn Lee. "Gail Godwin and Ellen Glasgow: Southern Mothers and Daughters." *Tulsa Studies in Women's Literature* 10.2 (1991): 287-94. Print.

Smith-Rosenberg, Carroll. "The Hysterical Woman: Sex Roles and Role Conflict in Nineteenth-Century America." *Disorderly Conduct: Visions of Gender in Victorian America.* New York: Alfred Knopf, 1985, 197-217. Print.

Thiebaux, Marcelle. *Ellen Glasgow.* New York: Frederick Ungar, 1982. Print.

Wagner, Linda W. *Ellen Glasgow: Beyond Convention.* Austin: University of Texas Press, 1982. Print.

Woolf, Virginia. "Professions for Women." *Collected Essays.* Vol. 2. Ed. Leonard Woolf. London: Chatto and Windus, 1966. 284-89. Print.

Wyatt-Brown, Anne M., and Janice Rossen, eds. *Aging & Gender in Literature: Studies in Creativity.* Charlottesville and London: University Press of Virginia, 1993. Print.

Growing Old and Searching for Identity in Anne Tyler's *Noah's Compass* (2009) and Umberto Eco's *The Mysterious Flame of Queen Loana* (2004)

A Contemporary Semantics of Aging

Helen Chupin

Today's fiction, when addressing the subject of age, struggles to develop new representations which reflect how people actually experience the process of aging and what consensual meaning, if any, is given to the words 'young,' 'middle-aged,' and 'old' in Western societies. In this article, I would like to analyze how novels by two contemporary writers, one American and one Italian, explore current and historical attitudes to this subject. More precisely, my analysis will concern *Noah's Compass* (Anne Tyler, 2009) and *The Mysterious Flame of Queen Loana* (Umberto Eco, 2004)[1]. The novels in question, different in story, in style and in country of origin, nevertheless share some remarkable resemblances in their representation of old age.

YAMBO AND LIAM – BOTH SHOCKED INTO OLD AGE

The protagonists of *Noah's Compass* and *The Mysterious Flame of Queen Loana* are men of approximately the same age – at the beginning of the novel. Gianbattista Bodoni, known as Yambo, the main character in *The Mysterious Flame of Queen Loana* is fifty-nine and Liam Pennywell, the pro-

---

1 | I will cite Geoffrey Brock's English translation of Eco's novel throughout my article.

tagonist of *Noah's Compass*, is sixty. Neither has retired: Yambo is a rare-books dealer in Milan and Liam a fifth-grade teacher in Baltimore. For both, a sudden event occurs at the beginning of the novel: Yambo has an undefined 'incident' – apparently a heart attack – and Liam is dismissed without warning from his teaching post. Both texts begin with a similarly unexpected situation which interrupts the normal sequence of everyday events and forces the sixty-year-olds to wonder to what extent this inter-ruption is due to their age and, more importantly, whether this represents a temporary or permanent change in their lives. A link between being dis-missed and Liam's age is certainly suggested by the juxtaposition of the two elements in the novel's incipit, "In the sixty-first year of his life, Liam Pennywell lost his job" (Tyler 3). Liam and Yambo are representative of many men in their late fifties and early sixties for whom it has been pointed out that such 'incidents' as "heart attacks, triple bypasses, high blood pres-sure, strokes" (Friedan 17) are common markers of transition from one life period (active adult) to the next (retired adult) (17), and a study of employ-ment patterns has shown that losing one's job for a person in his fifties or sixties often leads to permanent unemployment (Sewin and Stevens). In fact, in a random sample of sixty societies worldwide, anthropologists Anthony Glascock and Susan Feinman found that people were identified as 'old' for three main reasons: change of social/economic role, chronology, and change in physical characteristics. All three elements are present here. Yambo and Liam are, then, quite typical examples of men at the point of entering an age category which, if no longer clearly designated as 'old' by all, would nevertheless be given that denomination by most younger mem-bers of American or Italian society. Both find themselves looking at their reflections in hospital mirrors. Yambo sees himself as "[a] white, hollow face, a long beard, and two sunken eyes" (Eco 9). Liam is also surprised to see an old man when he, too, views his reflection while in hospital: "He saw first a flash of neck (old!)" (Tyler 28) where the use of the exclamation mark suffices to suggest the suddenness of this discovery. Losing his job might, he thinks, "be a sign" that it is time to enter what he calls "the next stage" (3) and he decides, "It's possible I'll retire" (53). In other words, both protagonists have, at the outset of their stories, under the influence of an unexpected event, begun to suspect that they may be (or be becoming) 'old.'

Their entry into what can be considered a transitional period is abrupt and unexpected. Eco uses the suddenness of Yambo's health problem to suggest this. Tyler's text accompanies the move from professional career to potential retirement with two levels of reactions. Liam was not expecting to be dismissed but, overtly, accepts it. He welcomes losing his job as an escape from his professional constraints, "the interminable after-school meetings and the reams of niggling paperwork" (3). The loss of salary is not seen as a problem by the naturally ascetic Liam. The consequent "paring down" of his expenses is met "with more enthusiasm than he'd felt in years" (4) and the ex-teacher moves rapidly and contentedly to a smaller flat. The entry into the transitional period does not at first appear as a negative shock. What happens in the first night spent in the new apartment can, however, be read as a metaphorical re-telling of the impact that this sudden loss has unconsciously produced in him. During the night, Liam receives a blow on the head from a burglar and, like Yambo, wakes up in a hospital room. Both texts, albeit in different ways, equate the psychological moment of transition to old age with a violent physical shock. In both, this shock displaces the protagonists from their usual spatial environments where they benefit from some form of authority (as a wealthy shop owner or as a teacher), and they find themselves on their backs, in hospital beds, with little potential for action, looking at old men in the mirror. From active members of society, both have been transformed overnight into passive victims. Entering 'old age' has been a sudden blow to both protagonists.

Loss of Memory

Both novels, each in its own way, incite the reader to reflect, not only on the fact that, at sixty, men are suddenly likely to be considered old, but also on some of the psychological effects of becoming old. Yambo's first dialogue with the doctor – significantly, the novel's incipit – when he awakes in hospital after his attack, reveals a problem:

"And what's your name?"
"Wait, it's on the tip of my tongue." (Eco 3)

Yambo's 'incident' has led to what the doctor easily defines as a case of retrograde amnesia. He has forgotten his name and, no longer capable of recognizing family or friends, he remembers nothing of his past life other than what he has read in his beloved books. The rest of the novel will take him on a quest to retrieve the memories of a lifetime, to recover his lost past. Liam also suffers from amnesia, albeit on a less grandiose scale than Yambo. Having lost consciousness for a few hours after the incident with the burglar, he wakes to discover that he remembers nothing of the night's events, "When he searched his mind for his last available memory, [...] all he could find was the image of going to sleep in his new apartment" (Tyler 14). Although this may seem a trivial loss of memory compared to that in *The Mysterious Flame of Queen Loana*, the protagonist here, too, will spend much time and energy attempting to retrieve the memory of the lost episode in his life during a large part of the novel.

Both Tyler and Eco insist on the specific nature of memory loss incurred. Yambo's doctor explains that it is a question of "the second type of explicit memory, which we call episodic, or autobiographical" (Eco 13). On the other hand, he specifies that his patient's "semantic memory, or public memory [...] seems to be working fine" (13), and Yambo quotes at length from a large number of books, providing a vast intertextual canvas on which the action of the novel is painted. Tyler makes a similar distinction between two different types of memory. Liam, a former philosophy teacher, prides himself on his "total recall" of "entire passages from the Stoics, in Greek if need be" (26). His cultural or semantic memory is, then, like Yambo's, still intact. The difficulty, here too, lies in the autobiographical memory: "remembering a personal event, he supposed, was somewhat different" (26). On the personal level, like Yambo, he "experienced an actual gap" (36). For Liam, it is not just a trivial question of a few minutes lost to oblivion: "I'm missing a piece of my life," he tells his former wife (Tyler 36). Similarly, Yambo hears the doctor inform him that he has lost "the episodes of [his] life" (Eco 13). So these two very different novels both present sixty-year-olds receiving a shock and undergoing a life change which the reader can link to their age. Subsequently they both suffer memory loss specifically concerning episodes of their own lives, not cultural acquisitions, and feel the need to recover their pasts. What are these novels telling us about what happens to men today at the age of sixty?

I would suggest that to try to contribute some form of answer to that question, we first need to analyze the connotations surrounding memory loss in both texts and secondly the different images of aging presented implicitly or explicitly by Tyler and Eco to understand how through narrative and metaphor they address some of the problems of according meaning to this time of life in contemporary society.

Loss of Identity

Although loss of memory in later life is easily associated with senility, dementia, and Alzheimer's disease in the public mind and, as such, represents one of society's greatest commonly held fears, this association is carefully avoided in both texts. Both insist on the excellent health of the protagonist's cultural or semantic memory, and their memory loss functions on a more symbolical level. Liam, for example, as he wonders how he behaved during what must have been a physical struggle with the burglar, needs to know what this revealed about him, whether he showed courage or cowardice (Tyler 26). Without this knowledge, he has the sentiment that he has "been excluded from [his] own experience" (48). Some form of fragmentation or disassociation has occurred within him, "His true self had gone away from him and had a crucial experience without him and failed to come back afterward" (49). Losing his memory, Liam has lost "his true self." As for Yambo, he has even lost the memory of his name, the clearest symbol of identity. Consequently, amnesia can be seen as a powerful metaphor in both novels for some kind of loss of identity striking a person as he turns sixty. It raises the question of how an individual's sense of identity may suddenly be challenged at this age.

This is a question concerning both the individual and society. Turning sixty may represent a specific age of life insofar as it often corresponds, in both public and private perceptions, to the first period of the three established by Sokolovsky – as those that follow fully active adulthood: "becoming old," "being old" and "fading into a stage of nonfunctioning senescence" (51). However, contemporary society provides no clear definition of this particular age in the life course. According to the findings of a number of sociologists and of observers of society's cultural attitudes to aging, the very lack of a clear definition is what best characterizes this stage. People of this age may be in excellent health or begin to have health problems linked to age. They may be professionally active or they may have retired. They may or may not have become grandparents. Their youngest children may or may not have left the family home. Blaikie, noting the "postmodern blurring of chronological boundaries [separating] each life-course stage" (177), insists on the "liminal status" of the "Third Age" or "middlescence" (mirroring the liminal or transitional nature of adolescence) and acknowledges that "there are no [...] procedures for the transition from mid- to later life" (184). For Cole, when one starts to become old, one "floats in a cultural limbo" (xxvi). This transitional period is one of anomie (Blaikie), of "the roleless role" (Hazan 184), both terms significantly expressing the notion of lack in their prefix or suffix. This vague representation of the time when one "becomes old" is in complete contrast, for example, with the later "firmly demarcated [...] dependency [of...] deep old age" (Blaikie 184), the equivalent of Sokolovsky's third period. If society has found that the only way to define this period seems to be as lack (of name, of role, of definition), one may wonder whether and how this is represented in the two literary texts studied here.

Time and space being integrally linked in a literary text, as Mikhail Bakhtin pointed out in his work on the literary chronotope, we need to examine spatial representations as well as temporal ones. Liam describes what he is experiencing in terms which soon slide, in typical chronotopical fashion, from the temporal to the spatial, when he notes, "this was the first time he had experienced an actual gap. A hole, it felt like. A hole in his mind, full of empty blue rushing air" (Tyler 26). Spatial parallels abound in Eco's text, too, concerning this new experience. Although Yambo has lived in Milan for many years, he now finds himself in "an unknown city" (27). He discovers that his whole being is dissolved in an all-encompassing fog. He is "suspended in a milky grey" where everything is devoid of precise color or form or meaning. With his typical love of the encyclopedic, Eco reinforces this image throughout the novel with quotations from tens of literary texts, all on the theme of mist and fog which becomes a dominant metaphor in the text. Both novels seem to suggest that the time of 'becoming old' is best represented as a place which is unfamiliar, lacks substance or definition: a hole, a gap, an undefined foggy area.

Their loss, I would suggest, is not only loss of memory but also a loss of a clear sense of identity at this time in their lives. Memory loss is clearly represented as the loss of some part of their past lives, of who they were. It also, interestingly, makes them question who they are, as if one cannot provide oneself with a clear sense of identity in the present without full acceptance and understanding of one's past. Both texts are marked by disorientation. The protagonists question who they are and how this period fits into their lives as a whole.

Cultural Segmentation of the Life Course

In fact, the protagonists' problem of what role they can play at this specific age of life is repeatedly linked in both novels to the broader question of the segmentation of the whole life course. This question of how one's life is demarcated into specific roles at specific times is both implicitly and explicitly addressed in these books. Liam's last thoughts before going to sleep on the night of the burglary, for example, represent a conventional segmentation: "He had accomplished all the conventional tasks – grown up, found work, gotten married, had children – and now he was winding down. This is it, he thought. The very end of the line" (Tyler 12).

Life is spatially represented as a line along which a set number of "tasks" are biologically or socially programmed: growing up is childhood's occupation, finding work, getting married and having children are the tasks allotted to productive adulthood. Then there is a period of "winding down," with no specific task to undertake. Unlike Sokolovsky, Liam suggests here that after sixty there is only one, not three stages of old age – and he has thus already arrived at "the end" ("This is it"). This global view of old age is also implicitly present in Liam's youngest daughter's comments about the old people she deals with at the dentist's office where she has a summer job, "I am so, so tired of old ladies [...] There's not a patient in that office who's under ninety, I swear" (43). The reader suspects that among the "old" ladies in question many may be nearer sixty than ninety, but that for the teenager, the life course is segmented into simply 'young' and 'old' with no differentiation between the different categories of 'old.' Many observers of today's culture in Western societies have remarked on the prevalence of this dichotomy in the way aging is perceived generally. It is this dichotomous and, ultimately, Manichean division of life into young/good and old/bad which has in part led to a fear of the aging process in American society, to the widespread view and fear of old age as total decline, and to what Gullette calls an "entire decline system" summed up as "innocent absorption of cultural signals, youthful age anxiety, middle-ageism, ageism – infiltrating our society from top to bottom" (15).

Eco's text also explores how life can be segmented into different periods, but it turns to historical representations of the aging process to do so. A description of the decoration upstairs in the old family home introduces intertwined images of historical portrayals of the life course. The illustrations on the wall show two of those allegorical staircases, one for men and another for women, that depict the various stages of life – the cradle and babies with leading strings on the first step; then, step by step, the approach to adulthood, which is represented by beautiful, radiant figures atop an Olympic podium; from there, the slow descent of increasingly elderly figures, who by the bottom step are reduced, as the Sphynx described, to three-legged creatures, two wobbly sticks and a cane, with an image of Death awaiting them. (Eco 98)

Such illustrations showing staircases (known variously as *la escala de la vida*, *Lebenstreppen*, *les degrés de la vie*, etc.) clearly depict a specific representation for each age of life, literally fixed in stone, and belong to a time when strict social rules of standard behavior gave each age of life a clear role to play. Today's Western societies no longer function in this way. The staircase places the fifty-year-old at the top of its symmetrical structure. Before fifty: ascension; after fifty: decline. Once again, there is a binary construction. In this textual description of a Spanish version of this popular trope, Eco adds another popular image to this iconographical grammar of the steps, just as symmetrical but not usually linked to age – that of the podium of the Olympic Games, where the gold medal winner is placed on the top step. The fifty-year-old becomes the champion, the 'beautiful,' 'radiant' winner. Never afterwards will he occupy such a position, says the illustration, nor enjoy such status. The reference to the Sphinx and thus to the enigma presented to Oedipus of the four-, then two- then three-legged creature that is Man, complicates the ten stages of life by placing over it the parallel motif of three stages – the infant, the adult, the old man, but it does not contradict its basic message. Beyond the fact that this superposition or superabundance of images and references is a clear mark of Eco's writing style, it also serves to reinforce the notion that society has traditionally viewed life after fifty as a decline leading to Man's final unchanging destination, present in a personified form: Death. This pyramidal structure, however, was far from the reality of everyday life at the time of its popularity. In the sixteenth century when these illustrations first began to appear, life expectancy was about half that shown in the pictures (Lucke et al 132). Very few people actually took fifty years to descend the second part of the staircase to death. With his reference to the Olympic podium (an invention of the modern era), Eco seems to suggest, however, that, although linked to both Antiquity and the Renaissance, this binary representation of aging is still prevalent in contemporary society, weighing on the sixty-year-old's own perceptions of his life, regardless of the changed perspective given by the new longevity of the over-fifty year olds today.

Both historical and contemporary segmentations of the life course present the period when one is aged sixty or over as a negative one of decline. Society seems to be saying that if 'being old' has been emptied of all positive meaning in rich countries, then the individual is faced with a binary choice: either he must consider himself as having arrived at 'the end of the line' and accept death, or try to stay forever young.

The Quest for Eternal Youth

One way of trying to retrieve youth is evoked diegetically in both novels. It has been noted that trying to find a younger female partner can be one of the "renewal activities" sometimes adopted by men in this age group (Sokolovsky 51). Both Liam and Yambo are tempted by this. Yambo is attracted to his young assistant and believes he may have been having an affair with her before his attack but as he remembers nothing of that time he now prefers to ignore this feeling of sexual attraction. Liam meets Eunice who is over twenty years younger than he, and a long-term relationship is envisaged by both until Liam puts an end to this possibility, having discovered that Eunice is not single. The attempt to retrieve youth through the surrogacy of a younger partner is, then, rejected in both texts.

This rejection of the quest for eternal youth is reinforced in Eco's text through the story of the cartoon character, the eponymous Queen Loana. As Yambo rediscovers the comics and books he read as a child in the family home to which he has returned in search of his memories, he comes across the story of *The Mysterious Flame of Queen Loana*. Its heroes, two young Americans, Tim and Spud, find themselves in a strange, lost land, a "mysterious kingdom" ruled over by the beautiful Queen Loana, priestess of the precious flame of immortality. Their aim is to obtain the flame for themselves. Tim and Spud's quest to bring back the magical flame fails lamentably, but this is presented as a relatively unimportant fact: "for our protagonists it is good-bye immortality, which must not be such a big deal, [...] in the end having lost the flame seems to matter very little to them" (252). Yambo now has the satisfaction of being able to remember the story – "I had reactivated the flame's name" but this is finally of little consequence to him: "The fog was still, as always, within me" (253). In both metaphorical and narrative terms, the quest for eternal youth is unfruitful.

BEING-TOWARD-DEATH

In the cultural construction of the life course that we have observed, the binary choice appears to be either to hold on to youth or to welcome the decline to death, so it is unsurprising that both novels explore the attitude of the protagonists to death. As he gradually remembers previous episodes from his life, Yambo comes to terms with death. Specifically, he recalls hearing certain passages on death from a well-known Italian book giving spiritual advice to young people[2] and even reciting its "Exercise for a Good Death" in the church of a monastery as a young man. Two pages are devoted to extracts from this text and notably to the description of the final physical stages prior to death. These memories bring him now "a serene consciousness of the fact that all men are mortal" and he concludes that "[t]hat lesson in Being-toward-Death prepared me for my destiny" (Eco 391). Yambo finds serenity in accepting the approach of death which indeed comes at the end of the novel with him succumbing to a second fatal heart attack.

As for Liam, at first he notes simply that in old age, there are no programmed tasks awaiting him, only decline, "winding *down*" (my emphasis), "the final stage," then death – "the very end of the line" (Tyler 12), confirming the binary division. Later in the novel, after a visit to his father, Liam, too, accepts death with serenity, realizing that "in the end we die like all the other animals and we're buried in the ground and after a few more years we might as well not have existed" and, paradoxically, "[t]his [...] made him feel better" (210). However, unlike Eco who offers no perspective other than an early, if well accepted, death to his protagonist, Tyler is to take hers on a longer journey, with acceptance of death only one step on the way to a more positive outcome.

---

2 | In the translation I am using here, this book is called *The Provident Young Man* but the Italian title (*Il Giovane Providuto*) is traditionally translated into English as *The Companion of Youth*. Written by Giovanni Bosco in 1847, it was reedited hundreds of times, provided spiritual advice for generations of young Catholics and included a part dedicated to "Esercizio della buona morte."

RE-CONNECTING WITH THE PAST

Although attempting to remain young is not viewed as a valid option, some form of a psychological return to youth and childhood is presented as necessary. To retrieve a sense of identity, both Liam and Yambo feel the need to go back over their past lives, to find the coherence and continuity which a clear notion of self can give. Becoming old is "the stage [to] reflect [...] on what it all meant" (Tyler 3). To do this, they are both required to set out on a psychological journey which, diegetically, takes the form of a physical journey to their parents' homes. Yambo goes back to his childhood home in Solaro. As he explores his former bedroom, the attic and a secret chamber, the text metaphorically enters the inner workings of his unconscious self. He peruses at length the books, newspapers and other memorabilia left over from the 1930s, 40s, and 50s, the time of his youth, with many of the images from these publications reproduced in the text, defined from the outset as an illustrated novel. In this long section, his quest for identity simultaneously takes the reader on a time travel journey back to Fascist Italy.

A similar effect of moving back in time is first given in *Noah's Compass* through the temporal markers in the description of Liam's father's house and garden motivated by Liam's visit. The house is located in "a neighborhood of unassuming little cottages from the 1940s" (198), "the flowers in the garden had a dated look" (199), and even the decorative dolls in the lounge wear "old-fashioned dresses" (200). Liam is moving backwards in time (in his father's discourse, he literally becomes "the boy" again) in a quest for meaning in his life, "hoping [...] for his father to say something significant, give some clue about his life" (207). Significantly, this visit takes place when Liam, having discovered that his recently met girlfriend is married, is comparing his own present behavior with that of his father during Liam's childhood. The parallel is clear – he is doing "the same thing," and says, "now I find I've been seeing another man's wife! [...] It's what happened when I was a boy – an outsider coming along and wrecking my parents' marriage" (187). His childhood memories of his father's abandoning the family return and, with them, the memory of the psychological wound this left him with.

However, neither for Liam nor for Yambo is the act of retrieval of the past an easy task. Eco expresses this difficulty in the large number of pages. Liam's difficulty to gain access to his past is expressed through imagery in an episode where his stepmother takes his hand to read his fortune but is troubled by the presence of the scar caused by the burglar during his struggle. This gives rise to the following dialogue:

"How do I read what's underneath it? I can't tell what's underneath it! I mean, your left hand is your whole entire past! [...]"
"If it's my past, why do we care? Liam asked. "We just want to know about my future."
"Oh, you can't read one without the other," Esther Jo told him. "They're inter-mingled. They bounce off of each other. That's what the amateurs fail to understand." (Tyler 204-5)

The need to integrate one's past into one's present life in order to be able to move forward is clearly expressed by Esther Jo, Liam's father's seventy-year-old second wife, who has offered to tell Liam's fortune for him. She cannot read his future without gaining access to his past.

Behind the physical scar lies the psychological scar dating from Liam's childhood. His father had abandoned the family to move in with Esther Jo, a young woman at the time. Even though he regularly visits him, Liam had never forgiven him for what he had done to their family and it is only now when his father explains the situation from his point of view – "I didn't desert, you know. I did play fair and square. I leveled with your mother and asked her for a divorce. I sent her money every month as regular as clock-work" (205) – that Liam is able to see the past in a new light.

Interestingly, both Liam and Yambo's attempts to understand their past lives are expressed through the metaphor of reading. For Yambo, re-reading the books of his childhood gradually enables him to reconstruct the events of his childhood and youth. For Liam, three images of reading one's life combine to underline the importance of this metaphor. First, in the fortune telling episode, it is the past in his hand that needs to be read but the lines are hidden. In an episode of personal reflection, he cannot read his own memories because his "mind was a blank [...] as blank and white and textureless as a sheet of unused paper" (41). Here, too, then, the lines of his past life are absent. Finally, in an episode with his young grandson, Liam re-reads the children's books that he used to read to his daughters when they were children and this briefly takes him back to when he was a young father. In the latter case, the memory is unsought for. It springs naturally to mind as Liam is, in fact, very much in contact with the present moment, aware of his sensory impressions, for example that his grandson's head "gave off a heated smell, like fresh-baked bread or warm honey" (218). It is, then, out of a strong connection with the present moment that Liam finds coherence with his past. In both texts reading and re-reading are presented as essential activities; both protagonists need to retrieve the lost texts of their lives.

CONNECTING THE PAST AND THE PRESENT, THE YOUNG AND THE OLD – THE PUER SENEX

What Liam finally remembers or realizes about his past life is that he, who "knew all there was to know about forgetting" the past (82), has also missed connecting with people in the present during most of his life. His amnesia concerning the burglary episode is nothing compared to this new amnesia, amplified to include his whole life. It is the close connection with his wives and daughters that he has lost. Only now can he look back and feel he understands at least this about his past.

> If the memory of his attack were handed to him today, he would just ask, is that it?
> Where's the rest? Where's everything else I've forgotten: my childhood and my youth, my first marriage and my second marriage and the growing up of my daughters?
> Why, he's had amnesia all along. [...]
> All along, it seemed, he had experienced only the most glancing relationship with his own life. (Tyler 241)

Only thirty or so pages from the end of the novel does the reader gain access to Liam's past life. Only after reconnecting with his feelings, thanks to Eunice, the married girlfriend, is Liam able to face recalling the time of his first wife's suicide and the difficult years that followed. Eunice, who at the end of the novel has no longer an active role to play in his life "really had turned out to be his rememberer" (250) and had played an essential role as a catalyst in the novel. Having reconnected with his past, and finding himself able to appreciate fully the moments shared with his grandson in the present, Liam can now imagine a future other than one of permanent decline. Finally, when offered a job, without really planning it, he says "Okay" (253). He accepts to babysit his grandson with the words, "Sure, bring him here" (215). When his daughter, Kitty, wants to come and live with him for a year, he, who others describe as having always been "so negative" (256), is able to say "yes to her" (255). It is finally neither by trying to remain young nor by considering himself as on the verge of death, but by saying "yes" to the present moment that Liam finds his identity at the age of sixty.

The final chapter sees Liam accepting his age. Only now does he notice that he has become "Poppy" for his grandson, and he begins his job at Bet Ha-Midrash preschool as "zayda," an assistant to the nursery school teacher. Tyler had carefully supplied the information much earlier on in the novel, apparently as an insignificant detail at that time, that "Zayda is the Jewish word for grandfather" (54). This double transformation into a grandfather does not now prevent him from taking on an active role not only in the family but also with the three-year-olds at the preschool. Making up for the fact that he has "never been present in [his] own life" (263), Liam now supplies the "texture" that was lacking on the "textureless page" of his mind by interacting fully with his young companions on the "Texture Table" where various activities are set up for the children. In so doing he seems to echo the words of one of the Stoic philosophers referred to earlier in the text, "What foolish forgetfulness of mortality to postpone wholesome plans to the fiftieth and sixtieth year!" (Seneca, Book III). Intertextually, the reference to Seneca brings to mind another segmentation of time – taken from a different perspective from those already mentioned, "Life is divided into three periods – that which has been, that which is, that which will be" (Seneca, Book X). Liam has in part rediscovered something of the capacity of a child to become fully involved in the present though, typical of many characters in Tyler's novels, he always remains somewhat haunted by past regrets and worried about future loneliness.

The need to return to the past and to one's childhood when on the threshold of old age is also crucial to *The Mysterious Flame of Queen Loana*, and Eco enriches this theme with a reference to *The Tale of Pipino, Born an Old Man and Died a Bambino* by Giulio Gianelli which allows him to express this need to break down the habitual barriers between child and adult in his own life, introducing a backward movement in time that he feels he must experience if he is to retrieve a valid sense of his own identity and to give meaning to the period of life he has entered at present. Once more, the idea is introduced through the reading of a book:

this book was about a pipe that had been left, still hot, on a table beside a clay statue of a little old man, and the pipe decided to breathe warmth into that dead thing to bring it to life, and thus an elderly man was born. *Puer senex*, an ancient commonplace. In the end, Pipino dies as an infant in his cradle and is carried up to heaven by fairies. It was better the way I had remembered it: Pipino was born as an old man in one cabbage and died a nursling in another. In either case, Pipino's journey toward infancy was my own. (Eco 147)

The "little old man" is presented at first as a "statue," a "dead thing," but, once brought to life, must move backwards in time, as must Yambo in order to gradually retrieve all his memories ("Pipino's journey was my own"), becoming a child in order to complete his life cycle. The idea is one which seems to have particular resonance in today's society, appearing in films as well as literary texts (Fincher, Minor, Coppola). The complimentary reference to the dialectical figure of the *puer senex*, commonly used in both Antiquity and the Middle Ages as well as in Jungian psychoanalytical theory, to express an alliance of youth and wisdom, the image of a being who is both young and old, brings to mind once more the necessity to connect one's life into an integrated whole.

CONCLUSION

The role played by culturally constructed perceptions in determining "how a given society metaphorically thinks about its elders" is important (Sokolovsky 51). Therefore, the similarity of the metaphorical representations of aging that we have found in *Noah's Compass* and *The Mysterious Flame of Queen Loana* should come as no surprise, the writing of both of these novels having been inevitably affected by contemporary trends in Western culture. Although one should be wary of reducing these texts to the single aspect studied here, a summary can nevertheless be made of their common metaphorical representations of the transitional age of 'becoming old.'

This appears, then, first, as a time for which men are poorly prepared, the metaphor of a physical blow to the head or to the heart being particularly apt to suggest their sense of shock when they realize they are entering this liminal age of life. It is, secondly, also evoked through the images of fog and empty space as a time for which there is no clearly defined social role. Thirdly, the consequent sentiment of losing one's individual identity is present metaphorically as amnesia in both novels. Fourthly, the need to look back over one's life in order to establish an identity which is independent of one's professional activity or of one's role as father is seen as re-reading the text(s) of one's lives, a remarkably suitable image for these writers, both of whom have many publications spread over their own lifetimes. Finally, this need to re-connect with one's life prior to adulthood and the psychological juggling necessary in order to realize continuity between oneself as child and oneself as old man emerges from both texts and is linked to journeys to the houses of the protagonists' parents, to stories of reverse aging and to the *puer senex* trope of Antiquity.

A rich metaphorical evocation of what it means to reach the threshold of old age is the result. These novels, though providing no clear solutions to the problems raised, help the reader to ask some difficult questions about how society views old age and about how individuals are forced to cope with their own representations of aging at this crucial time of their lives.

REFERENCES

Bakhtin, Mikhail. *Dialogic Imagination: Four Essays*. Trans. Caryl Emerson & Michael Holquist. Austin: University of Texas Press, 1981. Print.

Blaikie, Andrew. *Aging and Popular Culture*. Cambridge: Cambridge University Press, 1999. Print.

Burrow, John A. *The Ages of Man: A Study in Medieval Writing and Thought*. Oxford: Clarendon Press, 1986. Print.

Chan, Sewin, and Ann Huff Stevens. "Job Loss and Employment Patterns of Older Workers." *Journal of Labor Economics* 19.2 (2001): 484-521. Print.

Cole, Thomas R. *The Journey of Life: A Cultural History of Aging in America*. Cambridge: Cambridge University Press, 1992. Print.

Eco, Umberto. *The Mysterious Flame of Queen Loana, an illustrated novel*. Trans. from the Italian by Geoffrey Brock. [*La Mysteriosa Fiamma della Regina Loana*, 2004]. Orlando: Harcourt Inc., 2005. Print.

Friedan, Betty. *The Fountain of Age*. New York: Simon & Schuster, 1993. Print.

Glascock, Anthony and Susan Feinman. "Social Asset or Social Burden: An Analysis of the Treatment of the Aged in Non-Industrial Societies."

Ed. Christine L. Fry. *Dimensions: Aging, Culture and Health.* New York: Praeger, 1981. Print.

Gullette Morganroth, Margaret. *Agewise: Fighting the New Ageism in America.* Chicago & London: University of Chicago Press, 2011. Print.

Hazan, Haim. *From First Principles: An Experiment in Aging.* Westport: Bergin & Garvey, 1996. Print.

Lucke, Christoph, Margot Lucke, and Manfred Gogol. "Lebenstreppen – oder wie man den Alternsprozess, über die Jahrhunderte gesehen hat." *European Journal of Geriatrics* 2.3-4 (2009): 132-40. Web. 28 Nov. 2012.

Seneca, Lucius Annaeus. *De Brevitate Vitae.* Trans. as *On the Shortness of Life* by John W. Basore. London: William Heinemann, 1932. Kindle edition.

Sokolovsky, Jay. "Images Of Aging: A Cross-Cultural Perspective." *Generations* 17.2 (1993): 51. Academic Search Premier. Web. 28 Nov. 2012.

Tyler, Anne. *Noah's Compass.* New York: Alfred A. Knopf, 2009. London: Chatto & Windus, 2009. Print.

Films

Forever Young. Perf. Mel Gibson, Jamie Lee Curtis and Elijah Wood. Dir. Steve Minor. Warner/Icon, 1992. Film.

Peggy Sue Got Married. Perf. Kathleen Turner, Nicolas Cage and Barry Miller. Dir. Francis Ford Coppola. TriStar Pictures, 1986. Film.

The Curious Case of Benjamin Button. Perf. Brad Pitt, Cate Blanchett and Tilda Swinton. Dir. David Fincher. Paramount, 2008. Film.

Youth Without Youth. Dir. Francis Ford Coppola. Perf. Tim Roth, Alexandra Maria Lara, Bruno Ganz, Marcel Iures. Sony Classics, 2007. Film.

Man, Interrupted

Intersections of Masculinity, Disability, and Old Age in John Coetzee's *Slow Man*

Katharina Zilles

THE OLD AND AGING BODY FROM AN INTERSECTIONAL PERSPECTIVE

"While public policies contribute much to the social construction of old age, there is a strong perception in people's minds that ageing is really a bodily affair," as Gilleard and Higgs observe ("Ageing and its embodiment" 117). J. M. Coetzee's novel *Slow Man* provides a powerful narrative of aging corporeality which seems to reinforce the above statement. Bodies – including those written or told – are certainly a major site of the construction and concretization of age(ing)[1] and at the basis of the production of the age-other (Biggs), the effects of the passing of time being literally inscribed into their surfaces and performances.[2] Several categories of cultural differentiation are manifested and negotiated in and on the body, generating

---

1 | The used term age(ing) is to imply both the processuality of aging and the notion of age as an abstract category of cultural difference.

2 | In analogy with West's and Zimmerman's concept of "doing gender," Miriam Haller rightly suggests that there are cultural techniques of "doing age" which the individual performs to conform to age-related role models (Haller, "Undoing Age" 216-17). Adapting and performing physical features and behaviour ascribed to the old – be it intentionally or subconsciously – thus leads to an affirmation of ascriptions. Accordingly, by denying to perform in accordance with cultural expectations, techniques of "undoing gender" and "undoing age" can be realised (Haller).

a number of "bodyisms" (Winker and Degele 51), i.e. techniques of margin-alization on grounds of difference actualized on the surface of the body. This paper aims to examine images of age(ing) as represented in the cor-poreality of protagonist Paul Rayment from an intersectional perspective: age(ing) is seen as an interdependent category of cultural difference which is at the basis of the formation of both identity and alterity and explored in its concurrence with notions of masculinity and (dis)ability.

Age has been widely acknowledged as a category of social difference, but has rarely been analyzed from an intersectional point of view.[3] In fact, Gilleard and Higgs suggest that aging was a process of establishing same-ness across the boundaries of categories of difference which are dominant in the social life of the middle age: "The physicality that is the essence of old age seems to wipe away the imprint of class, gender and race that is so salient in earlier life" (Gilleard and Higgs, "Ageing and its embodiment" 117). As the analysis of *Slow Man* aims to show, however, the experience of age(ing) does not lessen, but may significantly alter notions and images of gendered identity with which it remains inextricably interwoven.

At the intersection of masculinity and old age, a category of potential hegemonic affirmation and a category of potential marginalization inter-act. Loss of physical abilities, health and strength as well as bodily changes related to age(ing) are associated with a loss of a person's incarnate cultural capital (Baudrillard 277), and numerous techniques and measures are of-fered to confront this 'decline' (Küpper 69) and prevent the old body from becoming invisible or marked as unattractive. With regard to the intersec-tion of age(ing) and gender, Susan Sontag states that "[e]very wrinkle, every line, every gray hair, is a defeat" (Sontag 36): losing the looks of youthful-ness means losing cultural capital, and this is supposed to affect women much earlier and more forcefully than men of the same calendrical age.

Images of masculinity and role models for men focus on men of middle age, "[...] as if men and masculinities simply 'ceased to exist' at some point before the onset of the last phase of their lives. Often older men, men with certain disabilities, and dying men are excluded from the category of 'men' and its analysis" (Hearns 112; my translation). For aging men, traditional images of masculinity as based on (economical) productivity, virility and agency provide specific challenges to identity. As the aging man encoun-

---

3 | Among the valuable exceptions are Hartung, *Alter und Geschlecht*; Hartung et al., *Graue Theorie*; Hearns "Vernachlässigte Intersektionalitäten."

ters the loss of social roles or physical abilities, his masculine self-identity needs to be reshaped and renegotiated. Aging – especially aging in the body – challenges masculine privilege: "Possibly, hegemonic masculinity is more likely to be problematised when frailty, disability, incontinence and other physical impediments, dependency and death are no longer ignored" (Hearns 114; my translation). When examining masculine corporeality with regard to age(ing), the intersection of age and gender with the category of ability becomes obvious and poses another challenge to hegemonic masculinity. Old age and disability potentially overlap since age-induced disease and physical decline can lead to decrease in mobility and ability: if the aging process is not interrupted by sudden death, some kind of disability will probably affect everyone at some point in later life (Garland-Thomsen 422). Both categories are based on constructions of "unusual corporealities" (Schmincke 13; my translation) whose aberrance may be functional (e.g. referring to incontinence or impairments of mobility) or aesthetic (referring to an outer appearance perceived as unpleasant or disfigured by age or impairment).

NON-NORMATIVE CORPOREALITIES: THE ABJECT, THE GROTESQUE, AND THE STIGMA

The otherness of the old and aging body is often signified by devaluing attributions. The concept of abjection as developed by Julia Kristeva can be understood as an aggravation of otherness based on corporeal difference. Abjection does not only refer to aberrance from the norm, but implies a drastic devaluation of the other who is labelled 'abject.' The mechanisms of othering which produce the abject are referred to as defilement (Kristeva 56-57). Originally referring to the maternal feminine – and here, the interconnectedness of gendered and age-related alterity shows – abjection encompasses fear of and disgust for the embodied other, especially when relating to a lack of control over the body's boundaries so that the insides of the body enter, and potentially contaminate, the outside world. Kristeva stresses that it is the fear of the Other contaminating the Self that is the basis of abjection, and the fear that the boundaries of the Self may be threatened: "It is thus not lack of cleanliness or health that causes abjection but what disturbs identity, system, order" (4). The concept is transferable to other bodies of difference, especially if they are marked by this lack of

control over physical functions and reliable delineation (e.g. by incontinence). Chris Gilleard and Paul Higgs conceive of abjection as a unique
feature of the "fourth age" ("Ageing abjection and embodiment" 135) which
is thus defined by radical corporeal otherness. The tense and problematic
relationship between the Self and the abject Other as hinted at by Kristeva
is especially clear for the category of age(ing): aging being an inescapable
process, the apprehension of becoming Other oneself is always part of the
abjection of old age.

The aspect of the delineation of 'unusual bodies' was problematized
much earlier by Michail Bakhtin in his study of body images and the grotesque. The 'grotesque' is to be understood as a special relationship of the
body and the outside world it interacts with: "[The grotesque] is looking
for that which protrudes from the body, all that seeks to go out beyond the
body's confines" (Bakhtin 92). It is thus located on the surface of the body
and in the negotiation of its boundaries, and encompasses the process of
the world 'entering' the body, and the body extending into it: "Eating, drinking, defecation [...], dismemberment [...] – all these acts are performed on
the confines of the body and the outer world, or on the confines of the old
and the new body. In all these events the beginning and the end of life are
closely linked and interwoven" (Bakhtin 93). The special relationship of the
old body and the outside world is qualified by time: the passing of time is
'written on the body' where it becomes concrete in wrinkled skin, sagging
muscles, hunches, hair loss, etc. The body, in age(ing) as well as in illness
or disability, may become less 'governable:' the control over its boundaries
and shapes decreases.

Finally, the embodiment of age(ing), especially the problematization of
"repulsive old age," is also related to the concept of age as stigma (Backes
147). Stigma refers to a sign not only of otherness, but of damage or disfigurement which is visible on the surface of the body. Besides pointing to
physical impairment, it symbolizes the impairment of identity. In his study
of the stigma and "the management of spoiled identity" Erving Goffman
describes the derivation of the concept:

[In ancient Greece,] [t]he signs were cut or burnt into the body and advertised
that the bearer was a slave, a criminal, or a traitor – a blemished person, ritu-
ally polluted, to be avoided [...]. Later, in Christian times, two layers of metaphor
were added to the term: the first referred to bodily signs of holy grace [...]; the
second [...] referred to bodily signs of physical disorder. (1)

Goffman's theory of stigmatization has been widely received within body and disability studies (Dederich 44) but is also fruitful for age(ing) studies if the physical signs of age(ing) are understood as visible labels of otherness which allow for exclusion and can be met with repulsion, disgust, contempt, or pity. In associating the stigma with "spoiled identity," Goffman points to the cultural practice of perceiving outer appearance as a reliable signifier of psychic and social conditions: identity, it seems, is communicated and negotiated primarily on the surface of the body (Goffman 4-5). The dominance of corporeality over individual identity in discourses on age(ing) has been termed "the mask of ageing" by Mike Featherstone and Mike Hepworth (Featherstone, "Post-Bodies" 227); Featherstone drastically terms the reduction of age(ing) and agedness to mere embodiment "the pornography of old age" (227).

From Standstill to Slow Motion: J. M. Coetzee's Slow Man

South Australia in the year 2000: the city of Adelaide, where the entire narrative takes place, is represented in many verifiable details, and since one character's age and birth date are given (Coetzee 120), the temporal setting can be calculated. It tells the story of Paul Rayment, a sixtyish single man who suffers a bad accident and the amputation of one leg and later falls in love with his Croatian day nurse Marijana, a married mother of three children.

The tension between a realist and highly referential narrative embedding and its disruption by self-conscious metafictional twists appears as striking when the narrative is then interrupted by the advent of Elizabeth Costello, a seventy-two-year-old Australian writer who claims to be the author of Rayment's story and has a disturbing knowledge of Rayment's past. A considerable part of the novel is thus concerned with the confrontation of the main character with another character who also functions as a by-proxy-author. The narrative is related through the focalization of its protagonist, thus entailing a limited and subjective representation of the events based on Rayment's perspective. His perceptions, thoughts and emotions are largely conveyed through psycho-narration and free indirect discourse. Rayment's privilege of seeing and perceiving the narrated world is called into question by Costello's intervention: claiming to have authored his story – and, consequentially, his perspective on it – she challenges the authenticity and validity of his perception.

The story of Paul Rayment starts in medias res with the accident that marks a radical caesura in his life. The accident signifies the beginning of old age and a diminished state of being for the protagonist which others him from his self-identity, as Hania Nashef observes: "The blow [...] results in a disfigurement that at once ages and shames the protagonist" (Nashef 149). His former Self, unmarked by old age and physical impairment, is used as the foil against which this alterity is negotiated. Information about this former identity is not provided from the beginning, but incorporated bit by bit as the story makes progress: Rayment – through his own focalization and in retrospect – is represented as a solitary but active man who takes pride in his independence, agency and mobility (Coetzee 25). Interestingly enough, these flashbacks are rare and short, mostly stretching over only a few sentences at a time – the protagonist's present experience and development is clearly privileged over the life narrative. Former caesuras in his life course, such as his divorce and, later, his retirement, are not represented as affecting his age-identity; his body is healthy and able. Although he is over sixty and retired, age(ing) has not been an important issue of reflection prior to his accident, at least he has never perceived it as a cause of social exclusion or functionlessness: "There was always more than enough to keep him occupied" (Coetzee 25). His cultural interests are varied; he is interested in film and literature, photography, and sports. In the pursuit of these activities he manages to establish coherency in his life cycle: his former professional work as a photographer is continued in retirement. It is in this state of contentment and self-sufficiency that the accident occurs, signifying the onset of later life as being and becoming Other.

In the following, the disruptive quality of Rayment's accident and mutilation, the following stage of disorientation and emotional upheaval and subsequent attempts at 'rehabilitation' are looked at as resembling an (incomplete) rite of passage.[4] Beginning with the truncation of his able body and his subsequent dissociation from a former unmarked age identity, the struggle for readjustment is never granted full closure. Although this pro-

---

4 | For a profound discussion of rites of passage in narratives of aging: Haller, "Altern erzählen" 102-03. For a discussion of the ritual as symbolic performance and the distinction of its three stages (dissociation - liminality - readjustment) see van Gennep 20-22.

cess is similar to an essential experience of dislocation and passage in his youth – his family's relocation from France to Australia – Rayment finds no resources to help him accept, and reintegrate into, the new and altered state of being he finds himself confronted with. Most of the narrative thus reflects the protagonist's struggling with this liminal phase and the quest for readjustment, the middle phase of passage.

THE DISRUPTED BODY

In the narrative examined here, age(ing) is no longer a linear process or progress as to be encountered, for example, in the midlife progress novel (Gullette), but rather represented as a sudden incidence which, without warning, fast-forwards the protagonist from midlife to old age. The first chapter of the narrative, just over a page in length, represents the accident which is going to change the protagonist's life and reflects the brief yet radical impact in its brevity. Subsequently, it becomes clear that he has been severely injured, and as a consequence to the damage done to his knee, one of his legs is amputated. The severity of the occurrence and the radical change to life as it was before is foreshadowed immediately after the accident has taken place: "The body that had flown so lightly through the air has grown ponderous, so ponderous that for the life of him he cannot lift a finger" (Coetzee 1). This sensation of ponderosity and passivity makes him feel that the events are "befalling" him (Coetzee 4), denying him active participation and agency (Jolly 98). In the narrated time that follows the event, the protagonist's life revolves around his maimed body: Although he has never taken a great interest in his body and its appearance (Coetzee 163), he is now confronted with his physical existence.

Rayment's loss of self-determination and agency is not only conveyed through the accident itself, but more explicitly so through his treatment in hospital. Learning that he might lose his injured leg in surgery, he is left without the opportunity to speak due to the medication he has received (Coetzee 5). Upon waking up, it becomes clear that the leg was indeed taken off. At this point, the topic of age(ing) is first addressed when the decision for the amputation is explained in the context of health economics: the value of the body as cultural capital, and the commitment to its treatment and care, depend on its calendrical age.

In a younger person they might perhaps have gone for a reconstruction, but a reconstruction of the required order would entail a whole series of operations, one
after another, extending over a year, even two years, with a success rate of less
than fifty per cent, so all in all, considering his age, it was thought best to take
the leg off cleanly above the knee, leaving a good length of bone for a prosthesis.
He (Dr Hansen) hopes he (Paul Rayment) will come to accept the wisdom of that
decision. (Coetzee 7; original parentheses)

Having had his cultural capital – the sound body – so drastically reduced,
he perceives himself as excluded and neglected:

[...] The nurses are kind and cheery, but beneath their brisk efficiency he can detect – he is not wrong, he has seen it too often in the past – a final indifference to
their fate, his and his companion's. From young Dr Hansen he feels, beneath the
kindly concern, the same indifference. It is as though at some unconscious level
these young people who have been assigned to care for them know they have
nothing left to give to the tribe and therefore do not count. *So young and yet so
heartless!* he cries to himself. *How did I come to fall into their hands? Better for
the old to tend the old, the dying the dying!* [...]. (Coetzee 12; original emphasis)

In his new state of impairment, he laments his old age and glorifies "the
old days, the days before the accident" (Coetzee 25) with an impressive
intensity. There is no textual evidence that Rayment has been so painfully
aware of his own age(ing) and vulnerability before the amputation. On the
contrary, the narrative stresses how normal, able and unmarked his body
was: "[h]e had never thought of himself as frail until he saw the X-rays"
(Coetzee 17) and "he was the kind of man who might last into his nineties"
(Coetzee 25). This un-awareness of the effects of time on his body, of mori-
bundity, had been one of the basic constituents of his formerly contented
life.

The accident constitutes a massive intrusion of the outside world into
his individual, private life – and, literally, into his body – which precipitates
an awareness of the impact of the passing of time onto the body. His 'truncated Self,' his maimed body, suddenly feels the impact of time running
up: it is, as Rayment becomes aware for the first time, subject to aging. The
loss of a body part is even interpreted as a smaller version of death: "A leg
gone: what is losing a leg, in the larger perspective? In the larger perspective, losing a leg is no more than a rehearsal for losing everything" (Coetzee

15). He imagines his organism as a team of supporters who "did for him what they could [...]; now they want to rest" (Coetzee 53). Unlike the usual, more formal and more strongly mediated representation of consciousness, his thoughts enter the narrative more overtly, and with more drastic diction, when he refers to his tedium vitae through another body image: "After sixty years of [...] pissing and shitting, then being harnessed for the day's haul, Paul Rayment's team will have had enough" (53). Here, a contemptuous image of the body is overevident: by reducing corporeality to metabolic function, the dysfunctional body is rendered entirely redundant.

The contempt Rayment feels for his maimed body is, in his perception, mirrored in reactions of other characters. The visible reduction and truncation of his formerly ageless body exposes him to "the pitiless gaze of the young" (Coetzee 13), thus separating him from the norm of the young and whole. The explicit mentioning of the concept of "gaze" as an instrument of othering makes clear that he perceives himself, as an old man in a maimed body, to be marked by profound difference and regarded with distance, even averseness.[5] Impairment and old age thus merge to one category of radical alterity into which Rayment irreversibly falls. The otherness induced by his disability is aggravated by, and in turn aggravates, his age-related otherness. His sense of personhood and identity is reduced to the same extent that his body has been both reduced and stigmatized by the amputation, literally cutting off a crucial part of his self-identity. Rayment himself suggests the connectivity of impairment with the passing of time by explicating the metaphorical potential of the incision, which comes to represent a turning point in his life and clearly divides his previous life from an uncertain future:

---

5 | This gaze which he even assumes from Marijana's six-year-old daughter Ljuba (Coetzee 187) frightens him enough to let himself be persuaded into a sexual adventure with a blind woman who cannot see his stump (Loimeier 229). His own judgement of the gaze of the young certainly reveals more about the process of othering himself from the young and whole than about the rejection he actually suffers from his onlookers, as Nashef notes: "Once again, self-consciousness prevails as he projects his own thoughts onto the child" (152). 'The young', as an assumed normative group who aims to exclude Rayment, can accordingly be read as the focalizer's own construct, which enables him to blame his self-alienation on social othering which he is subjected to.

> But in his case the cut seems to have marked off past from future with such un-
> common cleanness that it gives new meaning to the word new. By the sign of this
> cut let a new life commence. If you have hitherto been a man, with a man's life,
> may you henceforth be a dog, with a dog's life. (Coetzee 26)

This passage also shows the assumed relation of a visible impairment to
the inner Self: The stigma, as a sign of violation "cut or burnt into the body"
(Goffman 1) which refers to a moral disorder in its bearer[6]. Indeed, Rayment's physical violation can be viewed as stigma since it finally results in,
or brings out, depression, tetchiness, and an "unsuitable passion" (Coetzee
85) for his nurse.

After the concrete loss of a body part, his entire bodily and mental integrity seem at stake, he feels "time at work on him like a wasting disease,
like the quicklime they pour on corpses. Time is gnawing away at him, de-
vouring one by one the cells that make him up. His cells are going out like
lights", and at night "he can hear the ghostly creeping of his assaulted flesh
as it tries to knit itself together again" (Coetzee 11-12). The embodiedness
of old age, of finiteness, only becomes perceivable to Rayment after he has
been reverberated into physicalness by injury. Now he develops a longing
for disembodiment, imagining to "emerge on the other side [of the crema-
torium] as nothing but a shovelful of ash, almost weightless" (Coetzee 13).
He contemplates suicide as a possibility of getting rid of the body he can
no longer ignore and take for granted but which now continuously claims
presence through pain, subjection to gaze, and its unwontedness.

Interestingly, Rayment denies all possibilities to compensate for his
body's truncation and the trauma he suffered, whether by prosthetic provisions or by financial reparation. Upon the visit of an old friend, he states
that he has no intention of trying to symbolically reinstate a state of corporeal wholeness by suing the young man at fault for the accident. It seems
pointless to him: "'Too many openings for comedy. *I want my leg back, failing which...'*" (Coetzee 15). Rayment refuses the fitting of an artificial leg,
and is instead equipped with crutches and a walker, which he finds more
"honest" than a prosthesis. What looks like acceptance of the irreversibility
of his situation can also be interpreted as a lack of a practicable strategy
of coping with the social expectations towards his recovery. This reveals
the interesting body image he defends: In spite of the truncation and the

---

6 | About physical disability as stigma also see Waldschmidt 31.

estrangement he feels to his maimed physical Self, he does not want to complete or restore its functions with devices he considers as not being his own. He rejects the image of a modern body-machine: "It [the prosthesis] is out of Surrealism. It is out of Dali" (Coetzee 9); he prefers to make do with devices that are, in terms of medical technology, outdated. Thus, he is actively taking a position of being non-modern, non-up-to-date, othering himself in turn from ideologies of efficiency and functionality. In his struggle to come to terms with a body beyond repair, he resists the culturally desirable management and improvement of the corporeal Self.[7]

THE LIMINAL BODY

After his discharge, Rayment's 'new life' is reorganized around the needs of his impaired body and his avoidance of seeking its artificial replenishment. Whereas he thinks and speaks of the very intimate care of washing his genitals or inserting a catheter (Coetzee 6) in a factual, casual tone, his amputation stump becomes his most tabooed body part, the focus of what Hania Nashef calls the "resentment of the abject decomposing body" (154). Avoiding to think about (and thus to focalize on) it wherever possible, he only occasionally refers to the stump directly, either in a distanced and factual ("the thing," Coetzee 28) or sarcastic ("le jambon," Coetzee 29) manner. Ugly, obscene and disfigured (Coetzee 33), the stump is not only evidence of something lost, but also foreign matter no longer belonging to the body, inhuman and exotic like "some sightless deep-water fish" (Coetzee 28). What he tells Ljuba, his nurse's little daughter, is by no means his own conviction: "Is it true you've got a artificial leg?" [...] "No, it's the same leg I have always had, just a bit shorter" (Coetzee 55). In both its truncation and

---

7 | The collective ideology of managing the body is expressed by numerous other characters. Later in the narrative, for example, his stubborn rejection of the prosthesis leads his nurse to suggest that Rayment has the childish idea that his truncated leg might regrow after a while (Coetzee 62). Thus, the management of (or rather, the refusal to manage) his own body leads to further forms of othering the protagonist, this time by suggesting that he was behaving unreasonably. The comparison to a child (Coetzee 23, 60) is, as mentioned, a frequent strategy of producing age-related alterity and suggesting a reduction of the older person's mental ability and moral integrity.

its obscenity the amputation stump stands for Rayment's manhood and reveals that the impairment has also affected his masculine self-identity. Making clear that he no longer feels that he is a man but at best a "diminished man" (Coetzee 32), "a man not wholly a man [...] a half-man" (Coetzee 33-34), he alludes to a perception of having been castrated by the amputation as well as by the prevalent image of the old person as sexually neuter, although "not incapacitated" (Coetzee 37). At the same time, the repetition of the exotic, horrible and obscene qualities of his tabooed stump signify all too clearly a monstrous phallic organ, the uncovering of whose "naked face" makes Rayment "avert[...] his eyes" (Coetzee 28). Obscenity and repulsiveness are not limited to the stump, but seem to spread over and infect the rest of his body with ascriptions of abject agedness, which in its entirety is described as "smelly," "unlovely," and "obscene" (Coetzee 38, 107).

Before the accident, Rayment already had a distanced relationship to his own body, covering his bathroom mirror with a drape in order to be spared his own ugly, but most of all boring reflection (Coetzee 163-64). Never having had much regard for his own body, he now finds it even more difficult to build a relationship towards it, preferring to leave his body alone – not wanting a prosthesis and refusing any other help to reinstate its functions – and treating it as the Other of himself: "He still has a sense of being a soul with an undiminished soul-life; as for the rest of him, it is just a sack of blood and bones that he is forced to carry around" (Coetzee 32). His attitude to bodily pleasures is characterized by the need for control and a fear of losing it not only through bodily impairment but also through sexual pleasure, by getting caught in the "grip of passion" (Coetzee 46) – which according to Michael Marais serves as "a prelude to death" (197) – or by acquiring a contagious illness, "a comical but unavoidable affliction like mumps" (Coetzee 45). Although the body is regarded as the Other of the Self, the idea of the physical state influencing the state of mind is expressed:

The face that threatens to confront him in the mirror is that of a gaunt, unshaven old tramp. In fact, worse than that. At a bookstall on the Seine he once picked up a medical text with photographs of patients from the Salpêtrière: cases of mania, dementia, melancholia, Huntington's chorea. Despite the untidy beards, despite the hospital nightshirts, he at once recognised in them soul mates, cousins who had gone ahead down a road he would one day follow. (Coetzee 164)

Notably, the 'tramps' with whom Rayment identifies in anticipation are not only of unsound bodies and minds, they are also old. The use of the metaphor of the "road he would one day follow" and the mention of incurable degenerative processes (dementia and Huntington's chorea) are clear references to his horror of old age, which is presented as inevitable, abject, and degrading.

The concept of the body as the Other of the Self is especially observable in depictions of Rayment's body as grotesque and unruly – either by himself or by other characters. In Rayment's body, an unruly and obscene 'second phallus' has been created through surgery from a body part that was mutilated and lost its actual use. Being a remarkably dispassionate and sober-minded character with an alleged "aversion to the physical" (Coetzee 234), allusions to the grotesque quality of his truncated body present a challenge, even an offense, to his self-identity: that the tragic event of the accident resulted in a body perceived as comical is a further humiliation to him. The character Elizabeth Costello states that "[l]osing a leg is not a tragedy. On the contrary, losing a leg is comic. Losing any part of the body that sticks out is comic. [...] There was an old man with one leg / who stood with his hat out to beg" (Coetzee 99). The phantom limb receives, in its absence, an absurd degree of attention and hyper-presence (Sobchack 58).

Rayment's altered physical state of being also affects his experience and the semanticization of time and space. During his hospitalization, he is physically removed from the world he has formerly inhabited, and immobilized in his hospital bed. The surgical ward he finds himself in is depicted as an-Other, strictly confined space and perceived as surreal. The boundaries of this "land of whiteness" (Coetzee 13) are at first hardly distinguishable from the limits of the human body: "He tries to sit up but cannot; it is as if he were encased in concrete. Around him whiteness unrelieved [...]" (Coetzee 3). The loss of autonomous mobility he has not yet realized before his leg is actually amputated is thus foreshadowed through the physical confinement in the hospital ward. After the surgery, painkillers blur his perception of time and space, the sick room is only vaguely described as part of the "land of whiteness," the "zone of humiliation" (Coetzee 13) which can be entered by nurses and doctors at their own discretion but which he can neither lock nor leave. Thus exposed and caged at the same time, he waits for time to pass.

The protagonist's altered perception of space is attended by a change in the perception of the passing of time. By being spatially removed from the routines of the outside world, his sense of time is disconnected from the clock. Time is perceived in a most ambivalent way: moments of pain and humiliation are reflected in great detail and by stretching discourse time (e.g. Coetzee 13), whereas his body seems to feel the impact of time running out in high speed: "The clock stands still yet time does not. Even as he lies here he can feel time at work on him [...]" (Coetzee 11). The image of "time working on the body" is obviously an image of physical aging, the acknowledgement of which is triggered by the injury and immobilization of his body. The first instance of the close connection of time and space (and their relation to aging) in the novel can actually be found in the title: the attribution of slowness refers to spatial mobility in relation to time. Being 'slowed down' is also a common metaphor of age(ing), referring not only to the decrease of the body's mobility but also to a disconnection of the aging person from the temporal structure of professional life, and to the limitedness of future development. At the same time, age(ing) denotes a linear progress towards the end of life which is aggravated and accelerated by frailty and impairment, just as experienced by Paul Rayment. This double-edged image of age(ing) – as both winding down *and* accelerating the life course – is mirrored in his ambivalent perception of spatiality and temporality.

As spatial mobility and self-determined structuring of his time are denied to him, agency becomes limited to imagination: Rayment's mobility is confined to escapes into memories of his childhood in particular (Coetzee 11) and his life course in general, of which he critically takes stock, calling it *"a wasted chance"* (Coetzee 19; original emphasis). He fantasizes about his future, or rather, its limitations, namely death and the possibility of being committed to an "institution for the aged and infirm" (Coetzee 17). His perception of limited space and time is summarized in a metaphor of imprisonment and lack of perspective: "[...] there is no future, the door to the future has been closed and locked" (Coetzee 13), his life course being perceived as truncated as his leg.

In the state of immobility, the body itself becomes a space in which the protagonist is confined: its boundaries limit the protagonist's agency. The body's outer shell as "interface between the Self and its contexts" (Sielke and Schäfer-Wünsche 15) is represented as a site of negotiating self-determination, as becomes clear in the face of Rayment's humiliation when these boundaries are violently crossed through the amputation surgery and, later, in the care work performed on him by various nurses. The 'grotesque' potential of the maimed body is concretized through the violent reshaping and, later, trespassing of the border between the individual and the outside world. Again, this body image is interesting with regard to Rayment's masculine self-identity: the representation of the body as available and penetrable contains attributions of femininity. Later in the narrative, his male body is represented not only as abject, but also as leaky, a concept formerly used to describe the 'uncontrollable' boundaries of the female body especially with regard to menstruation and childbirth (Shildrick):

Does being unable to control one's bladder count as an emergency? No, clearly not. It is just part of life, part of growing old. Miserably he surrenders and urinates on the floor. [...] Now here he is, a helpless old man in urinous pyjamas trailing an obscene pink stump behind him from which the sodden bandages are slipping. (Coetzee 214)

The representation of Rayment's body as incontinent – protruding into and soiling the outside world – signifies not only a lack of control over the body but, moreover, contains ascriptions of eviration and agedness. The body is becoming – similar to Featherstone's and Hepworth's concept of the "mask of ageing" (Featherstone, "Post-Bodies") which conceals individual identity – a prison which confines identity and limits the inmate in agency and self-determination.

Back in his flat, the image of spatial confinement is repeated, yet this time in familiar surroundings. For months into his acquaintance with nurse Sheena and, subsequently, Marijana, there is no mention of a venture outside his flat except for weekly check-ups in the hospital and one visit to the public library. His own rooms have lost the quality of being a private refuge as they are now entered daily by different nurses – again, while he cannot cross spatial boundaries at his own discretion, he has no means of shutting out the outside world and protect his privacy; and finally "welcomes those days when [...] no one arrives to take care of him" (Coetzee 25). Siddharta Deb observes: "He has always preferred being left to his own devices but the modern world, having first crippled him, now demands to be let in as a care-giver" (par. 2).

In this confined space, literally locked in with his fears and musings, he begins to suffer from depression which he refers to as to a part of the interior, or a housemate: "The gloom seems to have settled in, to be part of the climate" (Coetzee 25). The outside world only exists in his memory now: "The universe has contracted to this flat and the block or two around, and it will not expand again. A circumscribed life" (Coetzee 25).[8] Like the experience of time, the perception of space is ambiguous: though circumscribed around a fixed base, Rayment feels "unstrung" (Coetzee 27) from the world he inhabits. Being confined to a limited indoor territory without access to the public sphere also relates to a gendered experience of space: he is now denied the stereotypically masculine privilege of freely venturing outdoors (Würzbach 50) – a privilege he considered a vital part of his lifestyle (Coetzee 25) – and suffers from the fact that the space that encages him is freely accessible for others while he tries to preserve a space of his own in memory and daydreaming.

With the advent of nurse Marijana, another person begins to inhabit Paul Rayment's personal space whom he willingly admits, and who provides a sufficient connection to the outside world and structuring of time – in contrast to former nurses and caregivers, whom he regarded as intruders. Elizabeth Costello and Drago Jokić (besides the briefly visiting Marianna and Margaret McCord) are two more characters who enter Rayment's private space and even set up house in his flat long before he is himself able to leave it again. Michael Marais relates to this situation under the term of 'hospitality' which suggests a free agency and willing invitation from the side of the host and does not quite capture the ambivalence of being spared loneliness and abandonment on the one hand and giving up control over the boundaries of personal space on the other. This becomes clear when Rayment offers a temporary shelter to Marijana's son Drago, hoping for a "quiet growth of intimacy" between them, and is disappointed: "In fact, he feels that Drago is pushing him away" (Coetzee 180) by annexing Rayment's flat just as Elizabeth Costello did, and inviting his own friends. In realizing that "I might as well be a stick of furniture" (Coetzee 181), he acknowledges the fact that he is no longer master of his own space. With the exception of Drago's prolonged visit, the spheres of old and young bodies are clearly demarcated. The young women 'demanding to be let in as caregivers' come for professional reasons (including Marianna, whom Rayment pays for an intimate encounter) – visitors who come for reasons

---

8 | The term 'circumscribed' can be read as a metafictional allusion: not only is Rayment's altered life limited by spatial and temporal confinements, it is also limited by the (in)adequacy of verbal representation.

of their own are Rayment's age mates (Margaret McCord) or seniors (Elizabeth Costello).

The state of being powerless in one's own space lasts until the very end of his novel, when Paul is persuaded by Elizabeth Costello to venture outside his home to visit Marijana's house in Munno Para, after months of only leaving his flat when it was unavoidable. "A real expedition," Elizabeth Costello calls it. "The dark continent of Munno Para. I'm sure it will take you out of yourself" (Coetzee 241). This quotation shows again how Paul's spatial confinement is a symbol for the confinement of his inner Self. The world outside his flat has become a dark continent ruled by modern convictions and ideologies he no longer wants to put up with, and his flat has become a refuge to a time past, a place where remnants of the past are assembled,[9] including himself (Coetzee 47-48, 51). Facing Elizabeth Costello, though, this metaphor is rejected by Rayment: "'If we visit Munno Para it will not be in order to take me out of myself' [...]. 'There is nothing in me that I need to escape from'" (Coetzee 241). During his visit to the Jokić family he makes a first attempt of regaining mobility and tries out the recumbent bike Drago has built for him with the help of his parents. Although Rayment thinks to himself that he will never use it again (Coetzee 256), Loimeier judges this scene "a moment of disenthrallment" (226; my translation) from the spatial and psychic confinement he has been suffering. After returning to Coniston Terrace with Elizabeth Costello, the ending is open and the repossession of his flat remains unnarrated. The end of the narrative, his bidding goodbye to Elizabeth Costello outside the front door, suggests that there will be no more uninvited guests into the house. This final closure of the private space against intrusion from the outside might also denote a process of healing or at least scarification of his injury: The cut on his leg marks the place where the outside world has entered and violated the integrity of Rayment's old body. At the end of the novel, this violation, made visible in the ugly stump he was left with, is no longer at

---

9 | The interior of Rayment's apartment points out in many respects that its resident belongs to an older generation: he possesses an outdated computer with no access to the internet (Coetzee 177-78), a book collection and a collection of black-and-white photography from Australia's later colonial history which is, in anticipation of his death, intended to be bequeathed to the State Library (Coetzee 49).

the center of attention – a development potentially pointing at the possibility of closure.

Bodies of Others

There is one other aged and aging body in the novel which is described in detail: that of Elizabeth Costello. First of all, Rayment conceives of her as an old woman: "a woman in her sixties, he would say, the later rather than the earlier sixties, wearing a floral silk dress cut low behind to reveal unattractively freckled, fleshy shoulders" (Coetzee 80). His skepticism is first alerted when Costello asks him to convince her of his physical substantiality – "We are not ghosts, are we?" (Coetzee 81) – and subsequently unsettled when Costello begins to recite the beginning of the novel itself:

'The blow catches him from the right, sharp and surprising and painful, like a bolt of electricity, lifting him up off the bicycle. Relax! he tells himself as he tumbles through the air, and so forth.' (Coetzee 81)

This *mise en abyme* points far beyond the mere bodily presence of Costello: here she is revealed to be metafiction made flesh, an abstract concept incarnated in the plain physical presence of an older woman otherwise physically weak and insignificant. For Rayment, Costello's parasitic annexion of his story, her (d)evaluation of his role and agency in it, and her subsequent attempts to alter his future, raise the question of the possibility of self-determination. On top of his previous loss of physical wholeness and agency, her physical advent in Rayment's apartment begins to threaten the formerly safe mental spaces established as response to his spatial confinement and exposedness.

Besides her metafictional functions, Costello's feminine corporeality offers itself as a correspondent to Rayment as a representative of masculine age(ing). Rayment has no feeling of solidarity with her at first but merely perceives her as a perpetrator. Images of abject agedness are used to refer to Costello as the Other: she is described as physically repulsive, and of ill health, with a bad heart, grey hair and skin, and blue-veined and "wasted" calves (Coetzee 82, 84). His mention of Costello's ugly legs points to a comparison of the old woman's physique with Marijana's healthy, attractive body: her legs are mentioned several times as the physical feature which intrigued Rayment the most (Coetzee 50). Linked to the devaluing descriptions of her body are typical, negative ascriptions of agedness which add up to the stereotype of the cantankerous old crone: Costello is depicted as domineering, viperish and intrusive. Only occasionally do the two aged characters seem reconcilable – through common experiences of aging and contrastive juxtaposition with images of youth, some sameness is established: "It is the first exchange that he and the Costello woman have had that he would call cordial, even amiable. For once they are on the same side: two old folk ganging up on youth" (Coetzee 191).

Behind Rayment's frequent depictions of Costello's aging female body as abject is an attempt to subvert Costello's power of deconstructing his identity: by devaluing and 'othering' her corporeal presence, he marginalizes at least her bodily existence, thus receiving a rudimental compensation for the marginalization and disempowerment he has suffered through 'being written' by her. In return, Costello rubs salt into the wound of his own problematic body image:

Where else in the world, at this late stage, are you going to find affection, you ugly old man? Yes, I am familiar with that word too, *ugly*. We are both of us ugly, Paul, old and ugly, As much as ever would we like to hold in our arms the beauty of all the world. It never wanes in us, that yearning. But the beauty of all the world does not want any of us. So we have to make do with less, a great deal less. (Coetzee 236; original emphasis)

At this stage of their acquaintance, Costello reveals the desire which is part of her appropriation of Paul Rayment: she wants to live with him in companionship; at best, she wants his love. For this purpose, she alludes to his fear of death: "'Adelaide is too much like a graveyard. [...] Come and live with me in Carlton instead'" (Coetzee 231). Rayment, however, reacts with repulsion to the idea of sharing his life with a woman whom he regards as abject and tetchy. With this confession of her neediness and affection – and, not least, of the wish for physical affection – part of the spell of her power is broken, and Rayment recognizes that "[s]he is not a higher being" (Coetzee 234). When, in a last surge of imperiousness, Costello tries to threaten Rayment into accepting her invitation, he can no longer be intimidated. At the very end of the novel, after Rayment's relationship with the Jokić family has ended, she repeats her offer, but this time it resembles a plea: "And this is your last word, do you think? No hope of budging you?" (Coetzee 263). Rayment scrutinizes her closely: "In the clear afternoon light he can see every detail, every hair, every vein. He examines her, then examines his heart. 'No,' he says at last [...]" (Coetzee 263). Costello, in Rayment's perception, has been humbled and reduced to just an old woman; within the narrative, she is now just another character of the novel. The confession of her affection and neediness implies a confession of being old, lonely, and afraid of death. Old age and its corporeality, as becomes evident here, have reduced her to her humanness. Their common experience of age(ing) has rendered the characters equal at last, but sameness will not be established.

The 'message of aging' – that physical existence is moribund, frail, and vulnerable – is clarified and exemplified by the irreversible maiming of the body: the mark of disability points to the marks of age(ing); one category of otherness brings along, and shapes, another. After the physically devastating accident becomes a catalyst of aging, the protagonist ends up without a self-contained and closed image of later life: the life story of the protagonist ends in a liminal state as the narrative deserts him in an open ending. The "end of a long day" as announced rather optimistically by Elizabeth Costello (Coetzee 262) does not signify closure but uncertainty. His 'coming of age' remains unaccomplished since he fails to find and adapt to a new age role which would resolve the process of becoming Other.

REFERENCES

Backes, Gertrud, and Wolfgang Clemens. *Lebensphase Alter. Eine Einführung in die sozialwissenschaftliche Alternsforschung.* Weinheim: Juventa, 1998. Print.

Bakhtin, Michail. "The Grotesque Image of the Body and its Sources." 1965. *The Body. A Reader.* Ed. Mariam Fraser and Monica Greco. London: Routledge, 2005. 92-95. Print.

Baudrillard, Jean. "The Finest Consumer Object: the Body." 1998. *The Body. A Reader.* Ed. Mariam Fraser and Monica Greco. London: Routledge, 2005. 277-82. Print.

Biggs, Simon. "The difficulties of putting oneself in the place of the age-other and the promise of intergenerational sustainability." *Netzwerk Alternsforschung. Archiv: Kongresse.* Universität Heidelberg, Mar. 2011. Web. 30 Jan. 2012.

Coetzee, John M. *Slow Man.* 2005. London: Penguin, 2006. Print.

Deb, Siddharta. "'Into the Hall of Mirrors.' Siddharta Deb reviews *Slow Man* by J. M. Coetzee." *The Telegraph* 4 Sept. 2005. Web. 25 May 2011.

Dederich, Markus. *Körper, Kultur und Behinderung. Eine Einführung in die Disability Studies.* Bielefeld: transcript, 2007. Print.

Featherstone, Mike. "Post-Bodies, Aging and Virtual Reality." *Images of Aging. Cultural Representations of Later Life.* Ed. Mike Featherstone and Andrew Wernick. London: Routledge, 1995. 227-44. Print.

Ferring, Dieter, Miriam Haller, Hartmut Meyer-Wolters, and Tom Michels, eds. *Soziokulturelle Konstruktion des Alters. Transdisziplinäre Perspektiven.* Würzburg: Königshausen & Neumann, 2008. Print.

Garland-Thomsen, Rosemary. "Andere Geschichten." Ed. Helma Lutz, Maria Teresa Herrera Vivar, and Linda Supik. *Fokus Intersektionalität. Bewegung und Verortung eines vielschichtigen Konzepts.* Wiesbaden: VS Verlag für Sozialwissenschaften, 2010. 418-25. Print.

Gilleard, Chris, and Paul Higgs. "Ageing and its embodiment." *The Body. A Reader.* Ed. Mariam Fraser and Monica Greco. London: Routledge, 2005. 117-21. Print.

—. "Ageing abjection and embodiment in the fourth age." *Journal of Aging Studies* 25 (2011): 135-42. Print.

Goffman, Erving. *Stigma. Notes on the Management of Spoiled Identity.* 1963. New York: Simon & Schuster, 1986. Print.

Gullette, Margaret Morganroth. *Safe at Last in the Middle Years. The Invention of the Midlife Progress Novel: Saul Bellow, Margaret Drabble, Anne Tyler, John Updike.* Berkeley: University of California Press, 1988. Print.

Haller, Miriam. "Altern erzählen. 'Rites de passage' als narratives Muster im zeitgenössischen Roman." *Soziokulturelle Konstruktion des Alters. Transdisziplinäre Perspektiven.* Ed. Dieter Ferring, Miriam Haller, Hartmut Meyer-Wolters, and Tom Michels. Würzburg: Königshausen & Neumann, 2008. 95-117. Print.

—. "Undoing Age. Die Performativität des alternden Körpers im autobiographischen Text." *"Für Dein Alter siehst Du gut aus!" Von der Un/Sichtbarkeit des alternden Körpers im Horizont des demographischen Wandels.* Ed. Sabine Mehlmann and Sigrid Ruby. Bielefeld: transcript, 2010. 215-33. Print.

Hartung, Heike, ed. *Alter und Geschlecht. Repräsentationen, Geschichten und Theorien des Alter(n)s.* Bielefeld: transcript, 2005. Print.

—, Dorothea Reinmuth, Christiane Streubel, Angelika Uhlmann, eds. *Graue Theorie. Die Kategorien Alter und Geschlecht im kulturellen Diskurs*. Cologne: Böhlau, 2007. Print.

Hearns, Jeff. "Vernachlässigte Intersektionalitäten in der Männerforschung: Alter(n), Virtualität, Transnationalität." *Fokus Intersektionalität. Bewegung und Verortung eines vielschichtigen Konzepts*. Ed. Helma Lutz, Maria Teresa Herrera Vivar, and Linda Supik. Wiesbaden: VS Verlag für Sozialwissenschaften, 2010. 105-24. Print.

Jolly, Rosemary. "Writing Desire Responsibly." *J.M. Coetzee in Context and Theory*. Ed. Elleke Boehmer, Katy Iddiols, and Robert Eaglestone. London: Continuum, 2009. 93-111. Print.

Kristeva, Julia. *Powers of Horror: an Essay on Abjection*. New York: Columbia University Press, 1982. Print.

Küpper, Thomas. "Natürlich künstlich glatte Haut." *"Für Dein Alter siehst du gut aus!" Von der Un/Sichtbarkeit des alternden Körpers im Horizont des demographischen Wandels*. Ed. Sabine Mehlmann and Sigrid Ruby. Bielefeld: transcript, 2010. 69-87. Print.

Loimeier, Manfred. *J. M. Coetzee*. Munich: edition text + kritik, 2008. Print.

Marais, Mike. *Secretary of the Invisible. The Idea of Hospitality in the Fiction of J. M. Coetzee*. Amsterdam: Rodopi, 2009. Print.

Nashef, Hania A. M. *The Politics of Humiliation in the Novels of J. M. Coetzee*. Abingdon: Taylor & Francis, 2009. Print.

Schmincke, Imke. "Außergewöhnliche Körper. Körpertheorie als Gesellschaftstheorie." *Marginalisierte Körper. Beiträge zur Soziologie und Geschichte des anderen Körpers*. Ed. Imke Schmincke and Thorsten Junge Münster: Unrast, 2007. 11-26. Print.

Shildrick, Margrit. *Leaky Bodies and Boundaries. Feminism, postmodernism and (bio)ethics*. London: Routledge, 1997. Print.

Sielke, Sabine, and Elisabeth Schäfer-Wünsche, eds. *The Body as Interface: Dialogues between the Disciplines*. Heidelberg: Winter, 2007. Print.

Sobchack, Vivian. "Living a 'Phantom Limb': On the Phenomenology of Bodily Integrity." *Body & Society* 16.3 (2010): 51-67. Print.

Sontag, Susan. "The Double Standard of Aging." *The Saturday Review*, September 23, 1972. 29-38. Print.

Van Gennep, Arnold. *Übergangsriten*. Frankfurt: campus, 2005 [1909].

Waldschmidt, Anne. "Behinderte Körper: Stigmatheorie, Diskurstheorie und Disability Studies im Vergleich." *Marginalisierte Körper. Beiträge zur Soziologie und Geschichte des* anderen *Körpers.* Ed. Imke Schmincke and Thorsten Junge Münster: Unrast, 2007. 27-43. Print.

West, Candace, and Don Zimmerman. "Doing Gender." *Gender and Society* 1.2 (1987): 125-51. Print.

Winker, Gabriele, and Nina Degele. *Intersektionalität. Zur Analyse sozialer Ungleichheiten.* Bielefeld: transcript, 2009. Print

—. "Raumdarstellung." *Erzähltextanalyse und Gender Studies.* Ed. Ansgar Nünning and Vera Nünning. Stuttgart: Metzler, 2004. 49-71. Print.

Würzbach, Natascha. "Einführung in die Theorie und Praxis der feministisch orientierten Literaturwissenschaft." Ed. Ansgar Nünning: *Literaturwissenschaftliche Theorien, Modelle und Methoden.* Trier: Wissenschaftlicher Verlag Trier, 1995. 137-52. Print.

Too Old To Rock?

Rushdie's Vina Apsara "Surging into Her
Mid-Forties Full of Beauty and Courage"

Dana Bădulescu

CHERCHEZ LA FEMME: RUSHDIE'S FLAMBOYANT CHARACTERS

Salman Rushdie has always been interested in exploring femininity, feminine issues, and representations of women across cultures and age. In "Women Beware Women," an article published in *The Guardian* in 2001, he warns against a growing tendency towards 'masculinism' in Indian society due to the availability of ultrasound tests to determine the gender of unborn children in order to reduce the number of girls being born in the country. He explains that in his writing he has "repeatedly sought to create female characters as rich and powerful as those" (par. 3) he has known. Rushdie considers this focus on women a normal and natural preoccupation for a writer. As in his generation girls outnumbered boys by two to one, Rushdie nostalgically recalls in the same *Guardian* article that coming "from a sprawling Indian family dominated by women," (par. 1) he grew up surrounded by a pair of "formidable" and "irresistible" aunts (par. 1), three sisters, and a league of female cousins, "few of whom resemble the stereotype of the demure, self-effacing Indian woman" (par. 2). Instead, Rushdie describes these women as "opinionated, voluble, smart, funny, arm-waving persons – lawyers, educators, radicals, movers, shakers, matriarchs" (par. 2). What Rushdie means is that women are not only very interesting and challenging company who will not listen to you unless you can really stir their interest, but they are also exemplary citizens and reliable friends. It is this personal background that irrevocably oriented Rushdie towards female characters, and by comparison he continues to say in "Women Beware Women" that "The men in my books are rarely as flamboyant as the women" (par. 3).

Rushdie's approach to women may be controversial and sometimes irritating, but the fact remains that he has always responded to the female as an irresistible power and used his finest writing skills to rise to the provocative task. The magnetic feminine power in Rushdie's writings is highlighted by various places such as countries and cities, which become rich metaphors for various stances of womanhood. More often than not, India is figured as a mother in *The Moor's Last Sigh*, or in the 'disorienting' story of *The Ground Beneath Her Feet* as the male character's first love never to be forgotten, no matter how hard one may try and despite the bitter-sweet experience it offers. The narrative emphasizes this lack of orientation in different instances, for example, when Vina Apsara lives in permanent danger of falling into "cracks and rifts," "the divisions in her soul" (*Ground* 339) until she is literally swallowed up by a terrible earthquake. However, before "the ground beneath her feet" (a recurrent image in the novel) shakes and she disappears into the unfathomable abyss, Vina Apsara, who acts as Rushdie's Eurydice, experiences a different form of "disorientation: loss of the East" (*Ground* 5). The Orient thus provides orientation not only for Vina, but by extension virtually for everyone. Vina's "disorientation" is also caused by the loss of her symbiotic lover Orpheus, whose archetypal part is played in the novel by rock 'n' roll singer Ormus Cama, "her sun" (*Ground* 5). In the same novel, England is seen as a clutching lover called "Tar Baby" with a strong grip that never lets go, which Ormus, the Orphic character in the novel, calls "stuck love" (*Ground* 276). Encouraged by Vina, Ormus manages to free himself from Tar Baby's strange embrace, and flees to America, "Langston Hughes's country that never existed but needed to exist, with that, like everyone else, I was thoroughly in love" (*Ground* 419), although having developed "double vision," (*Ground* 325) he also sees America's drawbacks. Since his transcultural imagination steps across frontiers to project places of the mind, Florence adds to the erotically charged imaginary map charted by Rushdie in *The Enchantress of Florence*. The tone and diction of the narrator's description of the Italian city in its Renaissance glory days is as a not to be resisted seductress where even reading about it is irresistibly seducing:

'Imagine a pair of woman's lips,' Mogor whispered, puckering for a kiss. That is the city of Florence, narrow at the edges, swelling at the centre, with the Arno flowing through between, parting the two lips, the upper and the lower. The city is an enchantress. When it kisses you, you are lost, whether you be a commoner or a king. (Rushdie, *Enchantress* 176)

Rushdie's consistent preference for female characters helped him refine his skills from one novel to the next. The writer is not merely interested in representing the appeal of young women, but instead to portray womanhood in its entire complexity. He explores archetypes and cultural representations of women across age and cultures, adapting the characters' age as the models require and giving archetypes as many twists as it takes to translate mythical patterns into contemporary forms so that his readers can relate to them.

WHO IS VINA?

The novel opens in a hotel room in the Mexican city of Guadalajara, where Vina is shown strongly shaken by a recent nightmare. The first passage in the book is a vivid account of a fantastic sacrificial ritual "in which she had been the intended victim" (*Ground* 3). It takes just one more line and the intrigued reader sees her body "naked and writhing, over a polished stone bearing the graven image of the snakebird Quetzalcoatl" (*Ground* 3). Just before her throat is slit in the dream, she wakes up soaked in perspiration to find by her side "a naked mestizio male in his early twenties," whom she barely knows, seized with spasms "identical to her own dream writhings" (*Ground* 3-4). Already in the grips of this strange mixture of dream/fantasy and reality, the reader's appetite for such unusual scenes needs fueling. The fuel comes in the next lines, which are a briefing on the events leading to this scene: Vina, the star of rock 'n' roll "had surrendered herself to this nobody, this boy less than half her age" (*Ground* 4). The next passage covers the testimony of the chauffeur, who though alarmed by "the ferocity of her appetite" "speaks with reverence of her naked body," whispering into the journalists' ears "about her swarming and predatory nudity as if it were a miracle, who'd have thought she was way the wrong side of forty" (*Ground* 4).

The scene is set by an ironical analogy on St. Valentine's Day 1989, the year when Rushdie himself received what he called "my unfunny Valentine" ("My unfunny Valentine" 28). The first line also indicates that this is to be the last day of Vina's life, and thereupon the story moves back- and forward in time, also going beyond 1989. It is unfolded by a photographer, Umeed Merchant, better known as Rai, who although three years younger than her is half-hopelessly-half-hopefully head over heels in love with Vina.

Rai, who is Vina's lover and confidante, tells us Vina's life story. Vina was born as Nissa Shetty to a Greek-American mother, a reader of books and dreamer, and an Indian father, who abandoned them. She grew up in a shack in the middle of a cornfield outside of Chester, Virginia. When her mother re-married John Poe, Vina became Nissy Poe and had a rather unhappy life as a child in America. Eventually, her mother killed all the members of her new family sparing only Nissy for unknown reasons, although the girl suspected it was because the mother had discovered her talent, her beautiful voice. During the year spent at her mother's distant relatives in Chickaboom, near the Finger Lakes in Western New York State, she discarded the name Nissy Poe and took the family name offered by her uncle Mr. Egiptus; "she became Diana Egiptus without regret" (*Ground* 109). After this one year, however, having been rejected by Mr. Egiptus, she was sent to India. When she arrived in Bombay, she was twelve years old, and there she finally met Ormus Cama and Rai, as she seemed to have been destined to. She did not live with her Indian relatives for long. Her relationship to Piloo Doodhwala was affected by the news he gathered of her dating Ormus, "a grown nineteen-year-old man with movie star good looks and a whispered success rate with the girls" (*Ground* 111). Forced to leave the Doodhwalas after a huge scandal, she arrived on the doorstep of Rai's family, with Ormus not far behind. The Merchants took her in, accepting Ormus' word that they were not having a sexual relationship. Moreover, Ormus swore that he would not touch her until she had turned sixteen. They were both changed by meeting each other in the sense that "he became the meaning of her life, and she of his" (*Ground* 112).

This mythically resonant story of love, which seems to be doomed from the start, employs the pattern of 'star-crossed lovers.' Within the novel, Ormus and Vina are separated for long periods of time, and Ormus is portrayed as "the lovesick floating romeo [who] sings to his unheeding love" (*Ground* 280) pining for their reunion and painfully missing his love. Vina, however, does not hear his 'appeal' because "she's in America and doesn't know he's floating off the coast of England, damp and yearning, and calling out her name" (*Ground* 280).

In India, Diana changes her name again, and from then on goes by the name of Vina Apsara. Meeting Ormus, the Orpheus of rock 'n' roll, who from the moment of his birth gave many indications of his precocious talent, "not only the chord progression of his finger movements but also the syncopated drumming of his tiny feet against his crib and the perfect pitch-gurgles that went up and down the musical scale" (*Ground* 46), Vina starts fulfilling her own destiny as a legendary voice. Rai explains the rich significance of her name "too good for this world" (*Ground* 55). Vina means "lyre" and Apsara, from *apsaras*, means "a swanlike water nymph" (*Ground* 55). The nymph analogy adds to Vina's mythically resonant figure. The nymph cult was widespread in Greek, and later in Latin and Italian culture. There are several categories of nymphs and myriads of connotations attached to them, ranging from nasty to fragile and vulnerable femininity. Modern representations of nymphs start from the depiction of mythological nymphs as non-human females who mate with men or women on their own free will, and are completely outside male control. Thus, modern connotations are applied to women who are believed to behave in a similar way. Modern psychology added a further aspect to these connotations coining the term nymphomania, which refers to a woman's desire to engage in sexuality often enough to be considered clinically significant. Rushdie, through his protagonist Rai, draws this analogy to nymphs as a foreshadowing of Vina's lust for men. At this stage of her life, Vina is also described by Rai as an "under-age nymphet" (*Ground* 96), and comparisons are made to Lolita. Rai explains that the Lolita analogy is a break with Indian cultural taboos, as "of course in the 1950s there were no girl tarts in Kamathipura working eighteen hours a day, and child marriages never took place, and the pursuit of the very young by lecherous old humberts – yes, we'd already heard of the new Nabokov shocker – was utterly unknown" (*Ground* 112).

"There was no Self-Effacing Vina to set against Vina of the Screamingly Stretched Extremes"

Vina is not one, but as many as she wants to be, as many as all the others make her be and see her as. Like a league of other Rushdie female and male characters, she does not belong to one culture, to one creed, or in her case to one man. She is what Rai the narrator calls in this novel a "non-belonger" (*Ground* 72-73). In junk vocabulary, Rai evokes her as "all of these and more," and so she is "Professor Vina and Crystal Vina, Holy Vina and Profane Vina, Junkie Vina and Veggie Vina, Women's Vina and Vina the Sex Machine, Barren-Childless-Tragic Vina and Traumatized-Childhood-Tragedy Vina, Leader Vina who blazed a trail for a generation of women and Disciple Vina who came to think of Ormus as the One she had always sought" (*Ground* 339). In addition, Rushdie portrays Vina as the talented singer, his imaginary legend of *rock 'n' roll* and he presents in this character layers of a stereotypical *femme fatale je ne sais quoi* image, which he successfully builds and then dismantles at the same time. The figure of Vina acquires archetypal and mythical dimensions through reiterated references and allusions to a medley of mythological entities, whose combined significance in the newly created context of her character seem to be virtually inexhaustible. Very often in the novel, Vina is called a "goddess," but alternatively she is "the goddess, the Galatea with whom the whole world would fall, as Ormus fell, as I fell, in love" (*Ground* 122), or Rati, the Hindu goddess who pleaded for Kama's life and softened Shiva's heart (*Ground* 148; 323-324). When they perform together, Vina "is the *Argo*, and Ormus sails in her" (394), as Vina is associated with Eurydice (*Ground* 54; 497-500; 547). When she dies in a devastating earthquake, Ormus has to embark on an Orphic quest to the underworld to bring her back through his music. Vina is not only associated with Eurydice, but also with the Indian earth mother and Persephone (*Ground* 479), "the greatest of women, who hold up the earth from below as mighty Atlas holds up the sky" (*Ground* 496). Rather than being herself unknowable, Vina has this permanent longing for having "a glimpse of the unknowable," and it is music which, "through the gates of perception" transports her "to the divine melody beyond" (*Ground* 123). In this mythological key, Vina's insatiable sexual appetite and loudmouthed noisy presence on stage reference orgiastic Dionysus (*Ground* 46; 61).

INVERTED GENDER ROLES

By daringly casting Vina in the role of a "female Dionysus" (*Ground* 61), Rushdie gives the myth a twist, which adds to Vina's transgressive and 'liquid' character. Vina, "rag-bag of selves, torn fragments of people she might have become" (*Ground* 122), is in her life and beyond it "the symbol she had constructed" (*Ground* 162). Even if she dies at forty-four, or maybe all the more because of her tragic death, Rai evokes Vina as "our Lady of the Stadiums, our arena Madonna, baring her scars to the masses like Alexander the Great rousing his soldiers for war" (*Ground* 20).

Evidence of her exceptional power and versatility are the names she has taken and buried and the conscious creation of her fabulous megastar popularity out of the mythically resonant fragments of her identity despite the unstable "ground beneath her feet." When she twice turns down Ormus' marriage proposals, although she knows he is the man she loves most, Vina does so because she knows he will not be the only man in her life. All she knows is that everything changes, and later she learns how fast it changes, since "nothing stays the same for five minutes" (*Ground* 369). Her infidelity is in fact her response to this *Zeitgeist* of change, impermanence and uncertainty, and thus her sexual flimsiness makes her an effigy of her times. She demolishes taboos and steps across the lines of gender, sex, race, and culture. She brings life to her performance and her performance to life, she shouts out her most intimate private life in public until the last boundaries fall.

When she turns down Ormus for the first time, she is sixteen. For four years she had been dreaming of their first night together and implored him to touch her. Although aware of "the twofold nature of man," both Vina and Ormus believe in "the living flesh" (*Ground* 146) It is in the name of "the flesh, the living flesh" that they "will drive people mad with desire, with music, will leave behind them long trails of destruction and delight" (*Ground* 146). If music draws them together, their natures drag them apart. In Ormus' view, which is bent to a form of asceticism, Vina's sensuality keeps them apart. Very early in her life at the age of twelve, Ormus makes of Vina's under-age youth a strong argument against the physical union towards which they both aspire.

When sixteen-year-old Vina, after their long awaited first night together, flatly turns Ormus down and is driven out of the merchants' house on account of her inappropriate behavior, she travels to America without any second thoughts, leaving both Ormus and Rai behind. Years pass, Ormus goes to England, where he swears to himself that he will work hard to be worthy of her and then find her, but he has a terrible accident. He falls into a long coma until she comes, like goddess Rati, to rescue him. Reunited, they go to America where he proposes to her for the second time. She is twenty-seven years old and "she loves him, she loves him to hell and back, but she won't put it in writing and sign her name to it" (*Ground* 369). She sees marriage as a form of captivity. Vina has her own clear opinions according to which "monogamy is a manacle, fidelity is a chain" (*Ground* 369). This is what determines her, "A revolutionary not a wifey will she be" (*Ground* 369).

When ten years later she finally accepts to marry Ormus, Vina is "in her thirty-something prime" and Rai remembers that she has become "not just America's Sweetheart like Mary Pickford long ago but the beloved of the whole aching planet".[1] Despite anything else that may change, Vina is as determined as ever to remain free even in the "manacle" of marriage and she tells Ormus, "I'll marry you, I'll spend the rest of my life with you and you know I will love you. But don't ask me for high fidelity. I'm a lo-fi kind of girl" (*Ground* 412). Rai's fascination with Vina seems to grow with the passing of years, and he records this mature period in Vina's life with a new set of praises for her increasingly flamboyant beauty, "I remember Vina on fire with the dark flame of her adult beauty, flaunting on her ring finger, another man's sparkler and platinum band, and, on her right hand, a cherished moonstone too," which is the ring Ormus gave her on her sixteenth birthday (*Ground* 413).

On Vina's and Rai's last night together, Vina is forty-four, her body more electrifying than ever. The chauffeur driving Vina and her one-night *amour* less than half her age to the hotel confesses to the journalists that he "would have done anything for such a woman," he "would have driven at two hundred kilometers per hour for her if it were speed she wanted," he "would have crashed into a concrete wall for her if it had been her desire to die" (*Ground* 4). Rai, who had followed her all the way to Mexico, devotes a whole paragraph in the narration to her breasts, which remind him of the breasts of Helen of Troy, which "were so astonishing that when she bared them to her husband at the fall of Troy, Menelaus was unable to do her harm" (*Ground* 459). When in her usually talkative mood after sex, Vina raises the issue of age for female singers and points out that in contrast to female artists, male singers can grow old without any career problems, although women are the ones "re-writing the book" (*Ground*

---

1 | Mary Pickford was a Canadian-born U.S. motion-picture actress, 'America's sweetheart' of the silent screen, and one of the first film stars. At the height of her career, she was one of the richest and most famous women in the United States. ("Mary Pickford." *Britannica Online Encyclopedia*. Web. 30 Nov. 2012.)

460). Aware of her "artistic worth" despite or even more due to her mature age, Vina compares her generation of singers to the new wave of female artists with their explosive attitude and their "rage," and then wonders, "To whine about guys, to complain about mom 'n' pop?, [that] just wasn't in it" (*Ground* 460).

Age is intimately related to gender, and despite her sleepiness, Vina challenges the androcentric order, where there is always "a man pulling our strings" (*Ground* 460). Voicing her opposition to this patriarchal system, Vina bitterly complains that "a man is for power and a woman is for pain" (*Ground* 460). Ironically, the example that serves her argument at this point is the myth, which endorses the novel, where she is cast in the role of Eurydice. She asks rhetorically, "Orpheus lives, Eurydice dies, right?" (*Ground* 460). Rai's answer reiterates a thought he has recorded in his narrative account, when he glosses on an interesting inversion of gender roles in their triangle of love:

It occurred to me that in the field of love and desire Vina was just behaving like a man; showing herself capable, like most men, of loving wholeheartedly and simultaneously, halfheartedly, betraying that love without guilt, without any sense of contradiction. She was capable not so much of a division of attention as of multiplying herself, until there was enough Vina to go round. We, Ormus and I, we were her women: he, the loyal wife standing by her philandering husband, settling for him in spite of his roving eye, his wanderlust; and I, the simultaneously wanton and long-suffering mistress, taking what I could get. That way round it made perfect sense. (*Ground* 433)

With that connection in mind, the reader might feel tempted to exclaim, as Rai does, "Yeah, but you're Orpheus too" (*Ground* 460).

Posthumous Vina – Too Old to Rock?

Any approach to *The Ground Beneath Her Feet* may as well take into account that the novel also makes fun of the reader. After all, Rushdie's 1999 book is a postmodernist novel, which embeds its own theory and criticism. Rai does a remarkable job when he blends *rock 'n' roll*, slang, chit-chat, and junk vocabulary with highbrow theory and criticism. This is what makes the novel entertaining and funny, but also virtually resistant to a traditional literary critical interpretation.

After her death, Vina becomes a cultural icon. Rai calls it "Vina Divina" (*Ground* 478-512) and a whole chapter covers it. Never at a loss for words to praise Vina and wonder at her phenomenal character, Rai argues that although she was no Callas, but "merely a 'low-culture' popular entertainer," "this posthumous goddess, this underground post-Vina, queen of the Underworld, supplanting dread Persephone on her throne, grew into something simply overwhelming" (*Ground* 479). As a matter of fact, the measure of "overwhelming" is given by Rai's always *ben trovato* analogies, "Dying when the world shook, by her death she shook the world, and was quickly raised, like a fallen Caesar, to the ranks of the divine" (*Ground* 479).

In this novel, Rushdie evokes both a low- and high-brow tongue-in-cheek approach to Vina's death, as for example, when Rai presents "a great American intellectual's essay", "Death as Metaphor," in which he argues that Vina's life, not her death, was the liberating force" (*Ground* 483). There is also "a recently ordained woman priest, deducing that the Vina phenomenon reveals the world's spiritual hunger," (*Ground* 483) and there are the protests of the Islamist women seeing the Vina phenomenon as an apocalyptic sign of the end of "the decadent and godless Western world" (*Ground* 483). More than two pages of the chapter are taken up by this parade of literary criticism and cultural studies fad. There are fierce intellectual debates around this hot topic in the literary criticism and in the drama panel (*Ground* 484). The novel seems to exhaust itself and its own reflections, containing them as an ocean contains tributaries, streams, rivers and seas (*Ground* 482-85). Is there anything for anybody left, high- or low-brow, to say?

Fishing in the low-brow average people's reactions section of this huge collective tribute to Vina, one comes across a fat English woman's, "boasting mendaciously on the time she told Vina she was too old to rock" (*Ground* 483). The English woman, however, does not understand the narrative. Of all the 'mirrors' reflecting Vina's 'divine' figure, Rai's is by far the prevailing 'looking-glass.' Vina never seems to be "too old to rock" in most of her contemporaries' eyes, and certainly the "female Dionysus" is not too old to rock or to seduce or to keep in her grip as many men or any man of any age as she may fancy, or any public for whom she may perform. It is true for Ormus, because he eventually retreats completely in his "otherworld," (*Ground* 436-37) and stops staging shows. Vina has to fight "her daily bout against self-doubt and existential uncertainty, the universal bogeys of the age" (*Ground* 438), but "at forty-three she was nowhere near ready to quit," as Rai remembers (*Ground* 439). At forty she is "fabulous" (*Ground* 323), and in the remaining four years before she dies, her charisma, her flame, and also her determination to set new marks, to live her life to the fullest never dwindle. On the contrary, as years go by and there are problems, Vina seems to grow stronger, more and more aware of her worth and more and more stylish. Rai recalls that "her style, these days, is late-eighties ultraglamour, no more hippie (or radical) chic. Très movie star, with an extra shock'n' roll twist of outrageousness" (*Ground* 458). At the same time, she grows increasingly "disoriented" (450). Ormus is, literally and metaphorically, her 'Orient(-ation).' He is an Indian, even if a rather 'un-Indian Indian,' he is her music and he is, more than anything, the love of her life. Losing grip of Ormus and not knowing how to save him from his obsessions, Vina is left without a benchmark, but not without will and resources. Rai recalls her conflicting mood in that period, "She said she was disoriented, confused, she needed time to think, all that. Yes, she was thinking of leaving him. She couldn't bear to be there anymore. She couldn't bear to leave him. She couldn't stay" (*Ground* 450) Although she is plagued by uncertainties and contradictions, she is never stuck in them but always ready and willing to move on. This is how Vina is described at forty-four, and to the other fabulous and glamorous Vinas Rai wants to remember, he adds her at this age, "I want to remember her the way she was then, surging into her mid-forties full of beauty and courage, alone and scared but heading back out there, looking for her life" (*Ground* 450). Musing on the significance of the posthumous Vina cult, Rai draws his own conclusion, "*Maybe it's better this way. For ever young, right? Well, young-looking, anyway. Pretty fucking fantastic for a woman of her years*" [italics in the original] (*Ground* 486).

Maybe there is just one detailed description in the novel of Vina looking her age at forty-four, when she leaves the hotel room alarmed by the mestizio's spasms. Rai, who is not only her confidante, her lover, and the one who tells her story, but also a photographer, "who would not dream of photographing her in such delicious and scandalous disarray" (*Ground* 5). Rai's narrative, however, does portray her at such a moment where she is caught in the earthquake seized with terror. This is the last Polaroid truth about Vina. She looks her age, because she is terrified, and she is terrified by tremors within and without, which seem to take hold of her and drag her down. Raï's tone in this ekphrasis is divided between shock and adoration. Noticing the obvious signs of Vina's aging in those last moments, Rai is at the same time fascinated by her imperishable, even if now clearly withering, beauty, "her whole self" is

momentarily out of focus and worst of all looking her age ... her tangled fountain of wiry dyed red hair quivering above her head in a woodpeckerish topknot, her lovely mouth trembling and uncertain, with the tiny fjords of the pitiless years deepening at the edges of her lips, the very archetype of the wild rock goddess halfway down the road to desolation and ruin. (*Ground* 5)

The moment, echoing Dante's lines in *Divina Commedia*, is all the more electrifyingly tragic because she is *nel mezzo del camin di sua vita*, when she tries to make a new start, a solo career without Ormus. Rai accounts for her state of mind as follows:

[...] so it wasn't really surprising that she was disoriented and off balance most of the time, and lonely. It must be admitted. Public life or private life, makes no difference, that's the truth: when she wasn't with him, it didn't matter who she was with, she was always alone. (*Ground* 5)

In Rushdie's world of magic realism, the earth shakes because the archetype of the wild rock goddess is in distress, and it is the end of Vina's life. In terms of living and aging, however, Vina experiences no trace of conflict. For her, living is singing and loving, and she never shows any signs of exhaustion. On the contrary, as Rai recalls and describes her throughout all the stages of her life, with age Vina's hunger for life increases. Apart from Raï's reiterated statements meant to confirm this, Vina herself bursts into one of her "flamboyant" retorts, "I'm a hungry woman. *I want more than what I want*" (*Ground* 328). The tragedies and troubles of her life ignite her desire to rise above them, and if the good things in her life can at the same time be the worst, she does not seem to take heed of that. "Discontinuity," in Raï's account, "is the wooden horse at the gates of Troy" (*Ground* 441). Rai sees himself as "a discontinuous being." Being an Indian living in America never to return to India, he "must believe" and by believing he has truly become "an American, inventing [himself] anew to make a new world in the company of other altered lives" (*Ground* 441). Rai calls it "metamorphic destiny" (*Ground* 441), and Vina has the same "metamorphic" propensity. Vina is 'life flame incarnate, living life and taking it to extremes,' if one tried to paraphrase Rai. She does not die of rocking at forty-four; she dies because of external forces that rock her.

THE GROUND BENEATH HER FEET AND VINA'S "LIQUID" CHARACTER

This is a novel about "the ground beneath her feet" and it gradually grows into an ocean of stories about the ground beneath everybody's feet. Literally, the ground beneath Vina's feet shakes, she is swallowed up and 'disappears.' Her body is not found and that gives grounds for speculations on television that she might still be alive somewhere out there. "Two wild-haired New Quakers" burst into hysterical mystical diatribes that "she will cometh again, [...], maybe from a spaceship?, maybe from a chariot of the gods?, to liberate us. Like Buddha Jesus, man, she liveth" (*Ground* 485).

Metaphorically, the novel hyperbolizes the idea that the ground beneath everybody's feet in those (and our) times is shaken by tremors. There are earthquakes everywhere in the world, ranging from mild to devastating on the Richter scale, there are "cracks," "fissures," "faults" (also to be read as "errors"), and there are "frontier earthquakes" (*Ground* 501) because "stability is what's rare" (*Ground* 500) these days. The novel generously makes use of puns on earthquakes and every possible word related to it until its connotations saturate its world. In the novel's meta-language, this is "geology as metaphor" (*Ground* 203). In psychological and ethical terms, this geo-political "instability" translates as "guilty uncertainty," and they all come together in a package called the *Zeitgeist* of the late 20th century (*Ground* 443).

Rushdie captured this "instability" in a novel which was published at the end of the century whose last decades it chronicles. His metaphorical depictions of the century's *Zeitgeist* are strikingly similar to Zygmunt Bauman's in *Liquid Modernity*, a book published in 2000. The two texts echo each other. Bauman finds the best analogy for our "late modernity" in the features of liquids. Liquids "cannot easily hold their shape," and they "travel easily" because they "'flow', 'spill', 'run out', 'splash', 'pour over', 'leak', 'flood', 'spray', 'drip', 'seep', 'ooze'" (2). The sociologist argues that "these are the reasons to consider 'fluidity' or 'liquidity' as fitting metaphors when we wish to grasp the nature of the present, in many ways *novel*, phase in the history of modernity" (Bauman 2). Showing that modernity implied liquefaction from the very onset, but only to establish a new modern "solidity" and that the true phase of liquefaction occurred in the last decades of the 20th century, Bauman states that "the first solids to be melted and the first sacreds to be profaned were traditional loyalties, customary rights and obligations which bound hands and feet, hindered moves and cramped the enterprise" (3). "Liquid modernity" is a stage when solids whose turn has come to be melted are "the bonds which interlock individual choices in collective projects and actions" (6). Those bonds are institutions like family, class and neighborhood, which survive "like zombies" (8).

Bauman explains that "zombie categories" (6) is a term coined by Ulrich Beck in an interview on February 3, 1999. A few years earlier Beck had coined "the term 'second modernity' to connote the phase marked by the modernity 'turning upon itself', the era of the soi-disant 'modernization of modernity'" (6).

In this light, does not Vina's obstinate repeated refusal to marry Ormus read like a sign that she assumes the 'unbound' condition that suits the age? Her gesture makes sense if seen as an onslaught of the "zombie" institution of marriage and all the other moral "zombies" it implies. Bauman's encapsulating description of "liquid modernity" is that of a period when the inherent characteristics of modernity actually shape the world in which we live. Thus, modernity is, especially in its liquid phase, "transgressive, boundary-breaking, all-eroding" (Bauman 6). These are, according to Bauman, the characteristics of time, space, individuality, work and community. "Liquid modernity" is a phase in which nomadic habits get the upper hand, barriers are broken down, not just blurred or eroded, check-points are phased out and people "travel light" (Bauman 13). Frontiers are replaced, in Rushdie's novel, by a "membrane" (*Ground* 256-76). Throughout the novel, all sorts of frontiers are demolished. The ultimate frontiers in *The Ground Beneath Her Feet* "crumble before the sorcery of the tune" (*Ground* 55).

The "sorcerers" in the novel are Vina and Ormus. In a 'liquid' and 'liquefying' world, their characters are 'liquid.' Although Ormus is also a bundle of contradictions, desires and frustrations, a "non-belonger," a "rootless" (72-73) *troubadour*, the epitome of fluidity in the novel is Vina. She is not one but many, she changes names, looks, partners, places, she becomes, she re-invents herself, and she leaves room for the rest of the world to re-invent her after her death. That may be her 'secret' that does the trick. She does not grow old because she permanently changes and, like a liquid, she cannot be contained. Symbolically, she dies a 'liquid' death, which is ironically captured by Rai in his last picture of her:

In my last photograph of Vina the ground beneath her feet is cracked like crazy paving and there's liquid everywhere. She's standing on a slab of street that's tilting to the right; she's bending left to compensate. Her arms are spread wide, her hair's flying, the expression on her face is halfway between anger and fear. Behind her the world is out of focus. There is a sense of eruptions all around her lurching body: great releases of water, terror, fire, tequila, dust. The last Vina is calamity incarnate, a woman *in extremis*, who is also by chance one of the most famous women in the world. (*Ground* 466)

CONCLUSION

Vina is not the kind of woman affected by the passing of years. Her versatility and her power to always re-invent herself, her determination to break taboos, to transgress conventions and norms render her immune to aging. In Vina's case, age works to her advantage rather than the other way round. The older she grows the keener her perceptions become, and the more essentially she is her real self, from one stage of her life to the next. In the character of Vina Apsara, which becomes the prototype of the famous rock 'n' roll singer, Rushdie lionizes the figure of the rock 'n' roll and pop female star. He may not have intended it, but Vina's power to "surge into" a rather late maturity "full of beauty and courage" (*Ground* 450) is a fictional version of the never-too-old-for-the-show legendary queen of pop, Madonna, who is now fifty-four years old and as sexy as ever, despite, as it seems, some signs and signals of aging speculated by those who desperately look for them in order to hold them against her.

There are sociological and cultural implications for these women's prolonged youth in the sense that these stars' 'liquid' femininity is shaped by their times and it shapes the times in its turn. Their strategy of re-inventing their images and of creating fashions serves the purpose of constructing a public persona to suit their careers. The construction of this public persona does not only imply keeping it bouncing and staying young, but also hard work and a permanent risk of shocking established institutions, their representatives, the public and even their fans with what may pass for scandalous behavior. To a very large extent, they are 'women on the edge' whose purpose in life is to avoid not only the abyss of pathetic aging, but 'cracks' of all sorts.

However, while real-life Madonnas resort to regular workouts, intensive weight training and other extremely exhausting ways of physical exercise, fictional Vinas seem to naturally stay young through a gender transgressive inner strength and a "fabulous hunger for life" (*Ground* 124). Ruxandra Cesereanu argues that "in her maturity, Vina feels *as old as love*. Who else than a woman *as old as love* can bring Orpheus back to life?" (Cesereanu 165). This is in fact where Rushdie twists the myth: Vina is Orpheus. In other words, "the agent of this modernization of the myth" is Dionysiac orgiastic Vina Apsara (Cesereanu 166).

Rushdie may have had yet another design in mind when he projected Vina as a miraculously for-ever-young rock goddess. The writer confesses that rock 'n' roll meant a lot to him as a child growing up in cosmopolitan Bombay, where people coming to the city would bring along their music. He saw the genre literally travel with him when he moved to England at fourteen, where the Beatles, the Rolling Stones, the Who, and Pink Floyd became rock phenomena. A cultural aspect Rushdie purposefully evokes in this particular novel is how easily the music traveled around the world. That is of course a crucial element of liquidity, of melting/collapsing frontiers, which become the 'membrane' through which music travels in the novel. Rushdie takes that to be the first globalized cultural phenomenon at a time when the world had not been globalized. He is fascinated by the 'power' of rock 'n' roll and by its rebellious spirit. Rock 'n' roll is the soundtrack of his life, as jazz used to be the soundtrack of the 1920s. The writer remembers having grown up with rock 'n' roll and he notices that now his children listen to it, a longevity that he translates into fiction by portraying Vina's young and free spirit and her commitment to the genre, which keeps her young.

Vina's overwhelming success is not only that of an idiosyncratic exceptional woman, whose stature in the novel is magnified by mythical associations and whose public persona is lifted to iconicity while she is alive and to a cult after her death, but also that of "*an ordinary woman writ large, flawed yet worthy, strong and weak, self-reliant and needy. She was a rock goddess of the golden age, but she was, improbably, also one of us*" [italics in the original] (*Ground* 478), or so Rai wants us to believe when we read this extraordinary make-believe. The casually dropped, intentionally inserted word "improbably" is a reminder of the fictionality of Rushdie's world. Can ordinary women be as liquid as Vina, if they want to? How thin is Rushdie's 'membrane' between reality and fiction? Thin enough for Vina and others to travel through, one hopes. Rai, the narrator, may have another surprise up his sleeve for the story's readers, his other name Umeed, "you see. Noun, feminine. Meaning hope" (*Ground* 19).

ACKNOWLEDGEMENTS

This work was supported by the strategic grant POSDRU/89/1.5/S/62259, project *Applied social, human and political sciences* co-financed by the European social fund within the Sectorial Operational Program Human Resources Development 2007 – 2013.

REFERENCES

Bauman, Zygmunt. *Liquid Modernity*. Cambridge: Polity, 2006. Print.

Cesereanu, Ruxandra. *Gourmet: Céline, Bulgakov, Cortázar, Rushdie (Close Reading)*. Cluj-Napoca: Limes, 2009. Print.

Pederson, Kristina. "Is Madonna Finally Feeling Her Age?" *Mail Online*, n.d., last updated 17 November 2006. Web. 23 March 2012.

Rushdie, Salman. "My Unfunny Valentine." *New Yorker* 74.46 (1999): 28. *Academic Search Premier*. Web. 9 Dec. 2012.

—. *The Ground Beneath Her Feet*. London: Vintage, 2000. Print.

—. "Women Beware Women. Salman Rushdie on the scandal of the missing girls of India." *The Guardian* 5 May 2001. Web. 18 March 2012.

—. *The Enchantress of Florence*. London: Vintage, 2009. Print.

Contributors

Dana Bădulescu, assistant professor and postdoctoral researcher, teaches modernist and postmodernist British and American literature, literary theory, poetics and translation at "Alexandru Ioan Cuza" University of Iasi, Romania. As a POSDRU grantee she is doing research on Salman Rushdie's writing as emblematic for contemporary society. Since 2006, she has published several articles on Salman Rushdie. The article "Varujan Vosganian's Novel of Postmemory" has been published in the journal *Word and Text* (2012).

Helen Chupin is a senior lecturer at the Université Paris-Dauphine and a member of CICLaS (EA 4405). Her field of research is the contemporary novel in English and she is particularly interested in the American writer Anne Tyler, whose fiction was the subject of her doctoral thesis at the Université de Paris-Sorbonne (Paris IV). She is currently studying fictional representations of aging in the novels of other contemporary writers.

Emma Domínguez-Rué graduated from the University of Lleida (Catalunya, Spain) with a degree in English and obtained an MA degree from Swansea University (UK). She specialized in female invalidism in the fiction of Ellen Glasgow and completed her PhD at the University of Lleida in 2005, where she now teaches English. Her main focus of research is Victorian and Gothic fiction from a feminist perspective.

Marvin Formosa is senior lecturer at the European Centre for Gerontology, University of Malta. In 1998 and 2008, he lectured for the International Institute on Ageing (United Nations) in Thailand and Qatar. He spent time at the Ontario Institute for Studies in Education, University of Toronto,

Canada (2009-2010). He is on the editorial board of *Research on Ageing and Social Policy* and *International Journal on Education and Ageing*. His primary interests are older adult learning, social class dynamics, and social exclusion.

Heinrich Grebe is a researcher at the Institute for European Ethnology/ Cultural Studies at Philipps University of Marburg, Germany, working on the interdisciplinary research project "Living well in old age in the face of vulnerability and finality – an analysis of images of age and aging in public discourses and everyday practices" funded by Volkswagen Stiftung.

Eva Klein is an art historian at the *Department for Art-History* of the University of Graz, Austria. She holds degrees in art history and graphic- and communication design, and a PhD in art history. Her research interests include design theory, modern art and visual communication, especially advertising. She curated several exhibitions and is author of *Große Schau der Reklame. Zwischen Umbruch und Kontinuität. Graz: Unipress 2009.*

Ulla Kriebernegg is assistant professor at the Center for Inter-American Studies of the University of Graz, Austria. She studied English and American Studies and German philology at the University of Graz and at University College Dublin, Ireland. Her research interests include (Inter)American studies, interculturality, cultural gerontology and U.S. and European higher education policy. Her current book project focuses on intersections of age and space in Canadian and U.S. American literature and film.

Thomas Küpper is currently professor for media studies at Goethe University, Frankfurt. Previously, he was visiting professor for cultural studies at the University of Arts, Braunschweig, Germany. He does research on the portrayals of age in literature and media.

Karin Lövgren is currently a researcher for the interdisciplinary research project "Aging and Living Conditions" at Umeå University, Sweden. She has worked as an ethnologist for many years, mainly on documentations for museums, and researches, teaches and tutors at various Swedish universities. Her thesis deals with cultural conceptions of age, gender and aging. She analyzes representations of aging in popular press targeting women in late midlife.

Roberta Maierhofer is professor of American Studies and director of the Center for Inter-American Studies of the University of Graz, Austria, and Adjunct Professor at Binghamton University, New York. Her research focuses on American literature and cultural studies, intersectionality and theory, transatlantic cooperation and age/aging studies. In her publication, *Salty Old Women: Gender and Aging in American Culture*, she developed a theoretical approach to gender and aging (anocriticism).

Nora Melzer-Azodanloo studied law at the University of Graz, Austria, where she now works as a research assistant at the Department of Labor Law and Social Security.

Marta Miquel-Baldellou is an associate lecturer at the Department of English and Linguistics of Lleida University, Spain. She is also a member of the Dedal-Lit research group, focused on the conceptualizations of aging in the literatures of the English-speaking countries, and the European Network of Aging Studies. Her field of research focuses on Victorian literature and nineteenth-century American literature, especially authors such as Edward Bulwer-Lytton and Edgar Allan Poe.

Welf-Gerrit Otto is a researcher at the Institute for European Ethnology/ Cultural Studies at Philipps University of Marburg, Germany, working on the research project "Living well in old age."

Jürgen Pirker studied law and history at the University of Graz, Austria, and currently works as a research assistant for the Department of Austrian, European and Comparative Public Law, Political Science and Administrative Studies of the University of Graz.

Cynthia Skenazi is professor of French and Comparative Literature at the University of California, Santa Barbara. She is the author of *Marie Gevers et la nature* (Brussels: Palais des Académies, 1983), *Maurice Scève et la pensée chrétienne* (Geneva: Droz, 1992), and *Le Poète architecte en France: Constructions d'un imaginaire monarchique* (Paris: Champion, 2003).

Sharon-Dale Stone, PhD is professor of Sociology at Lakehead University. Her research focuses on critical disability studies and social gerontology. She recently published *A Change of Plans: Women's Stories of Hemorrhagic*

Stroke (Toronto: Sumach Press, 2007) and she is lead editor for the forthcoming book *Working Bodies: Chronic Illness in the Canadian Workplace.*

Julian Wangler is a research fellow at the Institute for Media Studies at the University of Tübingen, Germany. His dissertation focuses on media's representations of old age, perceptions, and potentials of influence.

Katharina Zilles is a member of the International Graduate Centre for the Study of Culture (GCSC) and the International PhD Programme for Literary and Cultural Studies (IPP) at Justus-Liebig-University in Giessen. Her PhD project, which is co-supervised at Stockholm University, is concerned with age(ing) as a category of cultural difference and its representation in contemporary Anglophone fiction. Her research interests include gender, queer and postcolonial studies, theories of intersectionality, and body studies.

Harm-Peer Zimmermann is professor at the Institute of Popular Culture Studies at University of Zurich, Switzerland and head of the cultural studies working group that runs the project "Living well in old age." He is also a member of the expert commission for the Sixth German Government Report on the Elderly "Images of Ageing in Society" (2007-2010).